STRUGGLES FOR LIFE;

OR, THE

Autobiography

OF A

DISSENTING MINISTER.

Y GRAIG YW FY NHRIGFA

"Be Thou my strong rock, for an house of defence to save me."—*Psalm* xxxi. 2.

London:

W. AND F. G. CASH, 5, BISHOPSGATE WITHOUT.
DUBLIN: JAMES McGLASHAN AND J. B. GILPIN.
EDINBURGH: JOHN MENZIES.

MDCCCLIV.

LONDON:
J. UNWIN, GRESHAM STEAM PRESS,
BUCKLERSBURY.

TO

HIS BELOVED WIFE,

ASSOCIATE OF HIS PILGRIMAGE,

PATIENT COMPANION OF HIS SORROW,

GRATEFUL SHARER OF HIS JOY,

OBJECT OF HIS FIRST LOVE,

AND

LIGHT OF HIS DOMESTIC CIRCLE,

This Volume

IS AFFECTIONATELY DEDICATED,

BY

THE AUTHOR.

PREFACE.

PREFACES rank among the "Curiosities of Literature." The preface to a discourse is intended to inform the hearer respecting the design of the speaker. The preface to a book should disclose the purpose of the writer. Frequently, however, the orator's "preliminary remarks" have no sort of connexion with his oration; and sometimes those of the writer may be omitted without injury to his work. Many readers, as a matter of fact, do pass over prefaces, as impertinent or unworthy of notice. They consider them somewhat in the light of lovers' promises, or in that of a chapman's harangue in relation to the extraordinary quality of the wares of which he wishes to get rid. Whatever be the cause, modern prefaces, compared with those that adorned the folios of former days, are meagre, insipid, and pointless. Since the following work was written and printed—for every reader knows that the preface, amongst its other anomalies, is the last thing penned—I have met with a fine exception to this remark. I refer to the brief, but most suggestive paper prefixed to the Autobiographic Sketches of De Quincey.   His remarks on "printing" and "pub-lication," though confined to a page or two, are worth the price of the valuable volume,*—a volume which I have read, for the first time, since the last sheet of this narrative was in type.

It would be no dishonour to any man, however high his rank in the priesthood of letters, to elaborate a thought suggested by Thomas De Quincey; but, at the same time, I owe it to myself to state, as a matter of fact, that I had *not* seen his sketch entitled, " The Nation of London," when I related my impressions on first visiting the Metropolis, and my subsequent thoughts about the insignificance of an individual in the centre of a great multitude.   " Everywhere else in England," says this most accomplished writer, " you yourself, horses, carriage, attendants, (if you travel with any,) are regarded with attention, perhaps even with curiosity : at all events, you are seen.   But, after passing the final post-house on every avenue to London, for the latter ten or twelve miles, you become aware that you are no longer noticed : nobody sees you ; nobody hears you ; nobody regards you ; you do not even regard yourself. In fact, how should you, at the moment of first ascertaining your own total unimportance in the sum of things— a poor shivering unit in the aggregate of human life ? Now, for the first time, whatever manner of man you

* Selections, Grave and Gay, from writings published and unpublished. By Thomas De Quincey.

were, or seemed to be, at starting,—squire or 'squireen,' lord or lordling, and however related to that city, hamlet, or solitary house, from which yesterday or to-day you slipped your cable,—beyond disguise you find yourself but one wave in a total Atlantic, one plant (and a parasitical plant besides, needing alien props) in a forest of America. These are feelings which do not belong by preference to thoughtful people—far less to people merely sentimental. No man was ever left to himself for the first time in the streets, as yet unknown, of London, but he must have been saddened and mortified, perhaps terrified, by the sense of desertion and utter loneliness which belong to his situation. No loneliness can be like that which weighs upon the heart in the centre of faces never ending, without voice or utterance for him; eyes innumerable, that have no 'speculation' in their orbs which *he* can understand; and hurrying figures of men and women wending to and fro, with no apparent purpose intelligible to a stranger, seeming like a mass of maniacs, or, oftentimes, like a pageant of phantoms."

Having, in the opening chapter, stated the design of the following narrative, a preface is scarcely required; but on a review of what has been written, I find that several facts and incidents, which might have had some little interest to the reader, have recurred to memory too late for their appropriate places. These relate chiefly to—studying the Hebrew language with the assistance of a German Jew—comparing various systems of theology—scenes and sequels of "open-air preaching" —and various other matters of personal and domestic interest; but it is, perhaps, well that memory was asleep, as, otherwise, the volume would have been needlessly large.

With one or two exceptions, the names of the places, and, without exception, the names of the persons, mentioned in the book are fictitious; but the facts stated are all substantially, and all but circumstantially, true to the letter.

The spirit of the book will, I trust, be found genial and healthy: for fault-finding, dogmatism, and asperity, have no attractions either to my taste or judgment; and as Bishop Hall hath it—" I never loved those salamanders, that are never well but when they are in the fire of contention. I will rather suffer a thousand wrongs than offer one; I will suffer a hundred, rather than return one; I will suffer many ere I will complain of one, and endeavour to right it by contending. I have ever found, that to strive with my superior, is furious; with my equal, doubtful; with my inferior, sordid and base; with any, full of unquietness."

THE AUTHOR.

December, 1853.

CONTENTS.

CHAPTER I.
INTRODUCTION.

CHAPTER II.
BIRTH AND INFANCY.

CHAPTER III.
EARLY YOUTH.

CHAPTER IV.

SCHOOL DAYS AND SCHOOLFELLOWS.

CHAPTER V.

NEW SCENES AND NEW FACES.

CHAPTER VI.

CLOUDS AND SUNSHINE.

CHAPTER VII.
EXPERIENCE OF A VILLAGE PASTOR.

CHAPTER VIII.
THE INNER LIFE.

CHAPTER IX.
LITERATURE AND THEOLOGY.

CHAPTER X.
A NEW FIELD OF LABOUR.

CONCLUSION.
THE PAST AND THE FUTURE.

CHAPTER I.

INTRODUCTION.

" Shadows and sunny glimmerings."—Wordsworth.

INFLUENCE OF MEMORY ON PERSONAL FEELINGS—EVERY MAN A
WORLD TO HIMSELF—PECULIAR PROVIDENCES SUGGESTIVE OF
LESSONS WHICH MAY BENEFIT OTHERS—INSIGNIFICANT ORIGIN
OF GREAT EVENTS—LINKS IN THE SOCIAL CHAIN—VALUE OF
AUTOBIOGRAPHIES—REPEATED REQUESTS TO WRITE—CAUSES OF
DELAY—CHARACTER OF THE CONTEMPLATED NARRATIVE—TRUTH
STRANGER THAN FICTION—JUSTIFICATION OF THE ANONYMOUS—
PLACES AND DATES—NAMES OF CONTEMPORARIES.

SPEAKING officially, such is my "text." Convinced that
honesty would greatly improve the world, I act upon the
conviction, by presenting an outline of what the reader
may expect in the introductory chapter of my personal
memoirs. His inability to predict how this outline may
be filled up—this skeleton clothed—this voluntary pledge
to say something on certain given topics, redeemed—is,
of course, no fault of mine. On the assumption of previous acquaintanceship between us, the case would have
been different; from the past, he could have drawn an
inference as the basis of a prophecy; but as it is taken
for granted that we never met before, it is no reflection,
either on his perspicacity or on my candour, to say that
he cannot know what I am about to write, and that I
cannot tell him, except he—*read on.*

B

Wise men have always considered the possession of high character a valuable thing. Poor men have sometimes valued it so greatly as to refuse to give it in exchange for golden luxury. Rich men have occasionally found its absence a terrible deduction from the homage which is generally paid to affluence. Criminals have been heard at intervals groaning a burning prayer for the once despised and irrevocably lost treasure. Moralists have exhibited its attractions so as to excite esteem, and create the wish to acquire it. And philosophers, compassionating the multitude who have not studied the art of generalisation, have unfolded character in its constituent elements, in the hope that the results of this analysis would attract some, on whom general eulogy on the benefits of a good reputation would be thrown away. That such labours are praiseworthy it were folly to deny, and ingratitude to overlook. But praise for a thing done well, does not involve the necessity of silence concerning the omission of a fact or influential principle, whose introduction would have caused it to be done better. If, for example, to the united operation of sincerity, integrity, purity, decision, and religious faith, in forming an estimable character, the influence of memory were added, I think the facts of experience would more than justify the addition. The experience of most men teaches that the action of memory on the feelings and habits is too powerful to be ignored in one's estimate of personal character. Recollection is, in the case of some persons, the voice of a good angel securing the return of ten thousand hallowed and happy events and associations which minister to present enjoyment, and soothe the mind with the gentle melody of gratitude and hope. Flowery fields, where one sauntered in former years in the company of a beloved companion, during that quiet hour which the summer dew chooses as the period of its advent, are brought before the eye in all their holy beauty. The idyl of the humming brook, the bleating lamb, and the warbling nightingale, falls upon his ear. The tones of a human voice, which once distilled music, again vibrate upon the heart, producing that indescribable sensation of pleasure which only young spirits can feel. A peculiar tree, an angle in the road, a heap of stones, or an old building, may awaken slumbering feelings, of which the individual, thus thrown back over half a century of his personal existence, is alone conscious. Around either of these, or any other object, there may cluster reminiscences which have a peculiar significance to *him*, and which exert a silent but powerful influence on his feelings, disposition, and conduct; and as he surrenders himself to its agreeable impulse, he will become a kinder, a milder, and a better man. He who has the halls of memory adorned with such life-paintings, will neither be an irritable companion nor a tyrannous master. The stream of life, however rough the surface over which it has rolled, will partake in some measure of the freshness of its spring. Even the wrecked vessel, laden with oriental spices, when dashed against the rocky shores of the western world, will impart odours to the storm.

Or memory may recall, after the lapse of twenty or thirty years of youth and early manhood—that invaluable period of being in which, if a man is to *do* anything in this tumultuous market-place called the world, it must be done, or left undone for ever—scenes of strangely mingled complexion, having all the colours of the rainbow, without its unity and beauty, and all the variety of a Persian bazaar, without its order and elegance. Alternations of hope and disappointment, satisfaction and grief, gladness and tears, friends and enemies, good providences and deranged purposes, may so mingle and mix as to defy specific classification; yet the effect produced upon the individual who is the subject of these memories—that is to say, if he be still striving for victory—will be of a training character, giving wings to hope and nerve to resolution, such as are indicated in the following

BIRTHDAY HYMN.

Lo! 'tis a sickly dream! departed years,
 Viewed by the lightning eye of memory, seem
A storm of sighs upon a lake of tears,
 With here and there a glancing fitful gleam.

The light that plays upon its surface shows
 Not what I was, but what I might have been;
The beams that glance at intervals disclose
 Unnoticed treasures which I should have seen!

'Tis now too late! forbidden to retrace
 The path once trod, I heave the fruitless sigh;
And wonder that the sovereignty of grace
 Hath not, exhausted, passed the trifler by!

O, had I never sinned! In such a case,
 How full of joy life's retrospect would be!
But then, my Saviour, thy benignant face
 Would lose the smiles that draw my heart to thee!

'Tis in the hour of sadness that the tones
 Of friendship fall, like music, on the ear;
'Tis when the living conscience sadly groans,
 Messiah's merits in their worth appear.

Let, then, the ghosts of my departed years
 Frown as they will, and point to serious loss;
Despite of them I'll sing my Master's praise,
 And point them all to His victorious cross.

Upon the sides of Calvary I'll rest,
 And tell the accusing spirits of the past,
The balm of peace hath dropped upon my breast
 A consolation that will ever last.

I'll bless the Providence that still sustains
    A life so barren in the field of truth;
And that, through scenes of mingled joys and pains,
    Hath led me up from infancy and youth.

I'll ask that manhood's vigour may display
    The ripe luxuriance of celestial grace;
And as my years foretel the close of day,
    The steps of Christ I'll more intently trace.

Then in the heavens, instead of dropping tears
    Upon the shortness of the pilgrim's road,
I'll bless the speed of birthdays and of years,
    That brought me home so rapidly to God!

And, once more, the power of memory may be a source of such unrelieved sorrow—as in the case of one whose early prospects have been blighted by terrible calamities—that its afflicted possessor may wish it paralysed; or it may be a perfect demon, recalling scenes of endurance at the recital of which the flesh creeps, or deeds of atrocious guilt committed, whose remembrance is intolerable to the actor.

"Don't!" said Cassy,—trying to draw away her hand from Emmeline, who was gently caressing it,—"you'll get me to loving you; and I never mean to love anything again!"

"I wish, friend, thee would leave off cursing and swearing, and think upon thy ways," said good Aunt Dorcas to Tom Loker.

"What," said Tom, "should I think of *them* for? Last thing ever *I* want to think of—hang it all!"

The truth is, as the Athenian philosopher long ago remarked, every man is a world to himself; and the thoughts, feelings, principles, and habits which make up the entire man are the inhabitants of that world—a world ever in motion, in active deeds by day, and still more active dreams by night. With the government of this individualism, this animated and conscious world, no stranger may intermeddle. It has its own laws and customs, and looks forward to its own destiny, as truly and independently as if it were the only subject entity in creation.

Yet, from this very fact, an individual becomes the depository of impressions, ideas, and truths which, involuntarily as it were, qualify him to become the teacher of others. The treasures which he has gathered become at once his qualification and his call. If peculiarly the ward of God—laid in helpless infancy at the feet of Providence, like the child Moses by the waters of the Nile—if convinced that his experience has been circumstantially different from that of the sons of his father's equals—or, if not this, that he has had a more vivid impression of ordinary lessons than his playfellows and schoolmates—he may, without a particle of either fanaticism or presumption, translate this conviction or impression into a summons to speak what he has seen and heard. If this be deemed too slender a foundation on which to impose a general principle, let the following considerations be duly weighed, and perhaps a different verdict will be given by the objector.

In the first place, there can be nothing injurious to the interests of society in a devotional recognition of Divine Providence overruling and modifying the circumstances of human life. It is true that lords many and gods many assume this authority, and claim the right of wielding this mysterious prerogative. But what reasonable advocate of these deities would be offended, if the suggestion be thrown out that their lordships "Chance," "Accident," "Fortune," and "Coincidence" are but conventional terms for the manifestations of the purposes of an Invisible Power, who worketh all things after the counsel of His own will? What if chance, accident, or fortune, be but the birth of an eternal thought, at a time and under circumstances of which the man thereby affected had not the slightest premonition? And what if coincidence be but the meeting-point of two sides of an acute angle which had their basis in the eternal foundation of all things? The supposition, at all events, is not likely to prove a buttress to any blighting heresy; and it is far more in accordance with the acknowledged dignity of truth, than any theory which pleads for the power of second causes, while they are avowedly detached from, and independent of, an Omnipotent First Cause. Now the man who takes this view of what *he* calls providential deeds, may without offence read in them a commission to teach to others the doctrine which he believes they have imparted to him.

Secondly, the recognition of social claims is characteristic of every benevolent mind. To live for the good of others is a noble consecration. If men generally would do this, how amazingly would the sum of human happiness be increased! But if a man habitually neglect or overlook the voices of his personal experience, the moral and mental capital with which he should advance the interests of his fellow-men will remain miserably limited. If, however, on the other hand, he feels that he is not and cannot be an insulated being, but a unit in the aggregate, a link in the chain, of humanity, he will consider the lessons which have been whispered into his ear as intended for proclamation upon the house-tops. It is a serious thing to live in society, and we cannot live out of it. It is a serious thing to live at all, and this constitutes the dignity and the glory of life. Our social and relative arrangements are eloquent with meaning. They are constantly telling us how this serious social life of ours may be made the well-spring of innumerable personal and relative joys. The weak look to the strong, the ignorant to the educated, the poor to the rich, the child to its parent. Is not that look a glance of deep meaning from the God and Father of us all? Why are *you* strong, or educated, or rich, or a parent, while *he* is neither? Among the glorious truths which fell from the lips of Him who "came not to be ministered unto, but to minister, and to give His life a ransom for many," there was one which none of the Evangelists have recorded; yet it is recorded as a veritable saying of His. "I have showed you all things," says Paul, in his valedictory address to the elders of the church at Ephesus, "how that so labouring ye ought to support the weak, and to remember the words of the Lord Jesus, how He said, It is more blessed to give than to receive."

And thirdly, a thing which appears to one man an unmeaning common-place may, in the judgment of another, be invested with deep significance, suggesting trains of thought too important to be hastily forgotten, and too closely connected with the realities of life to be separated from them without violence and guilt.

The thing, considered as such, may indeed be insignificant, as the falling of an apple, or the steam of boiling water from a tea-kettle, but who shall forbid the reflections to which it may give birth, or prophesy the magnificent results to which it may lead? "Great" is a relative term, predicated of a thing which may have required many years of scientific application to bring it to maturity; but all the power of which it is capable in its fully developed state, lay originally in the small germ from which it has sprung. Viewed in this light, which is probably the true light in which to examine the history of man and the phenomena of nature, I question whether it is strictly philosophical to denominate anything little. When the clouds and shades of the present shall have passed away, we shall probably find, under the clear light of Infallible Certainty, that many things which we now toss upon the flood-marks of time as trifles, or cast into the great lumber-house of the world as useless, were in reality gems in the eyes of angels, requiring only spiritual vision to detect their intrinsic beauty and worth. That there will be a reversal of the world's verdicts when the world's facts shall have become historical, may be safely predicted, without laying claim to supernatural guidance; and, possibly, from the fact that many of the links of the social chain are invisible at present, it may be found that the hidden and the noiseless were working out their part in the great problem of humanity as efficiently as the prominent and the famous,

" Whose distant footsteps echo
Through the corridors of Time!"

It has often occurred to my thoughts that a collection of memoirs, truthfully relating the external history, and describing the inner life of the individual writers, would be a valuable contribution to the world's literature. The external history should surround the inner life, as objects surround and are revealed by a sunbeam. The power of circumstances upon the man, and the extent to which the man's principles subjected circumstances to the main purpose of life, should be seen. Such a collection of autobiographies would form an inestimable library to the thoughtful student of human nature, and might tend to cast considerable light on the perplexing question concerning the part which man acts in forming his own history. Does he determine his own course in life, by a series of purposes gradually unfolded and expanded into action?—or is it predetermined for him, so that those volitions and deeds which he thinks his own are but the impulse and outgrowth of an irresistible power, to which he is completely subject without knowing it? Is he an actor, controlling, directing, and shaping the events which immediately surround his steps as he proceeds along a chosen path to a goal which he has also chosen?—or is he merely passive without knowing it, being led when he thinks himself leader—a mere passenger in a ship over which he has no authority, while he imagines himself the skilful pilot standing by the helm? Is he a crowned sovereign, having undisputed sway over the little *things* which are included within the limits of his little kingdom?—or is he, whilst fancying himself regal master of this little territory, the unconscious servant of the lowest of his servants?

Personal friends, who know my convictions respecting the value of such works, have frequently suggested that I might help to accomplish the thing desiderated. Reluctance to speak of myself has been the chief reason which has hitherto prevented compliance with the suggestion—for, in an autobiography, one is compelled to use the first person singular; but that difficulty can be evaded, without in the smallest degree deducting from the interest or truthfulness of the narrative, by withholding the writer's name, and slightly altering the orthography of the names of places to which he will have occasion to refer. This, and some other causes of delay, having been overcome, the result is—the work now in my reader's hands.

The work itself is not the child of fiction—not the creature of imagination—not in any way the offspring of fancy; but, strictly and literally, a consecutive narrative of facts and events of which I have been the subject, or which have come under my personal observation. Of men and things and systems I mean to speak freely and ingenuously, convinced that whilst opinions differ, it is unmanly in the holder of any given opinion to conceal or modify it, from the apprehension that it may chafe the edges of some venerable prejudice, or disturb the surface of some quiet lake of thought sleeping among the social or ecclesiastical hills of his native land. That there are many hollow places in the frame-work of society, no man who has examined its texture will deny. That in our privileged country there are many beautiful corruptions, like a jewelled mummy in the shrine of an Italian cathedral, the most vigorous Conservative will scarcely gainsay. And that among the lauded improvements of those who think themselves effectually separated from the condemned abuses of the past, there lingers much unsuspected evil which tends to make the "improvement" as repulsive as that which it displaced, it is at once easy and painful to prove.

The facts to which these sentences point will come up, *without* giving the book a polemical or party colouring.

There are also many good and true things floating on the surface of society, seeking in vain, like Noah's dove, a resting place for the sole of their foot; things at once beautiful and beneficent, which men, in their haste to live, pass by unnoticed, because the costume in which they appear, and the voice in which they whisper their message, are different from that to which the stamp office of conventionalism has affixed its patent label.

The facts to which these sentences point will also pass under review, *without* making the book the advocate of any extravagant theory.

Incidentally, rather than dogmatically, will opinions appear; they will grow out of the main subject, and cluster around it, as the branches spring from the stem;

and the memoir itself will remain unbroken, as memory and notes supply the facts of which it will be composed. Should any of the following incidents afford a fresh illustration of the axiom that truth is stranger than fiction, and should the reader consequently resolve henceforth to seek mental instruction in the ample fields of truth rather than in those of fiction, one important object I have in view will be realised.

With all this, I justify the anonymous appearance of the work. *Who* the writer of a book is, is a matter of very little importance; but *what* he says, may be of service to some wearied traveller over the rough ways of human life. He may even conceal places under appropriate synonymes, and yet invest the localities with much interest; and he may characterise his contemporaries so faithfully as to leave no doubt concerning the originals, without the familiarity of mentioning their proper names. All this, to a certain extent, is contemplated in the following pages, and you, esteemed readers, will allow me to say, in the words of an esteemed poet:—

> " Therefore I hope to join your sea-side walk,
>   Saddened and mostly silent, with emotion ;
> Not interrupting with intrusive talk
>   The grand majestic symphonies of ocean.
>
> " Therefore I hope, as no unwelcome guest,
>   At your warm fireside, when the lamps are lighted,
> To have my place reserved among the rest,
>   Nor stand as one unsought or uninvited !"

CHAPTER II.

BIRTH AND INFANCY.

" This is the place.   Stand still, my steed,
    Let me review the scene ;
And summon from the shadowy past,
    The forms that once have been."—*Longfellow.*

THE BAY OF CHURCHBANK—POVERTY OF MY PARENTS—FRAUDULENT
BANKRUPTS—LOSS OF LIFE—CONVERSATION BETWEEN MY PARENTS
—DESCRIPTION OF MY INFANCY—TALK AMONG NEIGHBOURS—
SUPERSTITION—BLACK CATS—THE QUARRYTON FAIRIES—ZYBIL
MOSS—REFLECTIONS ON MODERN CREDULITY—MRS. GORING—THE
STRATAGEM—JAMES CLANFIELD—THE PINCH OF SNUFF—THE SACK
—THE WOUNDED EYE—LEARNING TO READ—THE PROPHECIES—
VIRGIL, POPE, AND COWPER—THE LITERAL AND THE METAPHORICAL
—STRANGE IMPRESSION—ZELOTES—THE PARLOUR OF THE "FOX"—
JOSEPH NORISON—PICTURE OF JOSEPH—DIALOGUE—REMOVAL TO
WARSTON—FRESH DIFFICULTIES—THE SCHOOL—" PILGRIM'S PRO-
GRESS"—NERVOUS SENSIBILITY—STRANGE MUSINGS—THE DARK
LAKE—WILD THOUGHTS—THE THUNDERSTORM—THE BURNING
SHIP—THE RAINBOW.

THE water in the bay is famous for its clearness; even
where the largest ships can ride at anchor, you can see
the bright pebbles and the seaweed at the bottom.   As
you enter the harbour, there is a green terraced mound
on your left hand, evidently the quiet relic of what was
once a fortification or castle.   The only memorial of war
remaining on the spot is a venerable piece of artillery,
which probably, in some forgotten age, did service, as the

oldest inhabitant has certain traditions on the subject, derived from his grandfathers, which he will circumstantially relate to you for the small consideration of a pinch of snuff. The mound is the favourite resort of children, and you may see them in scores at this moment running around its green base, leaping from its terrace, riding on the old gun—whose iron throat they, or rather the children of a former generation, have long since affectionately choked with stones—and gamboling at pleasure, as children in all ages have loved to do, whilst their shouts and laughter come ringing across the smooth surface of the water, and enter your ear as you stand upon the deck of the vessel viewing the dream-like scene. On your right stretches a green shore, with here and there a patch of land well cultivated, while about a mile and a half inland, a lofty conical hill rises and bounds the view. Right before you lies the venerable old town, stone built, sea washed, evidently enjoying repose, and looking as if it had been accustomed to nestle in the bosom of that bay for at least half a dozen centuries. In the centre of the town, like a giant monarch standing among his subjects, the parish church lifts its lofty dome, which sends forth sweet sounds daily to the inhabitants from a set of the finest-toned bells in the Queen's dominions. The unusual size of this building, for the purposes of a parish church to a small population, is accounted for by the fact that it was at one time a cathedral. It was built in the early part of the twelfth century. Many a legend, curious and wild, hovers around the history of this noble structure. Beyond, and a little to the right, sleep the ruins of the bishop's palace. Sparrows, starlings and ivy flourish in the remains of the upper storeys, and rats and kindred vermin enjoy themselves in what were once wine cellars and kitchens, well replenished for ecclesiastical appetites by a people devoted to the ancient church of Rome. The town itself consists of one long street, as irregular as the stem of a gnarled oak, which shoots out at irregular intervals short lanes, that, like the street itself, at the time of which I write, were odorous with heaps of ashes, rotten fish, and all kinds of abomination, which were allowed to accumulate from month to month, much to the benefit of disease and the doctors. This is the ancient town of Churchbank. This is my native place.

I was born in Churchbank, nearly forty years ago, and never did more unlikely child live to man's estate; never did feebler infant survive the dangers of infancy and childhood, and weather the storms of subsequent life; and never had the son of poor parents more reason for fervent gratitude to that great and good Being who watches with peculiar care over the helpless, and leads the blind by a way they know not.

At the time of my birth, my parents were miserably poor. One small room in a mean house was all they could afford. My father was then in his fiftieth year, my mother being his second wife, and I was the second and youngest child. In early life my father had toiled with great energy, and being a man of superior intellect, of decided piety, and consequently of sober and industrious habits, he had acquired sufficient property to keep him and his comfortable in after life. He had placed his honest earnings in the hands of two merchant-traders of the place, looking to the interest to meet his moderate wants. His first wife, by whom he had no children, had been an invalid for many years before her death, and as my mother was a person of cheerful temper and good education, in every way fitted to make his home comfortable, he looked forward to the future, so far as this world was concerned, with composure and hope. But, poor man! his toils and hardships were not yet ended, although he had crossed the meridian of life. About three months before my birth, he was startled with the intelligence that both the traders, in whose hands he had deposited the fruit of thirty years' hard labour by land and water, had become bankrupts, and fled the country. They had left behind them literally nothing, and the capture of the fugitives was not so easy a matter in those days as it is at present. A crew of five fine young fellows perished in the attempt to reach the foreign ship in which it was supposed the fraudulent bankrupts had made their escape. There was lamentation in the little town that day, and seeds of sorrow were sown which have not yet entirely ceased bearing fruit. Two of the young men who suddenly found a watery grave on this occasion were brothers, nephews of my father, over whom, as their father was dead, he exercised a generous and much-valued guardianship. From respect to their uncle, they had volunteered this hazardous service. My father was stunned by these calamities. But the last bitter drop had not yet fallen into his cup. Unable to bear the shock of these tidings, my mother was suddenly deprived of health; and three months afterwards I was born into the world, the feeblest of poor infants. She never recovered her wonted strength; and when I recall the facts with which I was made acquainted, and recollect the extreme feebleness and sickness of my early years, I am often astonished that both mother and child were not laid in the same grave shortly after my birth. Had not my father been possessed of a strong will, at once chastened and encouraged by undoubting faith in the wisdom of the Divine arrangements, he had quailed, especially at his time of life, before these complicated and sudden trials. To begin life again at fifty, especially where there is such a gloomy cause for it as he had, and in the absence, too, of domestic comfort, is no such easy matter as those who have not tried the experiment may imagine. Often, in the days of my childhood, have I wondered at the equanimity of his spirit in the midst of great privations, and at his habit of positive gratitude under all circumstances. He *literally* obeyed the precept, "In everything give thanks." To the opulent, who stimulate their appetites by rich sauces, it would doubtless sound ridiculous enough to hear a man, whose scanty meal was insufficient to supply the necessities of nature, expressing thanks that he had very little appetite. But I have heard this often, and knew that the man who so expressed himself was as incapable either of falsehood or religious cant, as he was of waylaying and robbing his neighbour. Sometimes my poor loving-hearted mother would give way to bursts of grief when she thought of her two poor boys—the youngest of whom was, in all probability, if not mercifully relieved by an early death, destined to be a helpless invalid for life—and of the dark prospect before them, contrasted with the happy circumstances of her own youth, and of the first three years after her marriage. On such occasions the father, who felt not only for the children, but the husband who felt keenly for his sorrow-stricken wife, invariably acted the part of a wise consoler, who knew where he had placed his hope, and felt confident that he should not be disappointed. He would say, "Yes, my dear, so far as we can *see*, our poor boys, should they live, have only a life of poverty and suffering before them; but the future is not to be with us a matter of sight, but of *faith*. The children belong to God. He is able to provide for them, and I am confident that He will do it."

"But if this poor child should never be able to do anything for himself?"

"That does not alter the case," he would reply. "God's ability and willingness to take care of His creatures do not depend upon their health and strength; and as we are specially anxious about the feeble one, just because he is feeble, so it may be that God will specially care for him also."

"Well, well, I hope they will not be forsaken; but those bad men that robbed us—"

"Forgive them, dear, as a Christian should."

To return to myself. Fancy a child with water on the brain, causing the head to be so unnaturally large that a cap as large as one belonging to his mother is required to cover it; fancy the obstinacy of this disease, so great that all the medical skill of the town is unable to remove it; fancy the little sufferer completely given up to death—the case absolutely hopeless—his death-linen waiting ready to be put on, when it shall be satisfactorily ascertained—an exceedingly difficult thing, from his extreme debility—that he has breathed his last; suppose that on several occasions he is pronounced dead; that frequently, for the period of a fortnight, the only nourishment he takes is two or three teaspoonfuls of milk and water; and imagine all this to continue for two years and six months, he all the time so incredibly weak that he can never sit on his mother's knee, but has to lie in her lap or on his little couch; and suppose, finally, that it is certain that, up to this period, he has not grown an inch from the hour of his birth; and you will have an exact picture of the first thirty months of my existence in the world.

It is superfluous to remark, that the singularity of this case was the subject of curiosity and conversation in

Churchbank and its neighbourhood, both among the medical men who had given it up as hopeless, and among sympathising persons, who felt much for my tried mother. She was my only nurse; for whenever any kind neighbour came in to relieve her for an hour, the well-meant purpose was defeated, with one solitary exception, by my unhappiness in the hands of a stranger. The low moan and wail invariably rendered it necessary that the useless little bit of humanity should be transferred to his mother's lap.

Churchbank, and the county of which it is the chief town, were at that time overrun with superstition. The clergy of the Established Church were, with scarcely an exception, utterly unfit for their office; and Nonconformity was only just beginning to alarm the slumbering shepherds, and to call the wandering flocks to more healthy pasture. The old mythology, with its invariable concomitants, gross ignorance and gross immorality, exercised a far more potent influence over the so-called Christian people than the Gospel, with its light and virtue. Three-fourths of the population were unquestioning believers in witchcraft, not merely as an historical mystery, but as an existing power dwelling among them —crossing their path, blighting their fields, wounding their cattle, wrecking their fishing boats, thwarting their purposes, and crazing their offspring! Unlucky days were more numerous than saints' days in the Romish calendar. Black cats standing in the road, leaping a wall, running as if pursued, or, in fact, in any other possible or impossible feline position or act, were specially to be avoided by the spectator as ominous of some undescribed evil, which, from the utter impossibility of guessing what it might be, filled the mind with gloomy forebodings. Whether those cats which had the good fortune to wear sable livery understood their power, and entered into a conservative league to preserve their profitable monopoly, I shall not say; but it is certain the colour paid well. The man or woman who occasionally had the hardihood to refuse a slice of his or her best to any puss in ebony that might choose to look in about dinner time was considered an infidel person, doomed to some dread catastrophe. Of course, every kitten of the privileged colour was exempt from the terrors of the hydropathic cure; and, of course, black cats were a well-fed public nuisance. But I need not lengthen the catalogue of their immunities.

Many other illustrations of those superstitions might be given. I shall mention only one at present,—one in which I was *said to be* personally interested. The most perplexing part of my case to the good people of the town was, that I would not, or at all events did not, die. Had I died, there would have been an end of the thing; but no; in vain the doctors leave, in vain the shroud arrives, in vain the fortnight's fast! Add to this the mysterious fact, that though life continued, there was neither strength nor growth during the long period already named. The resolution of the whole affair into natural causes, namely, the debility of the mother, and the weakness of the child, to whom it was impossible to administer nourishing food, would not do. No, it was the work of an evil eye, or of witchcraft, or—

"No," said Zybil Moss, an elderly lady, whose perpendicular and circumference were three feet ten inches each—and who for the past quarter of a century had been suspected of the habit of promenading the hills and glades in grey cloak and hood, for certain mysterious purposes, when righteous persons were softly slumbering in bed—"no, 'tis the Quarryton fairies."

"The fairies! say ye so?" eagerly inquired Mother

Bot, a personage who always pretended to reject Zybil's doctrines as worthless heresy, but who was, nevertheless, charged by knowing gossips with being an accomplice of the mysterious Zybil. "The fairies,—the Quarryton fairies,—say ye, Miss Moss? Nay, nay, the bairn's safe enough frae them. This is one o' yere tricks—fie!"

"Fie! indeed," retorted Zybil—her capacious nostrils widening under the influence of offended pride—" and d'ye mean to insinivate, Bet Bot, firstly, that there are no fairies in Quarryton; or, farther, that they have not changed this bairn; or, nextly, that *I* don't know their plans?"

"Ye know a great deal, Miss Moss; some say more than ye ought, but—"

"Whoorp!" interrupted Zybil—a sound and pronunciation which it is impossible to describe on paper, but which had the effect of instantly silencing and dispersing even the most garrulous group of idle dames that might gather around her. After that positively alarming utterance, which I have often heard with dismay in my youthful days, no one ventured to continue the conversation. And many persons affirmed that as soon as it escaped her lips, or throat, or whatever other organ she employed to give birth to it, a curious rustling sound was heard, as if a flock of bats had suddenly whirled around the heads of the party.

I do not feel myself called upon to account for, or give an explanation of, these mysteries. But I will take this opportunity of saying, that those who received them as proofs of a supernatural interference in the affairs of men, considering the comparative darkness in which they were kept by a well-paid Establishment, whose duty it was to have enlightened them—and considering, also, the natural tendency of the human heart to surrender itself to the influence of superior powers, real or imaginary—were far less censurable than the tens of thousands in Europe and America who have given themselves up to the puerile delusions of spirit-rappings, table-movings, table-prophesyings, and similar reason-dishonouring absurdities. These latter have no possible excuse to plead for their preposterous folly. The Bible is widely circulated: religion is free. There is no persecution for the sake of opinion—so far, at least, as Great Britain and America are concerned. The press was never more fertile in intelligent and healthy productions. Education runs through the nations with electric speed; and the grand peculiarities of the Gospel may be known by every earnest man, no one forbidding him. Yet, with all this, follies unequalled in the days of Odin or Thor, and silly fables, unsurpassed in the dark years of the middle ages, are carrying the people away as with a desolating flood. How is this? Intellect boasts its march; rationality trumpets its triumphs; wisdom proclaims its victories; infidelity scouts the weakness of believers in the glorious old Book of God; and the doctors of the new philosophy parade their beautiful findings as a practical panacea for all the ills of humanity. How is this, then? I repeat. The answer appears to me, in all sober seriousness, to amount to a terrible charge against the Gentile nations, who have had an opportunity of knowing and worshipping the only true God, and who have allowed it to pass unseized. Reason has had, as in the days of ancient Gentilism, previous to the missionary journeys of the illustrious Paul and his companions, ample room to test and try its vaunted resources, and it has failed; failed to find out God, failed to benefit man, and failed to cast a single ray of light on the thousand mysteries of perplexed humanity. Refusing Divine light, the great Source thereof has left it to choose gross darkness. Rejecting truth, it has been allowed to believe a lie. A second trial has been given to human wisdom, and the result is folly— folly intense and pitiful, proclaimed by every journal of the civilised world to the four winds of heaven. Infidelity, so far as the inspired documents and the true Lord of man are concerned, has, with wondrous credulity, received and adopted—as the veritable axioms of the invisible world—mutterings discreditable to a ballad-singer, and impossible to a Sunday-school child. Reason, reeling from her centre by rejecting the Word of God, has given way before the cabalistic tricks of modern knaves, and exhibited to that portion of mankind which has dared to stand erect in its heaven-revealed faith, a picture of degradation, and a lesson of profound significance. And learned doctors, philosophers, and statesmen, the nobles of nations, and the leaders of the people, have gone beyond the superstitions and idolatries of paganism, by giving heed to seducing spirits, in human form, interpreting the rappings of impostors into the voices of departed souls, and worshipping, as gods gifted with prescience, pieces of common household furniture!

To heave a sigh, and say, " Alas! for man," is easy, whilst it is a kind of sorrowful relief to the benevolent heart. But what is the use of it? Men forewarned, and continuing obstinate, are foredoomed because of that foreseen obstinacy. These modern aberrations, or rather abnegations, of common sense, are the hand-writing upon the wall, symbolising the speedy advent of a new dispensation, which will chase into darkness and oblivion the accumulated follies of six thousand years. The popular talk about the development of intellect, so far as religion is concerned, is one of the myriad hallucinations that have afflicted the world for ages; and the sooner public instructors recognise the fact, and attempt to stop the rapid progress of intellectual imbecility, the greater benefit will they bestow upon their pupils. The truth is, that man knows nothing on this subject but what he receives from the Bible; and if he will not receive the doctrines of this book, he must be left to his own folly, the plaything of every impostor that may choose to seek his suffrages, and the helpless wanderer across a wilderness without the pillar of cloud by day and of fire by night.

I have said that there was one exception to the fruitless efforts of neighbours to assist my mother in nursing her afflicted child. This was in the case of an old lady of the town, in whose company, it appears, I felt singular pleasure. Mrs. Goring was about seventy years of age, at the time I first remember her—namely, when I was about entering on my sixth summer. She was then remarkably tall and straight for her years: she had acquired the character of a person of uncommon discernment, and of strict integrity. Having seen much of the world, her remarks were respectfully heard by all, and having the reputation of a prophetess, the oracle was often solicited to speak concerning future events. She had too much good principle, however, to take any selfish advantage of these weaknesses in her neighbours, but quietly gave advice where she saw it was needed, without seeming to claim any superiority over ordinary mortals; at the same time she took every proper opportunity of rebutting and holding up to ridicule the childish superstitions of the townspeople. When I had entered on my second year, and a day or two after the conversation just related between the worthies, Zybil Moss and Mother Bot, Mrs. Goring visited my mother, and kindly offered to nurse the invalid for an hour or two—an offer which, it is needless to say, was very gratefully accepted.

Having nestled the fragile affair in her lap, she addressed my mother thus—of course, the narrative was related to me years afterwards, as I cannot be supposed guilty of remembering what was said at *that* time— "Well, neighbour E——, do you think your baby gets strength?"

"I fear not," said my mother.

"His case occasions much conversation," continued Mrs. Goring, "and people are at a loss how to account for it; but I heard a satisfactory explanation of the mystery last evening."

"Indeed!"

"Yes, that respectable person, Zybil Moss—"

"O, Mrs. Goring, I did not think *you* would have listened to—"

"That wise woman, Zybil Moss, called on me to say, that she had discovered the cause of this poor child's illness. It seems the fairies of Quarryton took a fancy to your infant, and managed to elope with it, leaving this afflicted one in its stead, which originally belonged to—"

"Whom?"

"Zybil is silent on that point, but she is prepared to arrange the matter with the fairies, on condition—"

"Of money, I presume?"

"Not exactly that, but something far more ridiculous, from which, however, she hopes to reap substantial benefit. Shall I tell you what it is?"

"Yes, if you think proper; but I would rather know what you said to her," replied my mother.

"Both, then," added Mrs. Goring. "She proposes that on three successive Friday nights, as the town-clock strikes twelve, you lay at the root of the bloody thorn at the mouth of Quarryton Cave, a parcel of tea, sugar, and snuff, and a bottle of spirits, saying at the same time,

C

' Lal, tal, bal, bam, bat, rip, ro, bat.' You must be alone at the time, and you must not, on any account, look behind you as you return."

" Horrible !" exclaimed my mother. " And what did you say to the designing person?"

" Say? why I promised to persuade you to do as she proposes."

" Me?"

" Yes, why not? It is time the town was rid of this good-for-nothing mischief-maker. She has fallen into her own trap, and if you will be guided by me, she will soon be compelled to earn her bread honestly, or to go without. James Clanfield owes her a grudge for the wicked trick she played upon him, and he will be but too glad to assist you. Leave the rest with me ; and for your encouragement I will add, that this sick child, over whom you have so long watched, not knowing whether he was alive or dead, will not only recover, but will be a man of name and character, of whom many persons will yet hear. But the poor project of Zybil Moss has nothing to do with his recovery ; nor have the fairies anything to do with his illness."

" Will my child recover ?" eagerly inquired my mother, without waiting to question the authenticity of the oracle's prediction.

" He will, *certainly*," answered Mrs. Goring, emphatically.

Quarryton was a dreary, desolate-looking place, about two miles from Churchbank, and about one-third of a mile from the sea shore. It was covered with heath and stunted thorns ; and a curious cave, which had been discovered in the centre of the heath some years before, was popularly believed to be the dwelling-place of a thriving population of little creatures called fairies. The habits and customs of these mysterious beings formed the subject of many an incoherent fireside story on winter evenings in the neighbourhood. It seems they excelled in certain kinds of minute gymnastic exercises, such as leaping, vaulting, and dancing. They were mischievously clever at throwing small stones, casting dust in the eyes of travellers, and similar pranks; and, what is not a little curious, they were immoderately fond of running away with snuff boxes from the hands or pockets of persons who indulged in that dusty luxury. Whether Zybil Moss had acquired the accomplishment of snuff-inhaling from the gentry of Quarryton I have no authority for determining, but it is certain that she had few equals in the art, as James Clanfield knew to his sorrow. Honest James loved tobacco as sincerely as any subject of the Ottoman empire, only he preferred it in the form of powder. James also loved a blue-eyed maid, the daughter of a farmer in the near neighbourhood of the haunted cave. Love to this young lady overcame James's natural fears of the pigmy Quarrytonites, and with commendable perseverance he was often seen in a locality where gentlemen not in love would not have ventured to show themselves. In consequence of her suspicious habit of nocturnal rambling, the notorious Zybil had frequently crossed Clanfield's path, and on every occasion, as a matter of course, she had begged and obtained a pinch of snuff. Once or twice James thought that she managed to extract an unnecessary quantity from his box. The thought occurred to him that there was no absolute necessity for plunging her thumb and finger so very deep into his little treasure; and so, for the fun of the thing, and by way of testing honest Zybil's delicacy of touch, he filled his snuff box on one occasion with a prickly thorn from the heath, sprinkling it over with snuff sufficient to have satisfied any ordinary pair of nostrils. Punctual as a lover was James at the trysting place, where he hoped to meet with his blue-eyed Maria, and punctual as an unwelcome bill was the form of Zybil in crossing his path, and asking a pinch from his box. The request was granted, and —— Zybil screamed, and vowed vengeance. She kept her vow. Maria believed the cool falsehoods of the irritated woman, and discarded her innocent lover. Wounded thus in a tender part, Clanfield waited an opportunity of exposing Zybil's character, and was not a little gratified when Mrs. Goring put it in his power to do so. Choosing a trusty confederate, he went early in the afternoon of the following Friday to the bloody thorn, carrying with him the basket of required delicacies. Carefully removing the turf, he dug a pit about three feet deep, bearing the earth to a distance so as to prevent suspicion. He then replaced the turf, resting it upon weak sticks, strong enough to bear the weight of the articles which he placed upon the turf, but utterly insufficient to bear the weight of a human body. He and his companion then hid themselves within the door of the cave—the desire of entrapping Zybil overcoming the fear of the fairies—so as to see what took place, without being seen by any one outside.

Shortly after twelve o'clock, James thought he saw something approaching the famous thorn, the dark legend connected with which had often filled him with terror. He and his companion scarcely breathed. At the same time they fancied they heard unearthly sounds behind them within the cave. The perspiration oozed from every pore of their bodies; they half repented their rash act. Still, however, they kept their eyes on the approaching object, dimly seen against a clear midnight sky. At that moment a huge black cat rushed past them out of the cave, in answer to the well-known call of

Zybil, whilst she herself, ignorantly stepping on the deceitful turf to snatch her booty, fell with a scream into the pit prepared for her. Leaping from their hiding place before the wretched creature had time to collect her scattered senses, the two men picked her up and placed her in a sack which they had brought for this gallant purpose, and which one of them swung on his back, whilst they proceeded in silence towards Churchbank; the afflicted captive making doleful sounds all the way, much to the amusement of the companions, and especially to the gratification of the rejoicing James Clanfield, who foresaw in the night's adventure a restoration of the alienated heart of his deceived Maria. His resolution was, that from that sack the prisoner should not escape, until she confessed her duplicity in the ear of Maria, and in the presence of his companion and himself. The confession was duly made; the captive was liberated. James and Maria were shortly afterwards duly married; Zybil became a laughing stock to the town, and black cats were less feared than formerly.

When I had reached my sixth year an occurrence took place, which it was feared would terminate in the blindness of one of my eyes. Still weak, and always suffering from headache,—although otherwise the symptoms of my affliction were gradually disappearing,—I was quite unfit to take part in those boyish sports which promote strength and activity. I could only look on whilst others were actively engaged. On one occasion I was thus sitting alone, a silent witness of the sports of the neighbouring children, when a mischievous boy, notorious in the street for his wild conduct, threw a stone at me which hit me on the right eye, wounding it severely. I remember quite distinctly at this moment that nothing could induce me to remove my hand from the wounded eye. For three months, day after day, I kept my hand upon it. The quantity of water which constantly trickled from the wound was surprising. I believe, however, that that occurrence was the means of removing the water from my head, and that the warmth of the hand tended to draw it out. To the wanton act of that boy I trace, under an overruling Providence, my deliverance from a disease which might have caused physical helplessness, or mental weakness for life. Previously, my parents had tried to teach me the alphabet, but they found it so difficult to give me an idea of the difference between one letter and another, that the sorrowful fear came upon them that it would be impossible to give me education. This apprehension was the more distressing from the fact that they were educated persons themselves, and of course knew its value; besides, seeing my physical weakness, they were anxious that I should acquire knowledge, not for its own sake merely, but as a probable means of obtaining honest bread, should it please God to spare my life. Judge, therefore, of their surprise when, after the healing of the wounded eye, they found that my acquisition of the rudiments of education was extremely rapid. It seemed as if some slumbering power had been suddenly awakened, some undiscovered faculty at once called into action. It is a fact, that in a few months from that time, I could read a chapter in the New Testament, not only without difficulty, but correctly and even fluently. And in a very short time I read with ease the whole of the Old Testament Scriptures. And not only so, but I remember distinctly that the books of the prophets, especially those of Isaiah and John, had a peculiar fascination for me. Chapter after chapter would I read unbidden. Indeed, Isaiah became my attraction, and neither for play nor food would I willingly leave that glorious composition. I used to read aloud; and old Jacob Brown, who lived next door, as he sat stitching and hammering at his trade of shoemaker, used to say in reference to my readings, "Ah! Tommy 'll be a parson, Tommy 'll be a parson! That's certain! Tommy's born for a parson!" I shall never forget, though it is impossible to describe the emotions produced in my young heart, at the age of seven or eight, by the ninth, eleventh, and sixtieth chapters of the evangelical prophet. The sixth and seventh verses of the ninth chapter used to throw me into a kind of rapture which no language can indicate. "For unto us a child is born, unto us a Son is given: and the government shall be upon His shoulder: and His name shall be called Wonderful, Counsellor, the mighty God, the everlasting Father, the Prince of Peace. Of the increase of His government and peace there shall be no end, upon the throne of David, and upon His kingdom, to order it, and to establish it with judgment and with justice from henceforth even for ever. The zeal of the Lord of hosts will perform this." The sixth and three following verses of the eleventh chapter especially afforded to me unmingled delight. I used to stand at a low table, with the family Bible open before me, and read them aloud; after which I would strut about the room repeating them in tones of triumph, as if I perfectly comprehended their meaning, and could dispute every inch of ground with the metaphorical theologians, who teach that these sublime sentences are to be understood as figurative descriptions of what the Gospel will effect in changing rude and wicked men to humble and loving saints. The passage to which I allude is—" The wolf also shall dwell with the lamb, and the leopard shall lie down with the kid; and the calf and the young lion and the fatling together; and a little child shall lead them. And the cow and the bear shall feed; their young ones shall lie down together: and the lion shall eat straw like the ox. And the sucking child shall play on the hole of the asp, and the weaned child shall put his hand on the cockatrice' den. They shall not hurt nor destroy in all my holy mountain: for the earth shall be full of the knowledge of the Lord, as the waters cover the sea." Of course I knew not then that the modern pulpit has abstracted the glory from those inimitable predictions, by affirming their metaphorical character; but to my young heart, brimfull of wonder and faith, there was no figure in them, but the grand utterances of literal realities about to take place at some future period of the world's history. Since then I have read Virgil, Pope, and Cowper, on the same fine theme; but with all their poetical beauty they have failed to bring back the exulting feelings produced in those early days.

"Ipsæ lacte domum referent distenta capellæ
Ubera, nec magnos metuent armenta leones—
Occidet et serpens, et fallax herba veneni
Occidet."—*Virgil.*

"The lambs with wolves shall graze the verdant mead,
And boys in flowery bands the tiger lead;
The steer and lion at one crib shall meet,
And harmless serpents lick the pilgrim's feet:
The smiling infant in his hand shall take
The crested basilisk and speckled snake;
Pleased the green lustre of the scales survey,
And with their forky tongue shall innocently play."—*Pope.*

"The lion, and the leopard, and the bear
Graze with the fearless flocks; all bask at noon
Together, or all gambol in the shade
Of the same grove, and drink one common stream.
Antipathies are none. No foe to man
Lurks in the serpent now; the mother sees,

And smiles to see, her infant's playful hand
Stretched forth to dally with the crested worm,
To stroke his azure neck, or to receive
The lambent homage of his arrowy tongue."—*Cowper*.

But whatever may have been the Latin poet's idea of the golden age, a passage of Scripture which has the power to call forth in the mere imitation such lines as these from our English bards, must be wonderfully suggestive and sublime. Of the effect produced on my mind by the sixtieth chapter I shall only say that it was one of unutterable admiration, and a strange longing to see and mingle with the magnificent scenes therein foreshadowed. The gorgeous scenery of the book of Revelation literally overwhelmed me. Often I sat down in my little chair in silent amazement, whilst tears ran from my eyes, and relieved my aching head.

On one occasion—and I remember it more distinctly than what took place in my own family circle yesterday—my mother left the house for half-an-hour. I was very weak, scarcely able to stand upright. I managed, however, to rise and read at the table a few favourite verses. Overcome by the exertion I sat down in a fainting state. I was then between seven and eight years of age. Whilst sitting in this state of utter helplessness, thinking that I should immediately die, I heard a voice—so at least I thought—saying in a soft but clear and distinct voice in my ear, but with this peculiarity that I fancied myself the speaker—" I shall not die but live, and declare the works of the Lord. The Lord hath chastened me sore: but He hath not given me over unto death." Instantly and involuntarily I lifted up my hands to heaven as if in prayer, and at that moment my mother entered the room. Seeing my strange excitement she ran towards me, exclaiming, "My child! what's the matter?"

"I thought I was going to die," I replied, "but now I am much better. I'm so glad you've come!"

"I was detained longer than I expected," she said, "but what made you anxious?"

"I feared you should find me dead."

"Dead! my dear child. Have you been reading?" she inquired, seeing the Bible lying open.

"A little," I said.

"Do you remember what it was?"

"Yes. In the tenth of John, where Jesus says, 'My sheep hear my voice, and I know them, and they follow me: and I give unto them eternal life; and they shall never perish, neither shall any man pluck them out of my hand.' And now, mother, don't be sad, for I know that I shall live."

My mother turned about, and put up her hand as if wiping away a tear.

These reminiscences are peculiarly interesting to me at this moment, as I look back through years never more to return. For, as Southey says,

> "Yet is remembrance sweet, though well I know
> The days of childhood are but days of woe."

My parents were in the habit of taking me with them to the place of worship which they attended. The minister, good man!—

> "An awful, reverend, and religious man,
> His eyes diffused a venerable grace,
> And charity itself was in his face—"

literally obeyed the command given to the prophet, "Cry aloud, spare not, lift up thy voice like a trumpet;" and the effect was, that I invariably returned from the service with an aching head. The voice of the orator rings in my ears sometimes yet! But excellent Zelotes—for so he deserved to be named for his fidelity, perseverance, and zeal, although Boanerges would better describe him as a public speaker—secured the affection and reverence of my heart, notwithstanding the pain he inflicted on the head. I shall have occasion to refer to this worthy man again, but I mention him here in connexion with an event which took place when I was entering on my eighth year.

My father came in one day and said to my mother, " Well, I have seen our minister about it, and he seems to think it a favourable opening, but advises me to see the farmer himself, and not to trust to any third party; and as I have just heard that he is in town at the market, I think we had both better go at once and see him." What all this meant I knew not. But speedily my mother took me by the hand, and we went to the market-place in the centre of the town. As we entered it we met a man who said to my father, "I was just going to your house to ask you to speak with Mr. Norison. He wants to see you. He is in the parlour of the Fox." To the "parlour of the Fox" we accordingly went. I had never been inside a public-house before, and the noise, and bustle, and number of people, somewhat alarmed me. I did not understand it, but I clung close to my mother's side. We were directed to the upper end of the room, where, at a side-table, sat three men talking very earnestly, all at the same time, and drinking a red liquid, which I afterwards understood to be rum. I was sorely puzzled to comprehend how they could understand one another when all were talking, and why one of them repeatedly struck the table with his hand. Our conductor introduced my father to the loudest talker of the three, whom he called " Mr. Joseph Norison." The other two retired to some little distance. Norison held out his hand, which shook a little, to my father and mother. We were seated, and the following conversation took place :—

Norison—" Ah! um! hic! glad yees cum, Mister Whats-i-may-call-'um! Understand horses? pigs? sheep? malting? Um! hic!"

" I know something about farming, Sir," said my father, " but it is some years since I had much to do with it."

Norison—" Ah! um, um, um! So I understand. Ye toonsfolks is—um, um, um!—poor farmers, he! he! hic! eh?"

" I suppose we are," said my father, drily.

Norison—" Glass of rum? Um, um! Yeer health; yeers, Mum," looking to my mother, who appeared to be in company she did not exactly fancy. " Health, youngster!" squinting towards me. Having uttered these benevolent wishes with incredible rapidity, Mr. Joseph Norison demonstrated his sincerity by lifting a wine glass-full of raw rum to his lips, which glass stood upon the table empty in the twinkling of an eye.

Before I report the sequel of the dialogue so intelligently begun, I may as well present you with a portrait of Norison. I do not know whether he ever " sat " to any artist, but as I have strong reasons for remembering the worthy—reason extending over five sorrowful years—I cannot be mistaken in the features. He was a tall, thin, cadaverous-looking person. His hair was closely cut. His forehead rose about an inch and a quarter above shaggy eyebrows. Where his right eye should have been, there was a hole with sealed lids. His left eye appeared like a little grey substance in the act of taking fire. His nose was thin and prominent, with a twist in the centre, as if had come in unfriendly contact with some hard substance, and deemed it prudent to yield to the shock. Out of his left nostril a small triangle seemed to have been scientifically cut. His mouth was large, the under lip exhibiting a tremulous motion, as if it had caught a fit of the ague; and his few remaining teeth stood like small bits of dirty indigo, fixed at irregular intervals. He had lost two fingers from his left hand; and his right leg, which was lame, lay under him as he sat, resting upon its side like half a coil of thick rope sheathed in cloth hanging from the chair. It was plain enough that he had been drinking freely on this occasion; but his mode of speech, which I have correctly indicated, was not the result of his libations at this time. He always spoke thus, with the addition of oaths and curses, which, although at the expense of strict fidelity, I do not choose to repeat. This is the proper place to add, that he could neither read nor write. Such was the gentleman who, moved by a strong desire to do good to the inhabitants of Warston, as he elegantly intimated, wished to engage my father as the overseer of his farm, and my mother as teacher of the youthful Warstonites.

" Yee's a trustworthy man? um!" said he to my father, after depositing a second glass of rum somewhere behind the indigo teeth, and venting an oath of undissembled surprise that my parents refused to drink. " A trustworthy man?—um! And you, Mum," to my mother, " is learned. Now, I'll make yee both a good—um!— offer. I'se often from home, buying and selling horses and tending markets."

" Yes, that he is," interposed the couple of kindred spirits, who had retired a little on one side, but who were strictly attentive to all that was passing.

" Tending markets; um! hic!" proceeded Norison, winking gratitude with his solitary orb for this seemingly unpremeditated confirmation of his veracity; " and I'll put everything, um! under yeer care — everything! Leave it all, um! D'ye see?"

" I should be happy to do my best for your interests," said my father; " but perhaps the responsibility will be too great if you are much from home."

" The—the—*what?*" said Norison, fairly staggered by the sound of the word responsibility, of which, as we afterwards found, he had not the remotest idea, either as it regarded his conduct towards God or man.

Without further continuing the conversation, I may say, in a word, that a few days afterwards my father agreed to the terms proposed to him by Norison, in the simplicity of his heart believing the promises of one of the most unprincipled persons that ever dishonoured the name of man.   My mother felt an unconquerable repugnance to this person, and predicted that nothing but disappointment and sorrow could issue from any connexion with him.   She was right.   Details I have no pleasure in giving, and shall therefore pass them over by merely stating, that after removing to the farm of Warston we found everything in wretched disorder—filth, waste, ignorance, barbarism, intemperance, and all the *et ceteras* naturally characteristic of the family of a notorious drunkard, horse dealer, and profane swearer.   All his promises to my parents were broken, and when reminded of them he denied them with horrid oaths.   I never knew a man, however bad, who had not some estimable quality, one little bright spot, upon which charity could rest for a moment, except Joseph Norison—" drunken Joe," as his servants honourably styled him.   But the fact afterwards came to light, that poor Joe himself, with all his cunning, had been outwitted.   He had fallen into the trap of his own avarice.   Desperately in debt, he was ever on the watch for prey.   One of his boon companions had assured him that my father, though seemingly poor, was possessed of considerable property, which he chose to conceal for reasons best known to himself. Joe handed a small "consideration" to his friend for this piece of information, and though my father assured him that his property was all gone, he disbelieved him, and rested not until, as has been said, he had induced him to remove to Warston, under the pretext that he was there to find useful employment as general overseer of the farm and everything therewith connected. Finding, shortly afterwards, that my father had spoken the truth, he poured his wrath against the deceiver upon the head of the innocent.

What was to be done now? There was plenty of work on the farm, but no wages. Trusting in God, my parents resolved to "make the best of a bad job." Seeing the children of the neighbourhood utterly neglected, the parents being mostly heathen, and the parish church and school being four miles distant, my mother thought she would adopt Norison's scholastic idea. By the assistance of some friends in Churchbank, from which Warston was eight miles distant, a small cottage by the side of the turnpike road was fitted up, and the intelligence was circulated that a day school was to be kept there. In a short time thirty or forty children were collected, at the rate of twopence a week each, but a more motley and unruly group never submitted their necks to the yoke of tuition. There was abundance of fish in the bays and around the neighbouring shores; in a short time my father, who was an expert and successful angler, obtained the use of a little boat, in which he spent many an hour, bringing home the finny treasures with a thankful and contented heart. I, too, began to find that I was no longer altogether useless. I was an excellent reader, and therefore a help to my mother in the conduct of the school. The fresh air and change of scenery had greatly improved my health, and by repeated solitary walks about the fields, the hills, and the sea-side, I not only gathered strength, but insensibly fell into the habit of musing long, and, as it appears to me yet, even consecutively on many subjects.

About this time Bunyan's " Pilgrim " fell in my way. I had already read the few books in our possession.   The character of my reading will be inferred when I name two or three of them:—Boston's " Fourfold State," Hervey's " Meditations," " The Crook in the Lot," Doddridge's " Rise and Progress," Baxter's " Saint's Rest," and a few others.   It will be thought these were sober enough studies for a boy not yet ten years old, but it is a fact that I took pleasure in them.   Hitherto, nothing approaching fiction had crossed my path ; my father would as soon have placed a barrel of gunpowder by his fireside as a novel on his bookshelf.   When Bunyan, therefore, came in my way, it was like the discovery of a new world. Columbus could not have exulted more when the western shores gladdened his eye.   Fancy, which had been a little excited by Hervey, now gave place to the higher attribute of imagination, which was liberally fed by the matchless Bunyan.   I revelled in the book, talked about it, dreamed about it, realised every scene and character with extraordinary vividness, and—what surprised my parents more than the excitement produced by the volume —perfectly understood that it was not a literal narrative but an allegory.   The introduction of this dirty old volume of the brilliant tinker to our house was rather amusing.   My parents had long known and valued the " Pilgrim," but they did not happen to have a copy in their possession.   One day, a strange-looking old woman called on my mother, and, with a mysterious air, said she wanted to have her advice about a book given to her by a pedlar in return for a night's lodgings.   She was " afraid it was a bad book, a pack o' lies," and, professing to be religiously anxious for the morals of her kindred, she would not let the suspicious volume lie about until she had obtained my mother's critical opinion. The chosen critic looked at the title-page, and a peculiar smile played on her countenance as she said to her enlightened visitor, " Will you kindly leave it for two or three days, for my little boy here to read? Look in, next time you pass this way, and he will give you his opinion." The poor soul was rather perplexed when the matter took this turn, and seemed to think the " Pilgrim" not so very dangerous after all, seeing that my mother wished *me* to become its reviewer.

My nervous sensibility was always painfully great, and several circumstances occurred shortly after our arrival at Warston which deeply affected me. By the wild and frightful stories which I frequently heard from the neighbours, my natural timidity was increased; and although my parents had instructed me concerning the goodness and love of God in Christ Jesus, yet there were certain dark and mysterious things which I ignorantly inferred from their Calvinistic creed, which caused me considerable pain and misgiving. I did not doubt that God was at once good and supreme, but then I imagined the wicked scarcely shared even in the protection of His government, and that Satan might have power to send witches, goblins, and other emissaries of terror far and wide. It occurred to me that the Evil Power, if under control, was still mighty; and that the control which was held over him had respect only to those who were chosen of God, and believers in Jesus. Now, could I have settled the question satisfactorily concerning my own faith, my apprehensions from the myriads of wicked agents with which superstition filled the land would have been removed; but as that was still a question, I was ill at ease. I wished to enjoy the safety of the good, but felt that doubt about the required character involved doubt respecting the desired protection. In this state of dismal uncertainty and foreboding I lived many months. I wandered about the hills and shores, musing on the mysteries of creation; sometimes I lay for hours on my back on some green spot, disturbed only by the passing of a bird or the bleating of sheep, and looking up to heaven, I wished to love God, and, if possible, to see some undoubted sign of His presence. I wondered much how a Being so great, and powerful, and good, who had created this beautiful world, and the surrounding heaven, sun, moon, and stars, could allow evil beings to exercise so much fearful influence over the minds and bodies of men; especially when I considered the great disadvantage of the latter, arising from their inability to *see* their spiritual adversaries. From the alleged practice of Satan in passing into the bodies of goats, cats, owls, ravens, and so forth, I imagined that he was not only unutterably wicked, but the vilest coward in existence, in making use of these dumb animals for the purpose of tormenting men. But suddenly the alarming thought struck me, that possibly his Bad Eminence might know the mental compliment I was paying him, and resolve on some terrible revenge. Again and again I heard my parents speak with pity of the people, and contempt of their superstitions; and of the fact, that a knowledge of the Gospel would exterminate all the tribes of ghosts and goblins; yet from the interest with which they seemed to listen to fairy legends, and apparently well-authenticated ghost stories, I was perplexed exceedingly. Unable to reconcile these things, my thoughts were only carried still further into the regions of spirit-world. The idea occurred to me frequently, that their verbal denunciation of the popular credulity was only a kind stratagem to keep me from dwelling on matters which might seriously injure my mind. Of course, from all this I passed into the old perplexing question of the origin of evil, little knowing at the time that it *was* an old perplexing question.

On one occasion I was lying by the side of a dark lake, in the middle of a wide heath, trying to solve this mystery. That lake was popularly believed to have been the scene of several tragedies; and to make the idea still more horrible, it was positively affirmed to be bottomless! Murders had been committed there on pedlars, for the sake of their money and trinkets, and their bodies thrown in, with stones to sink them. A certain squire, who was very cruel and unjust to his tenants, had ridden across this region on a dark winter's night, and lost his way. He met a strange-looking old man, who undertook to guide him. The squire gladly accepted the offer, but the horse was of a different mind; he, discerning beast! could not fancy the strange-looking old man at all, but snorted and plunged very uncivilly. Nevertheless, they proceeded together nearly a mile, when the guide said to the squire—" Now ride straight before you, and you will be *at home very soon.*" So saying, he touched the flank of the animal with his finger, at which he started as if a piece of red-hot iron had been plunged in his flesh, and sprang forward furiously. In a few seconds, horse and rider were in the dark lake; and, of course, as it is bottomless, they are rapidly sinking still! On the day to which I refer, I was lying on a green spot on the margin of this water, when after in vain attempting a solution of the question touching the origin of *evil,* my mind suddenly flashed to the question,—But what is the origin of *good?* Is not that as mysterious as the other? This thought was rapidly followed by another: Why is there *anything in existence at all?* Why not one universal blank; no God, no creation, no world? This thought increased in intensity. I vividly imagined *entire, universal, and eternal darkness and nonentity!* The hideous idea filled me with unutterable terror! I arose, trembling in every limb, and perspiring at every pore, and staggered homewards.

A night or two after this, a most appalling thunderstorm swept over our heads. I had no previous recollection of thunder. The storm began about eleven o'clock at night, and woke me out of sleep. I asked what it was. Peal after peal came with incredible rapidity, whilst the blue lightnings seemed to have set the heavens on fire. The thunder literally rattled like thousands of vast sheets of iron struck violently against each other by some superhuman power. Our little cottage shook as if about to fall and bury us in its ruins. The tempest continued for several long and terrible hours. It is impossible for me to give the faintest idea of my state of mind and feelings. My mother held me and tried to soothe me—but I felt that she was shedding tears, and trembled exceedingly, whilst I also knew that my father was on his knees in earnest prayer. Never shall I forget that night of terror; and even to this day, though I know, in the sublime language of Him who spoke out of the whirlwind, that God " maketh a way for the lightning of thunder," I cannot behold the symptoms of a gathering tempest without feelings of uneasiness. So indelible are the impressions made upon the young mind, just beginning to expand beneath the numberless influences and wonders of God's magnificent creation!

A fresh cause of excitement occurred shortly afterwards. A ship of the largest size had ridden at anchor for some time in the bay, about a mile from our house.

People had talked a good deal about this ship. They could not well understand why she lay so long, as favourable winds had occurred, of which, nevertheless, the captain had not availed himself. One dark evening the reflection of fire was seen on the horizon. People rushed out to ascertain the cause. There, on the bosom of the dark waters, lay the huge vessel, wrapped, from hull to topmast, in one vast shroud of glaring fire! For three days and nights the work of burning continued. If any effort was made to save her, it was entirely fruitless; but dark whisperings circled around that no such effort was honestly made—whisperings which, of course, stimulated my desire to know the origin and causes of things! The image of the burning ship now took possession of my mind, and, as usual, I extended it, and thought long about that time of terror when, in the dread language of Peter, " the earth also, and the works that are therein, shall be burned up."

The locality in which we lived was visited with heavy rains. A poor old widow, a neighbour of ours, who could not read, and who was very ill, lying, apparently, at the point of death, excited my sympathy. I took my little Testament with me one day, and went to her miserable hovel, and offered to read to her. She looked surprised, but at the same time thoughtful, and gladly accepted the offer. Among other portions of the sacred writings, I read the fourth chapter of the book of Revelation, in which occurs the description of a throne, surrounded by a rainbow. As I returned from this visit, a distance of about half-a-mile, a shower of rain fell, and then immediately I was startled by the appearance of a most magnificent rainbow. The colours were extremely vivid, and it appeared that I must pass directly under the glorious arch. Forgetting the wetting I had received, and everything else, I stood gazing like one entranced upon this sublime phenomenon. I recollected the promise of God to Noah—thought of the rainbow as a decided token of His presence and power—felt convinced that the evil things which alarmed me could not do me any positive harm, and resolved to trust in the protection of Him who made the rainbow!

CHAPTER III.

EARLY YOUTH.

" Whatever warms the heart or fills the head,
As the mind opens and its functions spread,
Imagination plies her dangerous art,
And pours it all upon the peccant part."—*Pope.*

JAMES BAKER, ESQ., J.P.—THE EVENTFUL MORNING—FEARS AND FAITH
—MY FATHER'S NARRATIVE—A CHRISTIAN—A JUVENILE FIGHT—
A SCRAPE—WRATH OF JOE—MR. ROBERT NELSON—REMARKABLE
DIALOGUE—I AM TAKEN TO TASK—GHOSTS AGAIN—THE RIVALS IN
BLACK—FRESH DESIRES FOR KNOWLEDGE—BUILDING A COTTAGE—
JOURNEY TO MOORNESS—STRANGE MISTAKE—"THE TRUTH"—
SOCIETY AT MOORNESS—RUSTIC LOVE—PRIVATE SECRETARY—
CURIOUS LOVE-LETTER—AN EXCITED LOVER—FAREWELL TO THE
LANGTONS.

ABOUT half-way between Warston and Churchbank stood
the residence of James Baker, Esq., J.P. This gentleman was agent for some Crown lands, and had the
power of letting certain portions thereof, at a nominal
rent, to parties disposed to build cottages, and reclaim
the long-neglected soil. Seeing the impossibility of
obtaining the means of living at Warston, where, through
the recklessness of Norison, everything was rapidly going
to ruin; and, especially, so far as we were personally concerned, the failure of the parents to pay for the education
of their children—a failure chiefly traceable to Norison
—my father resolved to apply to Mr. Baker for a few
acres of the ground referred to. After serious con-

sultation between my parents, this application was decided on, and a day fixed for the journey to Tankerhill Hall. We were in considerable trepidation as to the result. Would Mr. Baker grant a piece of ground, or would he not? seemed to be the absorbing question; although, in the event of his doing so, it was plain enough that my excellent father would only encounter fresh difficulties; for how was it possible for *him* to build a cottage and cultivate a piece of watery heath, where snipes and moor fowl had reigned supreme for many generations? The latter query, however, did not seem to trouble the good man. He had lived by faith for many years, and he saw no reason for departing from this rule of life at present. "To-morrow," said he, "will take thought for the things of itself. I will go and talk to Mr. Baker."

The eventful morning arrived. There was neither railway, steam-boat, nor stage; neither sailing packet, waggon, nor van; though, had there been either or all, my father would have chosen the venerable mode of conveyance which he adopted, namely, that which it is reasonable to conclude Adam took when he made the circuit of Paradise. Noon, afternoon, and evening arrived, but my father returned not. My mother became increasingly anxious. I was very unhappy. Completely under the dominion of a restless and morbid imagination, I thought and fancied all manner of hideous disasters; yet, strange as it may appear, I tried to console my agitated mother, assuring her that I was certain the cause of the delay, whatever it might be, would turn out for our advantage. Nor—though this mode of consolation was undoubtedly suggested by my tender love to her—did I doubt that it would be so. I fancied and feared evil; yet, by a strange and mysterious mental contradiction, of which, doubtless, many who will read this narrative have been conscious, I steadily believed that all was well with my father, and that his application had been successful.

The event happily scattered my fears, and justified the confidence I had expressed. At ten o'clock at night my father arrived, wet, wearied, and faint. A bit of cold fish, a crust of bread, and a cup of cold water refreshed him, and he related the day's experience thus :—

"I reached Tankerhill Hall at eight o'clock in the morning, and was told by a servant that Mr. Baker had gone to Churchbank an hour before, and would not return till twelve. To come back would be the loss of the entire day, and so I resolved to wait. I went a little way distant from the Hall, and sat down under a hedge. I had not rested long when a heavy shower of rain fell. Whilst sitting there a farmer passed, who, seeing me, stopped and inquired whether I would not go with him to his house, which was quite near, until the rain ceased? Of course, I gladly accepted the offer. He and his good wife were very kind, and it struck me that I should tell them my story. I did so. They had heard of us, and of Norison's conduct to us; and Mr. Underbrook, the worthy farmer, expressed surprise that I had not prosecuted Norison for his breach of engagement; but I said that I would leave all that concerned me to that good Providence which had thus far sustained me. Mr. Underbrook, on my mentioning our eldest boy* as being a pretty good scholar, said he should like to have such a youth to teach his family. The short of it is, James is engaged there."

"Engaged?" asked my mother.

"Yes."

"Then," exclaimed I, "I shall see James again!"

---

* I should have mentioned before that my brother was at school, twenty miles distant, with a relative of my mother.

" Yes, my boy," said my father, " I hope so, and that very soon; but I have more to say: would *you* like to go out? for Mr. Underbrook tells me of a Mr. Langton, three miles from Tankerhill, who wants a little boy to go errands, and promises to recommend you, if we think fit."

" Yes, I will go," I replied.

" *You* go from home!" said my mother, looking at me through tears; " and what will you do, poor child?"

" I will do whatever I am asked, if able; and if not, I will say so."

" There!" said my father, addressing my mother, " what do you think of *that?* Fear not. Tommy will do, if I am not mistaken."

" Well," said she, wiping her eyes, " and what about Mr. Baker?"

" At twelve, punctually, I was at the Hall, and saw Mr. Baker. He is very kind and humble. I believe him to be a really good man, and, from his conversation with me, I think he is undoubtedly what he professes—a sincere Christian."

" Thank God if we have found a *Christian* at last!" exclaimed my mother, on whose once fair and beautiful but now sorrow-stricken countenance a sweet smile played for a minute or two, as if a sudden rush of hope had emanated from that suggestive and honourable, but sadly abused name. The recollection of the deep impression which my mother's manner of pronouncing the term " Christian" made upon me at the time, together with many subsequent events of a somewhat similar character, led to the composition, years afterwards, of the following lines:—

> Who would not be a Christian? I have seen
> Men shrinking from the term, as if it brought
> A charge against them! Yet the honoured name
> Is full of gentlest meaning. Odours rise,

And beauty floats around it; from its eyes
Great tears of heavenly sympathy descend;
And mercy, soft as Hermon's fragrant dew,
Springs in its heart, and from its lips distils.
   I've seen it press an infant to its breast,
And kiss away his troubles; seen it take
An old grey-headed man, oppressed with years,
And wrinkled o'er with sorrow, and disclose
A prospect to his vision which hath made
The old man sing with gladness; seen it lay
Its soft hand gently on the blind and lame,
And lead them safely home; and seen it stoop
To the vile outcasts of society,
Whose character was odious in the streets,
And bring them back to virtue and to God!
   Hark! 'tis the loftiest name the language bears,
And all the languages in all the worlds
Have none sublimer! It relates to Christ,
And breathes of God and holiness; suggests
The virtues of humanity, adorned
By the rich graces of the Holy Ghost,
To fit them for the Paradise on high,
Where angels dwell, and perfect manhood shines
In the clear lustre of redeeming love,
For ever and for ever; and implies
A SON and HEIR of the ETERNAL GOD!

"Yes," continued my father, "I believe him to be a Christian, not merely from what he said, but from his manner, and his kind wishes. He inquired very particularly into my history and circumstances, and as I have no reason to conceal anything, I frankly told him all—not even omitting Mr. Underbrook's wish to have James in his family. When I had done, he smiled and said, ' Well, friend, I knew your history before. I have heard it all from my particular friend, your late pastor, who regards you highly, and is indignant at the way you have been used by the person who enticed you from Churchbank. I will allot you as much ground on Heathburn as I think you can properly manage, at a nominal rent for three years; and as I think it may be well for your eldest boy to try if he can be of any use to neighbour Underbrook's children, don't be offended if I offer to pay his travelling expenses home. So saying, he put a sovereign in my hand, shook hands with me, and hoped God would direct me."

My father sat back in his chair. My mother looked towards the fire-place, and said nothing, but I could perceive moisture beneath her eyes. I rose, after a few minutes' silence, and, softly laying my hand upon hers, said, in a whisper, " Mother ! did I not say that all would be good for us this day ?"

" You did, dear," she answered; " but how did you know ?"

" O ! I didn't *know*, I only believed."

" *Only believed !*" — she repeated — " only believed ! Happy reason. Never, never give it up, my child !" So saying she embraced me, and, after family worship, we retired to rest for the night.

Elated by these circumstances, though resolved to say nothing about them to Norison's sons, with whom I often met, and who, from sheer love of mischief, were in the habit of maltreating me, I was out early on the following day, and got into a sad scrape, which hastened our departure, at all events hastened mine, from the now hateful parish of Warston. Norison's time for sheepshearing was at hand. He and his farm servants had collected on a little hill, fronting our cottage, for this purpose. I went to look on. Whilst doing so, one of Norison's boys, a great, floundering, ignorant lad, came up to me and struck me. Enraged by this piece of wanton wickedness, I returned the compliment with such decision of purpose that my antagonist fell blubbering among the wool which had been taken from the sheep.

The father, seeing his boy in this predicament, limped towards me with his horse-whip—which he always carried with him, because, from his lameness, he generally rode on horseback—and tried to strike me, uttering at the same time a few of his choice oaths. I sprang aside so as to elude the blow, and ran as fast as possible towards home, calling out once or twice to the defeated and enraged pursuer, "Ah! ah! poor Joe! poor Joe!" I reached home quite alarmed for the probable consequences; told my mother what had transpired, and, as my father was not in, she begged me to hide myself for a little, as she well knew that Joe would not forgive, and that my father would probably be very angry with me.

In three or four minutes a scene occurred which I cannot better describe than by saying in a few words that Norison, followed by a troop of servants, rapped furiously at the door, which my mother opened, but dared him to enter. He poured out a torrent of oaths and foul imprecations, gnashing his teeth in impotent rage, and threatening the most summary vengeance, such as killing me, burning down the cottage, and similar benevolent purposes. My mother merely said, that, if I had used unbecoming language, she was sorry for it, and I should be chastised by my father, whose duty it was; but that he, Norison, should not cross the threshold of our door, and should not see the culprit. "But," she added, "what of your son, who severely struck my boy first, and began this quarrel?"

This very reasonable question acted like a spark of fire on gunpowder, and, if possible, aroused the wrath of poor Norison to a still fiercer degree of vehemence. He swore most fearfully, became black in the face, staggered, and fell. His servants lifted him up, carried him home, gave him two or three glasses of rum, and had the satisfaction of hearing him swear afresh—a conclusive proof that he had recovered.

There stood, about a stone's throw from the farm-house of Warston, a neat and somewhat elegant cottage, which, from its appearance, indicated both taste and substance. In this cottage lived Mr. Robert Nelson, a gentleman possessing a small independence. He was about sixty years of age, well informed, kind, good humoured, and the only man on the estate to whom the oppressed serfs of Norison could look for protection, as he was the only person in the neighbourhood of whom this accomplished personage stood in awe. The secret of Mr. Nelson's power over Norison was a mystery to the people; but it was manifest that that power was complete, and might have been used to the great advantage of the district, but for Mr. Nelson's indolence and love for the ludicrous. He seemed to think that if he thoroughly checked the farmer, there would be nothing to interrupt the monotony of life. But when his indignation was fairly aroused, and he walked over to the farm-house, with his oak stick in his hand, his eye-glass swinging in concert with the movements of his double chin, his step firm, and his lips portentously closed, woe to Joseph Norison! It was no small treat to the servants to see the whimpering, miserable cowardice of their master, when Mr. Nelson confronted him.

On the afternoon of this very day, the farmer, having quite recovered from his fit, was sitting sunning himself on a bench in front of the house, when suddenly the apparition of Mr. Nelson disturbed his equanimity. There were no electric telegraphs in those days; nevertheless, the tidings of his arrival reached the farm yard, the stables, and the kitchen, with incredible rapidity, and soon brought eager listeners on tip-toe, and " with 'bated breath," around the corners of the building. " Well, Joseph Norison," said Mr. Nelson, standing about six inches from the person addressed, and planting his walking-stick on the pavement with significant emphasis, " how long do you purpose taking yet, before you effectually learn the lesson which I have been trying to drive through your cracked scull for the last seven years ?"

Joseph, fortified by the red liquid which had restored him from his late attack of negro-colour, ventured to glance his solitary eye towards Mr. Nelson's lips, and said,

" Sir—um! hic!—I—I don't see what this—um!— means.   What lesson ?"

" Oh! don't you?   Then I have made no progress, as I had too much reason to fear, and must begin again."

" Ees, Sir," said Joseph, gathering confidence from Nelson's calmness, " I'se greetly 'bliged by um!—yeer 'tention and interest, um!"

Nelson—" I dare say, both interest and principal, eh? But I will have both from you, and that by a summary process, if you dare to molest, or say a word against, or disturb, or in any way maltreat those excellent people up yonder at the school.   You understand?"

Norison—" Ee, um!   What, what!   The little p— "

Nelson—" Hold, you fool of half a century old!   Don't make experiments on my patience *just now.*   It will be dangerous.   You understand THAT ?"

The tremendous shout with which " *that*" rang through the air and around the old buildings, making the eaves-droppers to start, and the sparrows to fly as if a fowling-piece had been discharged in dangerous proximity, instantly cowed Joseph.

Norison—" Ees, ees, Sir, what you wish, um! anything—hic! ees!"

Nelson—" What I wish? Very well. I have often wished you to learn a very simple lesson—namely, that it would be a libel on the donkey race to call you an ass; that it would be an unwarrantable excuse for your conduct to call you an idiot; and that to call you a blockhead would cause the wig on every barber's block in the kingdom to fly off with indignation."

Norison—" Ees, Sir."

Nelson—" Yes—very well. You admit all this. You admit that it would not be appropriate to call you any of these. Well, now listen. You are a tyrant, a scoundrel, and a coward; an oppressor of the poor, and a plague to your family. From sheer pity to them I have delayed selling you out, and sending you to the dogs to recompense you for the hundreds of dog-fights you have got up; but just try my patience again, by attempting to use *that* family as you have used many others, and your crocodile tears and disgusting whinings shall only add to the severity of my proceedings. Our Protestant church—but what a fool I am to name the church in your ears!—our Protestant church says there is no such place as purgatory. Well, I suppose not; but there is *another* place of still more awful character, where—though I am no parson—where, if you don't turn over a new leaf, you must of necessity find yourself; for *your* admission into heaven—when apoplexy shall strangle you, as it very nearly did this morning—I say, your admission into heaven is so perfectly preposterous, absurd, and ludicrous, that the idea makes one laugh outright. Good afternoon, Joseph—*Joseph*, indeed! What wiseacre christened the fellow by the name of that respectable gentleman?"

Norison—" Ees; good afternoon, Sir."

Mr. Nelson frequently spent an hour or two in our house, talking on various matters with my parents. He often said that for their sake he regretted that they ever came to Warston, where he himself resided, simply to see that the property of the farm was not absolutely wasted, as it was his only security for money he had lent to Norison; but on his own account he was pleased with the circumstance of our arrival, as it gave him an opportunity of chatting with intelligent people.

On this occasion he walked straight from the presence of the perturbed Joseph to our cottage. There was a queer smile on his large face when he entered. I saw at once that he had something to say, half comic, half serious. Bidding my mother good afternoon, and taking the seat she placed for him, he called me, saying,

" Well, my promising youngster, and so you are learning the way of the natives, are you? I am sorry to hear it. Fighting and calling names, eh? What have you to say for yourself?"

I explained the whole affair circumstantially. He listened with good-humoured attention, and then assuming an angry look, said,

" This is all very fine, sirrah; but I cannot allow you to frighten Mr. Norison this way, as I am the only person of whom he stands in awe, and I am too jealous to have my supremacy divided. A rival near my throne is out of the question. Remember that, and henceforth learn to curb your young spirit. The powers that be, sirrah! the powers that be; do you know who they are?"

" No, Sir, not exactly."

"Oh! you young Careless! Know, then, that Mr. Joseph Norison and Mr. Robert Nelson are the powers that be."

" I thought," said I, after a pause, " there was another —the ghosts."

" The ghosts !" he echoed, giving way to a hearty
explosion of laughter, " to be sure ; you are right ; I am
not supreme, after all. But what do you think ?" turning
to my mother; " I had an application of a serious kind
from Peter Gram, yesterday. Some of our honest people
have stolen poor Peter's wheelbarrow, and he applied to
me to raise the Devil to tell us where the barrow and the
thief may both be found. You know I have the reputation of understanding the black arts of free masonry,
and of being on intimate terms with a certain dark personage who is supposed to have a great deal to do with
this parish of Warston,—much more than the regularly
appointed and lawful clergyman."

" It would be well for the parish," said my mother,
" if the evil one had as little to do with it as the
clergyman."

" Well, at all events, the clergyman has the easiest
time of it. He does not labour half so earnestly as his
rival in black !" The speaker chuckled over his own
remark. I had crept close to my mother's side, and was
intently scrutinising Mr. Nelson's countenance, when
suddenly looking at me, he exclaimed, " What's the matter ? Are you unwell ? Poor fellow, how pale he is !"

I sat down, overcome by a rush of strange thoughts.
My mother gave me a little water, but I remained grave,
thoughtful, and almost silent during the evening. The
reader understands the secret of this. I had obtained a
new idea, a new link in the chain of mystery. A man
" raise" the evil one ! A respectable man on terms of
intimacy with *him !* That man also on terms of friendship with my parents ! Dreadful ! I was perplexed,
bewildered, and alarmed !

The events of the last few days had somewhat interfered with my usual musings, and with my strong desire

for knowledge. This occurrence sent my thoughts eagerly in the old channel, like waters, temporarily checked, rushing with increased velocity towards the great ocean.

> Hemmed in awhile, the furious waters roll,
> Like goaded coursers to the final goal;
> So mind, when checked, on latent passions feeds,
> And rushes onwards to ulterior deeds !

Thus I found it. "To know," became the verb of my existence, the ruling passion of my being. I had a craving for books, a craving which could not be satisfied. I was a good reader, a tolerable writer, and knew something of arithmetic; but these elementary acquirements tended only to whet, instead of allaying appetite. I had once and again heard that there was a school at Tankerhill, kept by a person named Jerome Brake, who was said to be a good man, and an efficient teacher. Respecting Jerome and his school I had many meditations, and not a few dreams; but I saw no prospect of placing myself at the feet of this wise man. Moreover, my father had spoken of Mr. Langton, and I had expressed willingness to go to him, and make myself useful to the extent of my limited ability. Should he call or send, I felt it would be wrong to draw back. Yet, Mr. Jerome Brake had my heart, and the imaginary bliss of his favoured pupils drinking the waters of knowledge at his feet in Tankerhill school occupied my imagination. Besides, how would going to Langton advance me? To get knowledge there, of the kind I desired, would be impossible; and I fervently hoped he would not send for me.

I mentioned all this one day to my parents. They were sad on account of their inability to comply with my wish. "But," suggested my mother, "suppose that Mr. Langton should engage you for three months, and give you a few shillings for your services. By that time we hope to remove to our little house at Heathburn, which is only a mile and a half from Tankerhill school, and thus you will be much nearer than you are now, and be able to pay school fees for a short time out of your own earnings."

This suggestion was as eagerly adopted as it was well-timed. I felt a degree of satisfaction, which I fear was nearly allied to pride, in the thought of paying for my own education; and I now became anxious for Mr. Langton's arrival. My father had begun to collect building materials for his contemplated cottage at Heathburn, and, with the aid of former settlers in the locality, cherished the hope of getting it ready before the severe winter set in. He walked daily to the scene of his labours, a distance of four miles, and returned at night, faring poorly, always exhausted, but never complaining. It was agreed that he should take one day to go to Mr. Langton's, which lay nearly five miles off in another direction, and take me with him. The eventful day came. I bade farewell to my mother, with aching heart and streaming eyes. We reached the farm of Moorness about noon. The house was a large, old-fashioned, straggling building, evidently erected at different times, with not the remotest conception of architectural symmetry, but solely with a view to convenience. Dwelling-houses, barns, stables, cow-sheds, and so forth, stood in admirable disorder, presenting a perfect labyrinth to the stranger. Even my father, who had often seen such places, was at a loss which was the habitation meant for the biped, and which was that intended for the quadruped portion of this social community. He surveyed the coast for some time, and then proceeded to the door of what, from its rather new and clean exterior, he judged a dwelling for the lords of creation. He rapped. Something between a grunt and a groan replied. Fancying that the voice meant to say " Come in," he opened the door. Our eyes fell upon a litter of pigs in the centre of the building, surrounding a large sow, who was grunting to her young in very endearing terms; while, in the corner, we espied some two or three horses at fodder. We were about to depart, when the door suddenly shut with violence, a rough grasp seized my father by the collar, and a rougher voice growled, " Thief! have you at last! Lost two already by your knavish tricks, besides fowls and corn! Shan't escape this time!" We were in total darkness. I screamed. My father tried to speak, but could not, from the eagerness of the fellow's gripe. A thought struck me. Creeping to the door, I pulled it open. When the light entered, the guardian angel of the premises instantly relaxed his grasp, and muttered something intended for apology. My father at once accepted it, but, at the same time, begged to assure the man that whatever he might think of his fidelity as a thief-catcher, he could not, conscientiously, praise his discernment.

This little adventure over, we were conducted to the human department of the establishment, and introduced to Mr. and Mrs. Langton, a worthy couple, whom I shall ever regard with respect and esteem, and who have, at this time, sons in different parts of the world, respectable merchants, whom I number among my personal friends.

The arrangement was soon effected. I was engaged to remain three months at Moorness, to do whatever I was required, to have plenty to eat, and, at the termination of the stipulated time, to receive the round sum of *five shillings.*

Mr. Langton was an office-bearer in the chapel which my parents attended. He recognised my father at once from this circumstance, as the vigilant man who had been stationed to keep watch over the interesting family of pigs had previously done. I remember Mr. Langton asking my father how it was that he came so far every Sunday to chapel. He replied, because he could not hear those who did not preach the truth. I had heard a remark of this kind frequently before, but, for some reason which I do not understand, it arrested my attention now for the first time.

"The truth,"—I reflected. Do not all clergymen preach the same thing? Are they not all servants of God? Can there be several Gospels? And how should hearers judge of the truth, and pretend that they know better than clergymen who are educated at College for the purpose of teaching others? And then the fact struck me that there were different religious parties— Churchmen, and various classes of Dissenters. My parents had given me some information on these topics, but the whole thing came upon me as new at this time. I pondered it much; and, after the trouble and longings of the first few days, in a strange place, among strange people, I determined to ask some one for light on the matter.

I had the happiness of seeing my parents once a week, from the fact that we met in the chapel every Lord's day, when my mother's health would permit her to travel so far; and when this was not the case, I was allowed to visit home on the evening of Saturday. My time at Moorness would have passed pleasantly enough, but for the restless longing after something—I could not tell what —something higher, future, mysterious. With the boys and lads on the farm I had very little mental sympathy;

but as it is the simple truth, I must say, even at the risk of something like self-praise, they all loved me for my constant efforts to do them acts of kindness. I often made peace between young belligerents, aided them as far as I could in their little difficulties, and derived especial pleasure from teaching them to read. There were several young men and women who could not write legibly, and when an opportunity occurred of corresponding with their relatives, so as to evade the crushing postage of those days, I was in great demand as an amanuensis. In fact, I was chosen private and confidential secretary to some half-dozen persons, each of whom had the fullest confidence that I would not divulge secrets. It may be imagined that sometimes very *delicate* matters were entrusted to my " honour." A new and totally unexpected field of knowledge was thus laid open before me. The region of love lay in enchanting novelty, in various directions, of which the old homestead of Moorness was the centre. The son of Mercury and Venus refused not to visit the clod-breakers and milk-maids. The beautiful winged boy, with his bow and quiver, found as genial employment in our rustic commonwealth, as he does in the mansions of elegance and wealth. Perhaps it would scarcely be correct to say of the young farmer, what Hypolito says of his friend—

> " —— He is in love with an ideal;
> A creature of his own imagination;
> A child of air; an echo of his heart;
> And, like a lily on a river floating,
> She floats upon the river of his thoughts!"

But though the farmer's fair one was more substantial than *that*, she both thrilled and filled his honest heart; she was all the world to *him*; and, though professed judges of female loveliness might have passed by Mary without a second glance, John saw in her that which subdued and elevated his heart, fired his ambition, prompted him to honest and persevering toil, and led him, even in his obscure and unknown walk in life, to feel that this earth is not all dreary and sad, but that the benign Father has thought of the sons of toil, and has provided for them seasons of joy, and sources of consolation, which gold cannot purchase, and which poverty cannot remove.

Some of the love epistles which I had the honour of writing were rich, both in style and sentiment, not to speak of love and promises, beyond imagination. My friends had no such thing as a "Model Letter-Writer" at hand. The book-shelf at Moorness carried no such volume; and I am certain, if you had put it into their hands, they would have flung it aside with disdain. Something with less elegance and more heart was desired. I would fain give a specimen of those earnest effusions, as I think I might do so *now* without any breach of confidence; but I cannot recollect a single perfect specimen. Professor Owen can rebuild a pre-adamite monster from two or three inches of bone; but I cannot re-construct an authentic ante-nuptial love epistle from memory. I remember, however, the case of a young man, who came to me mysteriously one beautiful moonlight evening, and asked if I would oblige him by writing a letter for him, and if I could see to do it by the light of the moon. We sat at an open window, Luna graciously patronising the enterprise by her most radiant smiles. In a short time, pen, ink, paper, and scribe were ready.

"Well, Pat," said I, "what shall I say?"

"Why, of course," replied Paterson, "begin with love."

"Hadn't you better name the party first?"

"The party? it isn't a *party*, you know—it's only Jess Brown."

"O! well, then, here goes:—' Dear Jess—' Shall I say Brown?"

"No, no! not Brown—love; dear Jess, love."

"Very well. ' Dear Jess, love.' What next, Pat?"

"What next? O, no jokes, now! *You* know; just put love here, love there, and love everywhere."

"Do you mean that I am to fill the sheet with the word love?"

"Yes, exactly; good! nothing better!"

"Nonsense, Pat; Jess will think you crazy."

"Will she? then do it; quick! quick! That's the very thing! I am crazy—crazy with love. Do!"

Here Paterson leaped from his chair, threw up his cap to the ceiling, danced about the room like a lunatic, knocked over everything in his way, and at last struck me on the back with such earnest affection that I felt the pain for several hours, exclaiming, " Bless you, Master Thomas! We all loves you. Such a scholard! Come, finish that letter, and—here's a bit of wax. Come."

"What *shall* I write, Paterson? Tell me, for the moon won't stay up all night to please either you or Jess Brown."

"What you like, so be there is love in it."

"Do you mean to leave it to me?"

"Joyfully!"

I immediately wrote as follows:—

" DEAR JESS,

" I am so deeply in love—in *love*—don't mistake me—with you, that I can neither eat, nor sleep, nor work, nor walk, nor do anything else. I am nearly, if not quite, mad.   Will you cure me by a short letter, saying that you are just in the same state respecting me?

" I am yours only and for ever,

" JOEL PATERSON."

I read this absurdity to him, asking, " Will that do, Pat?"

" Do!" he exclaimed, throwing his unfortunate cap once more to the ceiling; " do! there isn't a member o' King George's parliament that could equal it!"

" That I sincerely believe," said I, thoughtfully; " but will you really send this to Miss Brown?"

" To-morrow, if Jack Tramp calls here."

On the following day Jack Tramp did call; the important epistle was sent; the post-office was duly defrauded of sevenpence halfpenny; and in three months thereafter Joel and Jess were made one flesh.

By that time, however, I had left Moorness; had received my stipulated sum of five shillings; had gone to Heathburn; had seen my parents in their new house; had applied to Jerome Brake, at Tankerhill school; had been duly entered as a scholar; had commenced my studies of Lindley Murray; had seen my brother ruling copy-books and dictating lessons to Mr. Underbrook's family as their private tutor; and had felt the inspiration of new ideas, of which more anon.

I cannot, however, bid farewell to the family of the Langtons, without expressing an earnest good wish for them all.   The worthy couple, whom I first knew in their days of youth and health, the estimable parents of an esti-mable family, are now well stricken in years.   Yet, when last I heard of them, they were in good spirits, enjoying the green old age of a temperate and pious life, the affection of a neighbourhood where their example and conduct did much good, and the love of a noble-looking group of sons and daughters, whom they had instructed in the grand lessons of love to their fellow-creatures and to God. Long may they all live, and in due time may they meet in that happy world, where there will be no separations, for ever! And, were it not that it might appear somewhat affected, I would add a very hearty Amen!

CHAPTER IV.

SCHOOL DAYS AND SCHOOLFELLOWS.

"These trifling objects then my heart possessed—
These trifling objects still remain impressed;
So when with unskilled hand the idle hind
Carves his rude name within the sapling's rind,
In after years, the peasant lives to see
The expanding letters grow as grows the tree;
Though every winter's desolating sway
Shake the hoarse grove, and sweep the leaves away,
That rude inscription, uneffaced, will last,
Unaltered by the storm or wintry blast."—*Southey.*

CURIOUS DIALOGUE — MR. JEROME BRAKE — A TRIFLING ACCIDENT — POLEMICS—PALESTINE—MYSTERIOUS FEELINGS—THE REV. SMITH SMITH—"THE JEWISH QUESTION"—THE SONG ON THE MOOR—SAD SOLILOQUY — ABSOLUTE POVERTY — LITERARY CURIOSITY — THE WEDDING—THE REV. MR. WARPET—MADMEN AT LARGE—SONG— A NEW SITUATION—MR. AND MRS. ROLF—I RESOLVE TO LEAVE— THE DYING YOUNG LADY—THE TURNING POINT—FEARFUL STATE OF MIND—INTELLECTUAL AND MORAL CONVERSION—GREAT JOY— ALARMING TEMPTATIONS—MY NEW MASTER—THE EVENING SCHOOL — "THE SEVEN" — STUDIES — DEBATING SOCIETY — APPROACH OF CHOLERA—UNIVERSAL GLOOM—PRAYER—A FATAL EPIDEMIC—PERSONAL ILLNESS—FELICITY IN THE PROSPECT OF DEATH—RECOVERY.

"STAND!" said Mr. Brake.   At the word of command, the scholars rose.   The schoolmaster then, with evident reverence, offered a short prayer for the direction and blessing of God during the day. The prayer was marked by earnestness, and the new scholars, namely, myself and another, were particularly referred to. From that moment, I loved Mr. Jerome Brake. "A good beginning," thought I. After prayer, the owners of the respective copy-books were called. Presently all the scholars who could write were busy as scribes.

"Master Thomas!" said Mr. Brake. I arose and went to the desk.

"Have you put your cap in the proper place?"

"Yes, Sir."

"What do you wish to learn?"

"Geography and English grammar, Sir."

"These are five shillings a quarter."

"Very well, Sir."

"The practice of this Institution is payment in advance."

My five shillings were burning in my hand. I longed to get rid of them. I handed the sum to Mr. Brake. He received it with a gracious smile.

"Which books have you, Master Thomas?"

"I have 'Boston's Fourfold State,' 'Paley's Works,' 'Paradise Lost,' and——" *

"Stop!" said the schoolmaster, with evident astonishment, opening his mouth, which was a remarkably large member, and suddenly growing about six inches taller, as if an internal spring had been touched. I started back with surprise and fear, apprehensive that I had committed some indiscretion. He continued to stare at me, deliberately pushing the fingers of his right hand through his hair, and making the most grotesque grimaces, opening and shutting his large mouth, and darting up and down as if the imaginary spring-work had been set

* How, or where, I had received Paley and Milton, I cannot remember; but that I had read both is certain. My impression is, that they were given to me by a literary gentleman in the neighbourhood of Moorness.

actively in motion. I continued my retrograde movement, still keeping my eye fixed on the never-to-be-forgotten face of my teacher, until, suddenly kicking my heels against a form, I fell on my back on the floor, much to the delight of the assembled scribes, who sympathised with my misfortune by a low titter. At the same moment, I heard the voice of Mr. Brake slowly repeating, as if it were the last vocal effort he meant to make in this world—" Bos—ton, Pa—a—ley, Par—a—dise Lost! The boy's a —! Here, Thomas! Are you hurt?"

" No, Sir, thank you."

" Silence!"—addressing the giggling juveniles. " Do you mean to say, Master Thomas, or imply, or intimate, that you have brought the fervent Boston, and the immortal Paley, and the celestial Milton—always excepting his unholy republican propensities—to Tankerhill school with you, as elementary educational auxiliaries from which you anticipate assistance?"

" Sir?—I—I beg your pardon."

" Oh! perhaps you do not realise the literal import of my query in the exact form in which my phraseology hath exhibited it to your comprehension."

I looked about in despair, involuntarily moving my hand, as if I wished to lay hold on something by way of support.

Evidently enjoying the effect produced by his erudition, the schoolmaster, after a pause of a few seconds,— during which he looked as if he meant to read the secrets of my soul,—took pity on me, and said,

" Where are the volumes you have designated?"

" At home, Sir."

" Well, you will require school books. Shall I provide them for you?"

" If you please, Sir."

" That will do. Take your seat."

Mr. Jerome Brake was about thirty years of age, of rather low stature, and a dark complexion. One of his legs was some three or four inches shorter than the other; and when he was excited he always drew himself up by a sudden spring upon the longest, at the same time elevating his eyebrows, casting his eyes on the ceiling, opening his mouth, pushing his right hand through his hair, and uttering a singular ejaculation which sounded something like " Croush!" What particular signification he attached to this outlandish monosyllable I do not know, and need not conjecture. It was, however, frequently repeated in the course of the day; and whenever it greeted our ears we were sure to see the tall leg in requisition. He never exclaimed " Croush!" when resting on the secondary limb. In religion Jerome was a rigid Churchman, and in politics an equally rigid Tory. He held in abomination every ecclesiastical and political opinion which diverged a hair's breadth from his own. Having made up his mind that he was right, it followed that to differ from him was to be a heretic. But he was passionately fond of discussion, probably from the conviction that he was sure to conquer his opponent in argument. Whether this conviction was justified by facts I shall not say; but, in addition to the extraordinary style in which he indulged, it is certain that in his polemical enterprises he always managed to have the last word, and fairly demolished his antagonist by springing on the tall leg and shouting " Croush!"

There were some young men in the neighbourhood who were as keen in controversy as Jerome himself, and many long and animated discussions were the consequence. If the truth must be told, I was not a whit behind the rest in the eagerness with which I vindicated my chosen notions, and in the dexterity with which I tried to cover the enemy with defeat. I had not been long at school when Jerome discovered that, in matters relating to Church and State, I was a sad heretic. He looked upon me with considerable coldness for a time, mingled with something like a ludicrous anxiety for my conversion to his own views; but having learned from one of the young men that I could show cause, I was admitted to the fellowship of wranglers, my youth notwithstanding. Those intellectual combats took place after school hours, and ultimately led to the formation of an important Debating Society in the town of Churchbank, of which I shall speak more fully in due course.

My three months at Tankerhill school vanished as every quarter of a year does. In the study of English grammar I did very well. The verb "To love" was duly impressed on memory, and conjugated. Geography, however, excited a powerful influence on my imagination. A desire to see the world, and to behold the different countries, and tribes of men, filled my mind. The wish to travel became painfully strong; and the impossibility of gratifying that wish only added fuel to the spark which had been kindled. The East, the famous, celebrated, mysterious East, especially claimed my thoughts. To see Palestine, Bethlehem, Nazareth, Jerusalem, was my daily wish.* To describe the absorbing interest with which I regarded the City of David at that time is literally impossible. How is this, and what are the peculiar fascinations of the Orient world?

Civilisation, arts, letters, religion, arose in the East. The progress of man, like that of the sun, has been

---

* I may just say, in a note, that this desire remains unabated and ungratified to this day. Hope of seeing those lands has almost died; and the perusal of Oriental travels only tantalises instead of satisfying me.

westward. By the aid of a hoary antiquity, we can trace the stream of population to its Orient spring, and watch it gliding westward over hill and dale, mountain and valley, ocean and continent. It seems to have followed the track of the solar luminary, and to have been guided in its movements by the inclination of his beams. The sun appears to have been the first great traveller and discoverer. From his lofty path he saw what was concealed from the circumscribed vision of the plodders upon the surface of the earth; and, like a giant in the heavens, he pointed with his finger to great lands stretching far away, to new worlds upon which he would gaze before he " pillowed his chin" upon the far-off western wave. Men understood the signal; and finding the cradle-land "too narrow by reason of the inhabitants," forced their way through all the difficulties of primeval forests, howling deserts, and trackless seas. " Spreading westward" was the historic fact for many centuries. " Spreading westward" is the historic fact still; and, though America has been added to the great world of population, activity, and energy, the "far West" continues the object of desire. Let this passion be gratified a few years longer, and extremes will meet, if mighty seas forbid not. The globe will be surrounded, and the emigrant to the " far West" will find himself erecting his log hut by the side of the Orient's tent.

It would seem, however, that notwithstanding the migrations occasioned by the love of novelty, the necessities of existence, the driving pestilence, and the fortunes of war, men cannot forget the East. The lapse of ages, the rise and fall of dynasties, and the birth, growth, and decay of mighty empires are unable to erase from the *memory*—shall I call it?—of humanity that the *East* is its native place. There is deep meaning in this yearning

of the heart towards the birth-land of the race. It is
not the Jew only, but also the Gentile, who experiences
this strong feeling. Undoubtedly, the Bible has much to do
with this clustering of the affections around the scenes
of sacred story—this turning of the heart to the soil first
kissed by the rising light of day — this involuntary
sympathy with all that relates to the supposed locality of
Eden, and the home of the glory and disgrace of our
first parents—and this excitement of the emotions when
the Holy Land—the land of patriarch, prophet, and
Saviour—is named in our hearing; but sometimes, in
our wild day-dreams, we imagine that our acquaintance
with Biblical geography and story is *but the renewal* of
knowledge which has accidentally slipped from memory—
a recalling of events with which we were familiar, ere
yet we had lisped the sweet name of " Mother," or nestled
in her bosom for repose. Of course, this is a trick of
the fancy; but how to account for it is a problem, which
I may venture to challenge the whole constellation of
philosophers to solve. I would consider that man the
wisest of his generation who could satisfactorily answer
the following questions:—What is the origin of that
mental picture which, when we are placed amidst circumstances and scenery which are absolutely new in our
history, presents itself before us with the impression that
these circumstances and scenes are *not* new, and gives
the idea, notwithstanding our knowledge to the contrary,
that we had seen all this before ? How is it that, though
angry with ourselves for the notion, we are moved by a
strong effort to recollect the time when we *saw* these
scenes ? Is it the vivid realisation of a forgotten dream?
Or has the spirit the faculty of sight independent of the
body; and when the bodily presence is brought to the
spot which the spirit had previously visited, does it

tantalise its sluggish companion by the idea that this is only a fresh visit to a long-since familiar place? The idea I wish to convey is so subtle and ill-defined that I can scarcely hope to place it in the reader's possession; yet I think I shall be understood for all that, as, doubtless, the experience of others is similar to my own in this very mysterious matter.

But, dreams and visions apart, men are everywhere turning to the East with unprecedented earnestness, expectations, and longings. To ask the reason of this, would lead us back to the region of speculation; but the *fact* is unquestionable. The literature of travels increases with unusual rapidity, and the people do read and will read everything of the sort, good, bad, or indifferent, especially if it relate to the *East.* The thirst for knowledge respecting the manners, customs, peoples, climate, politics, religions, topography, and scenery of that part of the world is daily increasing. The supply is large, but it cannot satisfy the still larger demand. It is well. There is prophetic meaning in all this. Does it not indicate a secretly working Providence? Are there not grand predictions waiting fulfilment, which, perhaps, require, as a preliminary condition, that the eyes of western nations be fixed on the lands of sacred narrative, and especially on the inheritance given to Abraham, and to his seed after him? Indeed, that inheritance cannot be forgotten, so long as the Book of our faith—beautiful and blessed Book!—is the most popular volume in the world; is in the hands of millions, and in the hearts of myriads; and is the text from which, every first day of the week, thousands of pulpits are supplying information to listening throngs. That information, sweeping over history, doctrine, and prophecy, cannot avoid the land through which the famous Jordan runs, nor omit to

mention often the mystery-wreathed metropolis of old
Judea. Jerusalem shall be held " in remembrance !"
A glory awaits it yet, surpassing all its former splendours;
and the East—the land of poets and prophets, the magnet
of Christian hearts, and the scene of the marvellous
works of the Man of Sorrows —is destined to command the
attention of all the nations of the peopled globe. The
land whose hills and valleys first embrace the beams of
the rising sun, waits a light of immeasurably greater
splendour; and the man who believes *this*, whatever
interest he may take in other portions of the earth, is not
likely to lose sight of the country where Abraham, Isaac,
and Jacob dwelt in tents.

My teacher *did* believe this. On " the Jewish Question" he was more than in earnest. He was an enthusiast
on the subject; yet he supported his opinions by strong
reasons, and seldom failed to silence the opponent of the
national restoration of the Hebrews. One of his oppo-
nents was the Rev. Smith Smith, the clergyman of the
parish. Mr. Smith was a man of considerable ability;
had the reputation of being a kind neighbour; was
faithful in the discharge of his parochial duties, and
seldom took part in denominational struggles, excepting
on Church-property occasions, when, having the law on
his side, you always found him on the side of the law.
The parish church was very near the school. The juxta-
position was, I think, natural and proper. Does it not
suggest that education should be Christian?—that there
should be harmony between the clergyman and schoolmaster?—that, essentially, the functions of both recognise
the spiritual nature of man?—and that both require the
direction which is afforded by revealed and infallible
truth? On these points the clergyman and schoolmaster
were agreed, as well as on most others of either an eccle-

siastical or political character, but on questions relating to the future of the Jewish people they could not see eye to eye.

The minister held that the natural descendants of Abraham will be converted to Christianity by the preaching of the Gospel, and will then become identified with the nations, so that the distinction between Jew and Gentile shall cease and be forgotten, and all the world shall become influenced by, and remain under the influence of, pure religion. His descriptions of the happiness of mankind under this state of things were very fine, and almost amounted to poetry. To support his views, however, he found it necessary to turn into metaphor hundreds of very plain predictions, a procedure against which the teacher, notwithstanding his reverence for the minister, very earnestly protested.

Returning from school one afternoon, my thoughts were fixed on a discussion of this kind, to which I had just listened. I thought of the strange history of the Hebrew people; their privileges, their folly, their wickedness, sufferings, wanderings, and preservation as a distinct people. I thought of the departed glories of the metropolis of Judea, and very earnestly hoped that Mr. Brake's assurance, that it is destined to be rebuilt in greater splendour than ever, might prove correct. I had to pass over a moor of considerable extent; the weather was cold and wet, and the darkness was fast setting in. About the centre of the moor were the ruins of a shed. By whom or for what purpose this humble building had been erected no one seemed to know, but it was now in a state of entire dilapidation. As I passed on this occasion, I thought I heard a low sound proceeding from the shed. I listened, and heard a feeble voice singing in broken notes the following fine old lines:—

" O, mother dear, Jerusalem !
  When shall I come to thee ?
When shall my sorrows have an end ?
  Thy joys when shall I see ?

" When shall these eyes thy heaven-built walls
  And pearly gates behold ;
Thy bulwarks with salvation strong,
  And streets of shining gold ?

" There happier bowers than Eden's bloom,
  Nor sin nor sorrow know ;
Blessed seats ! through rude and stormy scenes,
  I onward press to you.

" Why should I shrink from pain and woe,
  Or feel at death dismay ?
I've Canaan's goodly land in view,
  And realms of endless day.

" Apostles, martyrs, prophets there,
  Around my Saviour stand ;
And soon my friends in Christ below,
  Will join the glorious band.

" Jerusalem, my happy home !
  My soul still pants for thee ;
Then shall my sorrows have an end,
  When I thy joys shall see."

That the voice was that of an aged female there could be no doubt, and from the long pauses I judged that the singer was in a state of exhaustion. I did not like to enter the shed suddenly, lest I should disturb her, as she doubtless considered herself quite alone. I therefore retired silently a few yards, and then returned coughing, so as to attract her attention. The device was successful. A poor, feeble creature, with a staff in her hand, appeared by the side of the broken wall. I said, " Good evening." She put her hand to her face, over which tears had been falling. I asked if she felt unwell.

" No, thank you, master," she replied ; " blessed be *His* name, I'm very well and happy, but a little tired. The good lady at the Hall has given me a bag of potatoes, and I'm trying to get them home. Would ye be so kind to help lift them on my back?"

I asked where her home was. She named the place—a wretched hovel on the edge of the heath, about a mile distant, which I had frequently noticed.

"Where is your burden?" I asked.

"In the shed," she replied, beginning to move towards it. I sprang past her, seized the bag, and threw it on my back.

"Come, mother," I said, "I'm going your way. I'll carry it for you." The unfeigned surprise of the poor creature actually surprised me in turn.

"No, no!" she said, "no, no; a young gentleman carry *my* burden!" and she attempted to seize it.

"Come," I said, "walk along quietly—I shall walk as slow as you like—but I mean to have my way, and I fear you're not strong enough to prevent me."

"Well," she said, "ye'll be rewarded, though not by Jane Renton;" and then, speaking to herself—as we travelled slowly over the moor—"he called me '*Mother!*' Yes—there was a time when my son—my boy—my own child—called me so. Yes, 'Mother.'—O! it was a name *I loved*, and—and, yes, I loved him that called me ' Mother;'—O Edward! I love you yet, and yours; and forgive you,—freely,—freely,—as I've been forgiven. Yes, yours I forgive and pray for—though your son, so like what his father was, twenty years ago,—fair and clever,—threw a piece o'turf at his poor grandmother this—this very day—and called her a poor beggar. Well, I am! Yes—how long? O good Saviour, give me—give me patience! '*Mother!*' blessings on the lips that said it!"

I could not avoid hearing this sad soliloquy. I did not like to interrupt her by speaking, and when, once or twice, I stepped a little quicker, I saw that she attempted to keep pace with me, which was too much for her. I therefore had to listen. She took much more time uttering the above, than the reader has taken in reading it. She moved her head slowly from side to side, as she spoke, her thin white hair trembling in the wind over her deeply-furrowed brow and face. Her clothing was miserably mean for the wet, cold evening, even if she had been thirty years younger. There are numberless sad sights in the world, and one of the saddest to my feelings is to see a grey-headed woman, of seventy years, walking feebly by road or street in a wintry day, covered only with a thin garment, which, from long use, seems to cling to the body, but which is incapable of securing necessary warmth. And this was the appearance of my poor companion.

We reached her sorry dwelling. The rain was now falling fast. I entered at her request, and saw poverty in its absolute sense. For a chair, she had a large stone. There was no table, and no substitute for it. What she termed her bed, was a little straw in a corner, over which a ragged coverlet was thrown. The roof of the old hovel was leaky, and when it rained, she moved the straw from place to place, to the spots where least rain fell. She had no fuel, but intended to go out again to search for bits of wood and patches of turf, that she might boil a few potatoes, which were the only article of food she possessed. And yet this old woman was happy. What made her so? What was the secret of her contentment? The song I had heard on the moor suggested the secret, and it was confirmed by her own aged lips; for taking from a crevice in the wall of her cottage a much-used copy of the New Testament, she handed it to me, saying, " Will you please read the seventh verse, fifth chapter of first Peter?"

I turned to the passage and read, " *Casting all your care upon Him; for he careth for you.* "

Reaching home, my parents handed me an invitation to a marriage feast in a neighbouring parish, which they had that day received. The literary attractions of this hymeneal epistle, together with the odd circumstances of the feast, induce me to relate the matter. The letter was as follows :—

" john turnley aund Mary Green preeseents thir Completents to Misteer and Mistrass aund tumass—and hee wull bee obleejed uff Thee wull Cuum Too thur weedinng tuMurow Wik next WeDnewsdy Att Twilf o'cloc Persizele.

" I em yurs Himble
" jon turnley Mary green."

As my parents were acquainted with the parents of the bride, they had resolved to go. It required very few arguments to incline me to accompany them. We had some little difficulty, however, concerning the *time* when this important contract was to be legally sanctioned, as " tu-Murow Wik next WeDnewsdy " was not remarkably explicit. Charitably judging that this haziness of information was rather the misfortune than the fault of "john turnley," we resolved to ascertain the exact day from the ready gossip of the district. This medium of intelligence required no red stamp from Somerset House—no "copy"—no "printing press"—and no editorial supervision. It was cheap, accessible, and ever ready; and it answered local purposes as well as if we had gloried in a miniature imitation of the *Times.*

I had twice or thrice seen the clergyman of Deercreek, of whose eccentric appearance and habits curious things were reported; and as the engaged couple belonged to his geographical fold, I hoped that the pleasure of again seeing him awaited me.   That hope was realised.

Mr. Warpet was a little man, whose small legs seemed to have been neglected when he nourished the rest of his body. He had broad shoulders and long arms; his head and face were large.   His hair, which was long and grizzly, did not look as if it were often disturbed with the luxuries of comb and brush.   He was about sixty years of age at the period referred to, and exhibited a figure partly ridiculous and partly frightful when he arrived at the house of the bride's father, where the wedding-feast was held.   He was late, too, and kept thirty hungry guests waiting much longer than they thought agreeable.   When Mr. Warpet at last made his appearance he was literally soaked in water, and covered from head to foot with mud and filth of every offensive kind.   His hat was gone, but his head was liberally thatched with steaming mire; his smallclothes had suffered from some unknown casualty, and one of the tails of his coat had been left on the road. Imagine the flutter and excitement caused by the introduction of this very unclerical-like apparition in the midst of a bridal party.   The male portion of the circle, after the first moment of surprise, lost all reverence for what remained of " the cloth," and, after half-suffocating themselves with pocket handkerchiefs, gave way to the most uproarious laughter.   The softer sex expressed the usual ejaculations, and hid themselves in different rooms with great celerity.   The afflicted pastor " smiled a ghastly smile," and faintly asked for a glass of water.

" Water, indeed!" shouted Mr. Green, when he realised the fact that his clergyman,—who had said wise and kind words to his daughter at church, two hours before, touching the duties of married life, — now stood before him—" Water, Sir? I think you have had rather too much of that! Under the circumstances, I should say a glass of brandy. Here, Sir,—do take it; off with it; there!"

Mr. Green evidently felt satisfaction at the use which had been made of his brandy, and, as soon as it had disappeared, he took hold of the pastor's hand and conducted him to another room, obviously for the purpose of improving the appearance of the outer man.

Whether it was an improvement or otherwise shall be left to the reader's imagination; but, half-an-hour afterwards, the clergyman and his kind parishioner took their places at the dinner table—the former attired in a suit of clothes belonging to the latter. I have already described Mr. Warpet. Mr. Green stood six feet two inches in his stockings, so that, obviously, the clergyman had ample room in his friend's garments. The cause of the catastrophe was now explained. It was the deed of an insane person. By some unaccountable negligence there was no lunatic asylum in the county. The relatives of insane persons allowed them to go at large, and many disasters and injuries resulted from the practice. Where the friends of the mentally diseased could afford it, they were placed under the care of clergymen, who were thus exposed to the dislike of the poor creatures who had been deprived of reason. It was currently reported, that, in several instances, the irresponsible power given to the clergymen over their hapless lodgers was not exercised in the mildest manner. Indeed, it is a well-known fact that restraint and force were, at that period, far more general in the treatment of the mentally imbecile than they are at present. The ameliorations in their treatment which more modern times have witnessed—ameliorations suggested by humanity, and the

wisdom of which has been verified by actual experience—
are exceedingly gratifying to every benevolent mind;
but, twenty years ago, the thought had not occurred—at
least, in the county of which Churchbank is the capital—
that anything short of physical force could be available.
It is gratifying to reflect upon the change to which I
have alluded. Kindness and gentleness, even with the
insane, are better than the contrary mode of treatment;
and that man is a real benefactor to his race who suggests
a plan by which those who are thus afflicted are taught
to confide in the sympathetic kindness of their fellow-
creatures.

Mr. Warpet gave us an account of the whole matter:—
how he returned from church to the parsonage—remained
there about an hour—left for the house in which we were
assembled—met near it poor George Fleck, who suddenly
sprang upon him, struck him, tore his clothes, plunged
him into a ditch, and would probably have killed him,
but for the timely arrival of two strong young men, farm
servants, who were passing at the time; and judging it
safer to come to Mr. Green's than return to his own house,
how he had done so, notwithstanding his sorry and melancholy appearance. We all deeply sympathised with the
good man; and as George Fleck was well known to
every one present as a person of gigantic strength—
generally harmless, but most dangerous in his anger—we
felt thankful that the worthy clergyman had escaped on
such easy terms. He had received no personal injury.
The excitement of fear soon passed away. He made
some very excellent remarks on the value of reason, and
its province; talked, as only a man of education and
intelligence could, on the various topics suggested by the
company; and left, at an early hour, under the guardianship of a couple of strong fellows, who were more

than a match for "all comers;" and, as soon as he departed, the poet of the parish volunteered the following song :—

> " On the new-married two,
> Let the sun and the dew
>   Of love and prosperity fall ;
> May they live, while they live,
> In abundance, and give
>   Of their stores at necessity's call.
>
> " Round their hearth be the birth
> Of joys, such as earth
>   Cannot mar by its querulous noise ;
> And as years furnish tears
> Both to Commons and Peers,
>   May our friends have a houseful of boys ! "

Here there was a hearty peal of laughter. " What, Smith," cried a voice, " no *girls ?* "

"'The fact is," replied the poet, who bore the remarkable name of John Smith, " I could not find a rhyme that would chime this time with girls; but when *you* marry, perhaps I shall."

There was evidently some sarcastic allusion in this which the company understood, for the laugh was turned against the owner of the voice.

" Twirls, or squirrels, would do," said another, " would it not, Mr. Smith ?"

"Of course," replied the poet, offended by this intrusion upon his province, " of course, either would do in the case of persons who prefer sound to sense, and bombast to real poetry !"

" Come, Mr. Smith," said the bridegroom, " lift your glass; singing is dry work. We are greatly obliged for your good wishes, and excellent song."

" Thank you; but I was interrupted; there is another verse :—

"When time, past his prime,
Sheds his silvery rime
    On their heads, like a halo of light;
May the new-married two
Have the sun and the dew
    Of love everlasting in sight!"

"Beautiful! fine!" exclaimed several persons at once.

"Why, it's like the psalms," remarked a critical old lady.

"The psalms!" echoed the poet; "do you mean Stern-hold and Hopkins' version, Ma'am?"

"Old Hopkins!" replied the lady in surprise, "*he* make verses! Ha, ha! he's only fit to swear at his master's poor dumb horses; but you're making fun, surely; I meant the psalms of *David.*"

*   *   *   *   *   *

I had numbered my fifteenth birth-day. Age and debility were rapidly doing their work on my dear parents. I often wept in secret that I could not make the evening of their days somewhat more comfortable. My brother had obtained a situation in Churchbank, and I urged him to look out for one for me. Our desire was to take lodgings for our parents in the town, that we might all live together once more, before they should be called to that country whence there is no return. After a time he was successful, and I was engaged as book-keeper, for a term of three years, to a general dealer in the town, at a very low salary. Mr. Rolf was a mild, take-it-easy personage, who saw no necessity for the hurry and excitement in which many persons live. He thought there was time enough and room enough for all mankind, and deemed a good dinner, and an hour's nap after it, the very essence of existence; but, alas! poor man, he was married, and he knew it; and so did I! I lodged with my employer. My fare was wretched both in quantity and quality. My sleeping-place was in a miserable attic, where the vermin disported at pleasure; and, from the warm reception they gave me, it was clear they considered me either in the light of an intruder, or in that of a windfall. I *felt* that the latter was the more probable conclusion. After the sleepless torment of two or three nights, I humbly represented the case to Mrs. Rolf, suggesting that a visit of the servant-girl to my bed-room, with a mop and pail of water, might be serviceable. Unhappy speech! There was a wet and dirty towel in the lady's hands, which speedily descended on my head and face with unerring precision and undoubted force. Pride, anger, and astonishment kept me silent. I left the room in no enviable mood, and went into the shop to attend to the duties of my desk. On the following morning, about five o'clock, I heard a voice at the foot of the attic ladder calling me. It was that of the servant.

"Mistress told me to call you to get up and clean out the cow-shed, and——" Here the poor girl stopped, as if ashamed of her message.

"Have you not made a mistake?" I asked; "are you sure Mrs. Rolf meant *me*?"

"Quite sure," she replied, naming several other most menial services, which were ordered to be performed by me before seven o'clock that morning—seven o'clock being the hour for opening the shop. My resolution was instantly taken.

"But *will* you do it?" asked Jane, doubtingly.

"Certainly," I replied, "that is, as well as I can. It is better to be up and doing than lying among these vermin."

The kind-hearted girl heard the last word; and, though in danger of a merciless scolding, if not of something worse, from her mistress, she managed to visit the attic in the course of the day, and to make it somewhat more tolerable. She had never been in it before, as I was compelled to make my own bed, such as it was. After breakfast that morning, Mrs. Rolf, addressing me, said, "How dare you allow the door scraper to remain uncleaned?" I was about to say that I was not aware that I was expected to clean it; but the explanation was anticipated by a gentle push from the lady, which sent me to the door scraper with involuntary quickness.

I led this life for nearly six months, and would have borne it with considerable patience, but for the fact that I could not get a moment for mental improvement. I had a little book in my pocket, which I read for two or three nights in my attic by the light of a small bit of candle; but this practice was soon discovered by my economical mistress, and henceforth I had to crawl to my dormitory in the dark. This was the most galling ingredient in my cup of troubles. I had frequently attempted to complain to Mr. Rolf; but I suppose he foresaw the sequel, for he invariably evaded entering on the matter. The truth is, he required no information concerning it.

When I had been nearly six months in this establishment, a young man in the town commenced business on his own account. He called me in one day, as I was passing his shop, and asked whether I intended to remain with Mr. Rolf. I replied, that I meant to leave him as soon as another opening presented itself. He offered to engage me on the same terms as those under which I had entered Rolf's employment, at the same time promising that no duty should be required of me except that of attending to the desk. Here was a break in the cloud, for which I felt sincerely thankful. I had resolved to leave, but to go back to my poor parents was out of the question; hence I bore patiently the ills of my lot. At times, Mrs. Rolf was as remarkable for her kindness, as she was at other times for her uncontrollable passion. An instance of this occurred when I informed Mr. Rolf that I intended to leave his employment; he, of course, told his wife, and she, of course, sent for me. With great earnestness she entreated me to stay, assuring me that Mr. Rolf thought highly of me; that she herself liked me very much; that I was quite a favourite with the children; and that she intended hiring a boy to do the extra work, to which the poverty of the times had compelled her, very much against her will, to put me. I listened to all this with ill-suppressed disgust, and told her that my mind was fixed; that I meant to leave, and that I would leave in ten days hence. She actually *wept,* and shook hands with me, putting a small piece of money in my hand. This was nearly too much for me; I was staggered for a moment, but two or three turns in the garden brought back my firmness. It there occurred to me that jealousy of the rival tradesman, to whom I had told her I was going, had something to do with it.

The following day the good lady was herself again. " Thomas," said she, " I did not mention to you yesterday that you cannot honourably leave us, as you were engaged for three years."

" Mrs. Rolf," I replied, speaking very deliberately, " I engaged to be Mr. Rolf's *clerk and book-keeper* for three years; to the discharge of those duties I agreed, but to nothing else. You *understand me ?*"

" Well, well, never mind; I hope you will find things better where you are going. My poor dear Ann has been asking very kindly for you to-day; she would like to see you. Will you go up stairs and speak to her ?"

I did not require to be asked again. Ann was the eldest daughter, a beautiful and amiable girl of fifteen, rapidly sinking under fell consumption. In fine days I had frequently helped her 'to walk a little in the garden. O, how I wished for strength to that fragile form. How thankfully she received every little attention or act of kindness I showed to her, I well remember ; and I believe I should have left the house months before, but for the knowledge that Ann esteemed me, and felt deeply grieved at her mother's conduct towards me. Dear, gentle Ann ! There she lay on the sofa, almost gasping for breath, with the fatal tint upon her face, and her thin white fingers resting upon an open book. Her lips trembled as I entered. I went close to her. She whispered, " Is it—really—true ? Are you going to—to—leave—us ?"

" No, Miss Rolf, not until you are better."

She opened her blue eyes, whose supernatural brilliance made me tremble for a moment, and looking earnestly in my face pronounced the word " *Better?*" very slowly.

" Yes, Miss Rolf," I said, " I certainly will not."

" But," she whispered, " I shall not recover. I am—dying. I am—going—to—my—Redeemer."

After a short silence, I said, " *Which is far better.*"

She gently pressed my hand with her white fingers, and said, " Thank you; this *is* kind, *very kind*. May you—be—happy !"

I kept my word ; in ten days after that she was better. The gentle spirit had gone to a holier region than that of earth. I wept over her grave, though there was nothing there but the broken casket; the gem was re-set elsewhere. Dear Ann !

*　　　*　　　*　　　*

The turning point in a man's history is, undoubtedly, the period of his spiritual enlightenment. Every other change, whether of opinion, or place, or of circumstance, sinks into nothing when compared with this. Through the mercy of God, that point in my history was drawing near. I had been, up to the period under notice, like many others who are trained amidst religious influences, an intellectual Christian, but nothing more; that is to say, I believed the Bible to be the truth of God, and I believed that Jesus Christ is the true Messiah, and the only Saviour of men. But the fact is, I had never doubted these things; my state of mind, therefore, instead of being the result of personal conviction and personal faith, was, more properly, acquiescence in the opinions of others; an adherence to the received doctrines, rather than a personal appropriation of the truth. My faith stood in the wisdom of men, rather than in the power of God. I could defend certain doctrines and certain theological opinions against gainsayers. Had I heard a man avow himself an infidel, I should have been filled with horror. Virtue and morality I considered extremely beautiful. For the vices of others I had no mercy; my own external conduct was generally irreproachable. Reading the Scriptures, and morning and evening prayer, were settled habits of my life. Under the ministry of the excellent Zelotes I had placed myself on my return to Churchbank. I greatly valued his teaching; paid strict attention to his sermons; attended his Sabbath school, first as a scholar and afterwards as a teacher; committed to memory large portions of the Scriptures, hymns, and catechisms, and was considered an excellent and exemplary youth. What more, then, was required? Everything, dear reader. With all this I was *not* a Christian, in the true sense of that much-abused term. I was ignorant of myself; knew not the depth of corruption which lay in my own heart; felt not the love of God as the animating motive to all acceptable service; and had no personal experience of soul-fellowship with a living Saviour. I was, to all intents and purposes, a self-

righteous Pharisee, though I loathed the very name.
I was leaning on my own righteousness, although I
thought the righteousness of Christ the foundation of my
hope. I was unchanged in heart, although I spoke frequently about the doctrine of the new birth. In one
word, I was morally ignorant of myself. If there was
light in the head, there was no real life in the heart. I
understood, but felt not. I looked upon Christianity as a
beautiful whole, but had not realised its distinct parts—
for doctrine, for reproof, for correction. It was, in my
eye, a finished system, but the design of that system, as a
power upon individual consciences, I had not felt.

The time arrived, however, in my sixteenth year,
when, by the instrumentality of a sermon preached by a
student, a stranger, I was shaken like a reed before a
storm. Never shall I forget that Lord's day. But, singular as it may seem, it is the fact, that I have no recollection, and never had, either of the preacher's text or his
subject; I only remember that I was absorbed in what
he said. I felt overwhelmed with terror, as if an invisible
hand had seized my soul, and was dragging it to judgment. I became faint; darkness seemed to gather around
me. At the close of the service I went home, as it were,
unconsciously. I spoke to no one, and did not dare to
lift my eyes from my feet, as I expected the earth to open
and swallow me. The commotion of my soul was altogether such as language cannot describe. I crept to my
room, locked the door, and fell upon my knees; but no
words came. I could not pray. The perspiration was
oozing from every pore.

How long I lay on my knees I know not; happily,
this fearful agony of mind did not last long, or I should
have died. Some hours elapsed—hours like ages; in
which I *felt* myself before the throne of righteous judg-

ment, and while the process was going on I was dumb. Had the salvation of my soul depended upon a word I could not have uttered it. But He who had smitten graciously healed. As if they had been slowly unfolded before me, there appeared these never-to-be-forgotten words:—" THE BLOOD OF JESUS CHRIST CLEANSETH US FROM ALL SIN."

I had read and heard these wonderful words often, but now they appeared new to me. I gazed, believed, loved, and embraced them. The crisis was past. A flood of tears rushed from my eyes; my tongue was set at liberty. I prayed, and perhaps it was the first time in my life that I really did pray.

For three days after this I was filled with indescribable joy. I thought I saw heaven, with its blessed inhabitants, and its glorious King. I thought He was looking on me with unutterable compassion, and that I recognised Him as Jesus my Saviour, who had laid me under eternal obligation. The world, and all its concerns, appeared utterly worthless. The conduct of ungodly men filled me with grief and pity. I saw everything in an entirely new light: a strong desire to fly to heathen lands, that I might preach the good news to idolaters, filled my heart. I longed to speak about the grand discovery I had made, and felt assured that I had but to open my lips to convince every one of the infinite grace of Christ, and the infinite value of salvation. And I thought my troubles over, and that, henceforth, the same scenes of joy and hallowed peace were to pass before my eyes, and fill my heart.

But, alas! I was mistaken. I had to come down from this mount of transfiguration—and a terrible descent it was! I had to learn the bitter lesson of my depravity, and to go through a fiery baptism. Many months of dark and fearful thoughts were before me. I have said that I had not previously doubted, and therefore, strictly speaking, I had not really believed. Temptations to sin beset me. Passions, of whose existence I scarcely knew, grew up within me like fierce giants, who would neither be controlled nor refuted. The more I prayed, the fiercer became the conflict. A real struggle ensued. Scepticism came down upon me like a pestilential cloud. Some evil voice followed me with the cry, that the Bible is false, Christianity a fable, Jesus not the Saviour, souls not immortal! All the past, it was suggested, was a delusion. I had only been in a dream. It was the fervid manner of the young preacher that excited me. I had never been converted. To yield to what was called sin could not be wrong, as the indulgence of natural inclinations could not be objected to by the Creator. Thus I was beset occasionally, and at intervals, for a long period. At other times, the thought that I had sinned away the day of grace would fill me with dismay, and terrible forebodings. I felt that I had been a greater sinner after my deep religious convictions than before.

I need not further describe my melancholy state of mind. Suffice it to say, that all this time I was enabled to keep close to the house and people of the Lord, openly to profess my faith in Him, and to persevere, though often with a heavy heart, in the path which my conscience declared to be right. Alas! the faults, the failings, the sins of heart and life; but the grand Scripture which relieved me on *that* memorable Sabbath-day is my relief and my plea in view of them all; a relief sufficient, and a plea that will not be rejected.

To return to my ordinary history. My new employer was an active, energetic man, who was resolved to make and drive a good business. Some of his plans, with this end in view, appeared to me far enough from squaring with the golden rule of Scripture. But it is needless to dwell on a case of this kind, as, unhappily, they are by far too common in the world.

Whilst in Mr. Davison's employment, however, I had my evenings to myself. There was a very able schoolmaster in the town, who so thoroughly devoted himself to the benefit of others, that after conducting a school of more than a hundred boys during the day, he spent his evenings in teaching young men in business and others who chose to avail themselves of the privilege. Mr. Anfield was a good classical scholar, and mathematician. I entered his evening school, and studied Latin and mathematics. Here I found my old friend and teacher, Mr. Brake, who had given up his school at Tankerhill, and removed to Churchbank, to improve his knowledge of Latin, and to learn the Greek language, under the eye of Mr. Anfield. There were five other young men attending these valuable classes, between whom, and Mr. Brake, and myself, a firm friendship sprang up—a friendship which was productive of valuable results to us all. We became so fully recognised as young men firmly attached to each other, and pursuing the thorny path of knowledge under difficulties, that we were popularly designated, " The Seven Friends," or, briefly, " The Seven." With peculiar interest I recall the faces and peculiarities of my six companions. Jerome Brake is still a schoolmaster in his native county. Walter Loxley succeeded Mr. Anfield, as teacher of the large school to which I have referred. James Brooke, the most loving spirit of the seven, went to college, studied for the ministry, entered the sacred profession, caught cold after preaching his third sermon, fell a victim to consumption, and was laid in an early grave. William

Wallis is confidential clerk in a large mercantile house in India. Harry Spencer is a successful engineer in one of the southern counties of England. John Andrews is a prosperous ship-broker in the city of London; and I am an unworthy labourer in the service in which my loving-hearted friend Brooke fell so soon. Such has been the way in which the "Seven" have been conducted. I have only seen one of them for the last fifteen years, and may never meet any of them again in this world. May we meet in a better!

In the pursuit of our studies we greatly helped each other. The disposition to do so reigned in our breasts. We were a little commonwealth, a band of true Socialists; but the idea occurred to us, that we might consecrate this friendship to still higher objects, and instrumentally do good to others who were beyond the circle of our little fraternity. A Society, regularly organised, for mutual instruction, and the study of the Scriptures, was suggested. The suggestion was soon realised. From this sprang a Debating Society, at whose meetings the public might attend as hearers. The questions discussed embraced a wide range of thought. Metaphysics, ancient and modern philosophy, history, social characteristics, church systems, and secular politics, all passed under review. All this required both thought and reading; and, as will be obvious to every one, it required great command of temper in the conduct of discussions, where unanimity of opinion was not to be expected. But as our object was not victory, but light and improvement, we succeeded admirably Our chosen motto was, "*Suaviter in modo, fortiter in re;*" and we endeavoured to keep it in mind. The meetings of our Society took place on a week evening, at a late hour, to enable clerks, shopmen, and others to attend. "The early closing" movement had not then begun its salutary operations; so that the poor youths, who stood behind the counter of grocer and draper from seven in the morning until ten or eleven at night, had few opportunities of nourishing the mind, or elevating the intellect with beneficial knowledge.

After a time, I suggested that a Sabbath-morning prayer-meeting, at seven o'clock, would, by God's blessing, be of essential service to us. The idea was favourably entertained by the friends, and carried out successfully. We met in each other's lodgings in rotation, when that was possible; and when it happened to be inconvenient, the vestry of the chapel was placed at our service by our kind minister, who rejoiced in our exertions, and wished us God speed. We were all engaged, with one exception, as teachers in the Sunday school; and I believe some of our scholars remember our names affectionately to this day.

When I had been about two years in the service of Mr. Davison, the inhabitants of Churchbank were filled with anxiety by rumours of the approach of Asiatic cholera. That alarming and devastating pestilence had swept over many cities and towns, sending apprehension and terror before it, carrying with it agony and death, and leaving, as its memorials, widows and orphans, lamentation, mourning, and woe. Everything that could be done to anticipate the arrival of the dreaded stranger, was done by the people of the town. The removal of nuisances, the opening and furnishing of a place as a public hospital, and other measures, were attended to in solemn earnestness. An extraordinary depression settled down upon the people—a cloud of melancholy seemed to cover the town. The pulpits rang with the cry, "Prepare to meet thy God!" Every new day brought

F

rumours more startling than those of its predecessor respecting the ravages and proximity of the mysterious foe. Had a besieging army, of irresistible power and without mercy, been at hand, the effect could not have been more alarming. Men looked at each other when they met, but smiled not. All were serious. Intemperance was greatly checked. The public-houses were nearly deserted, except by the utterly abandoned and hardened, who had lost fear because they had no hope; and to give a direction to this general feeling, there was a day of fasting and humiliation observed by all in the various places of worship in the town and neighbourhood. Earnest—*very* earnest—were the prayers presented to God that day, that we might all be saved from the pestilence.

We were saved! The fatal disease came within twenty miles of us, and carried away many; but it came no nearer. There was not a single known case in the whole district. But mark the sequel! Scarcely had the authentic intelligence reached us that Asiatic cholera was leaving our land, when the people seemed to forget their merciful exemption from the dire affliction, which had gorged so many burial grounds throughout England and Scotland. An unreasoning joy succeeded the gloom I have described. The thoughtless became more giddy than before. The sceptical smiled at the "false alarm." The drunkard returned to his cups with increased thirst. And, worse than all, not a few professors of religion seemed to fall into the error of believing more firmly in the power of prayer, than in the mercy of Him who hears prayer. That the really religious were permanently benefited, and that piety received an accession to its power, is also true; but the state of the town generally was decidedly worse than before. Six months afterwards, we were all surprised by an unusual mortality among the people. "Slight colds," as they seemed at first, terminated in ulcerated throats, inflammation of the chest, and death! Three days were generally the longest period between the attack and its fatal issue. Few that were seized recovered. No class, or rank, escaped. The holy and the unclean alike fell before the messenger of death. Nothing like it had been known in the place before. Every day witnessed funeral processions in the street. Shops were closed, business stood still, and fear sat on every face. The question every morning, for nearly two months, was simply— "Who has died?" Among my nearest friends, I may mention, for the sake of illustration, that the young wife of my brother—before they had been married ten months—and their infant were laid in the same grave; that at the very hour, and on the same day when she departed, the excellent mother of the young lady, who has since become my own beloved wife, breathed her last; that an aunt of mine suddenly died; that two or three esteemed acquaintances fell in one week; and that there was scarcely a street in which the blinds of the windows were not down, in token of what had taken place inside. Some time before this, we had taken our aged parents to the town, and we all lived under the same roof. They were not affected by the epidemic; but it laid hold on me, and for the period of no less than three months I suffered from it. A constant inflammation of the throat, with periodical prostration—prostration so complete, that my friends frequently thought I had breathed my last — characterised my illness. I remember particularly one occasion. I was lying on my back, utterly helpless. I was scarcely conscious of breathing. Several of my dear young friends, to whom I have so repeatedly referred, had come to see me for the last time—as all thought, and as I thought. They first prayed in a low voice, and then sat around the bed, watching for the last scene. My poor mother sat, with her head resting on her hands, weeping; my father was at her side, his few grey hairs surrounding his head like a crown of honour won in the battle of life. My sense of hearing was marvellously acute. I could not speak—could not lift a finger—yet I knew all that was said, and heard most distinctly the faintest whisper. I heard the sigh of my father, and the tears dropping from my mother's face. But I felt indescribably happy. Can *this* be dying? I thought. What perfect peace! I cannot compare it to any known experience. Shall I say it was like floating on the surface of a crystal stream, whose banks were fragrant with all the odours of a fertile summer? I heard the most soothing and enchanting music. Everything was calm as calmness itself. I had no pain, no anxiety, no wish—except it was that I should continue in that state of mental felicity for ever. It was not a swoon—for I knew all that was transpiring; and it was not a dream—for when any of my friends gently looked on my face, I returned the look with a faint smile of recognition. This exquisite sensation lasted about three hours, as nearly as I can recollect, when it gradually passed away, with the gradual return of a little physical strength. From that day, I recovered slowly. It was in the month of February, 1834; and on the 20th of June following, I left my native town, with a *few* shillings and *many* "letters of introduction" in my pocket, " with all the world before me where to choose, and Providence my Guide."

CHAPTER V.

NEW SCENES AND NEW FACES.

" Come, Disappointment, come!
  Though from Hope's summit hurled,
Still, rigid nurse, thou art forgiven,
For thou severe wert sent from heaven,
  To wean me from the world;
    To turn my eye
    From vanity,
And point to scenes of bliss that never, never die."

Kirke White.

MY SOLILOQUY—THE DECISION—PARTING INTERVIEW—DANGERS OF LARGE CITIES—ADVICE TO A YOUTH LEAVING HOME—ARRIVAL AT EDINBURGH—FEELING ALONE IN THE CROWD—A GUIDE—LODGINGS ON THE " SEVENTH FLAT"—DELIVERING " LETTERS OF INTRO- DUCTION"—THE S. S. C.—UNWELCOME ADVICE—DISAPPOINTMENT AND HUNGER—A NEW FRIEND—HUMANITY AND DIVINITY—NEW THOUGHTS—MORAL ANATOMY—CHARITY—AT SCHOOL, OUTSIDE THE COLLEGE—VIEW FROM THE CALTON HILL—LETTERS FOUR AND FIVE—A LUCRATIVE OFFER AS " LIGHT PORTER"—ELDER SCALES — FREDERICK SINCLAIR — PECULIARITIES OF DIFFERENT PERSONS—SERIOUS CONVERSATION—I AM ATTACKED WITH FEVER —RECOVERY — A PERMANENT SITUATION — THE " VOLUNTARY CHURCH" CONTROVERSY—I BECOME AN AUTHOR—THE " VETO" QUESTION—THE FREE CHURCH—IS A JUST RELIGIOUS ESTABLISH- MENT POSSIBLE?—THE JUNIOR CLERK—THE REQUEST TO PREACH MY FIRST SERMON—AGITATING THOUGHTS—THE STARVING TRA- VELLER—MY MARRIAGE—I STUDY GREEK—AN ECCENTRIC EDITOR —DEATH OF THE HEAD OF THE FIRM—I AM " AT SEA."

" WHITHER shall I bend my steps? To London? It is likely to prove a great whirlpool of excitement, anxiety,

trouble, and doubt; a wilderness of strange faces, strange
scenes, and strange heart-wringings; a great desert, in
which I shall be lost—perhaps ruined; for, by all accounts,
the stranger without a name, without friends, and especially without funds, is, in the Great Metropolis, like a
stray leaf in autumn, driven hither and thither, no one
knowing what he is, or what becomes of him. Besides,
London is too far off, and, even if I had introductions to
that huge city, it is beyond my power to travel to it.
Shall I think of Liverpool? It is a prosperous town.
It is full of enterprising merchants. There must be
constant changes going on. Possibly I may hear of an
opening in some mercantile house, where a clerk is
required. But no; Liverpool is all very well for those
who are wedded to pounds, shillings, and pence. I want
to go to some seat of learning. Oxford, Cambridge,
Glasgow, Aberdeen, Edinburgh; these are all before me.
Simpleton! what are you dreaming about? Twenty-five
shillings is the entire amount of your wealth; the sum of
your possessions! Ah! true; I forgot *that!* Well,
never mind. I have long wished to see Scotland—the
land of intellect, freedom, and daring; the land of mountain and flood; of imperishable names, and undying
moral heroism. I wish to breathe its bracing atmosphere;
to climb its rugged hills; to catch its thrilling spirit of
patriotism, and to sit at the feet of its renowned teachers.
To modern Athens I will go in the first instance, and
trust to God for the result."

Such was the substance of my soliloquy when, per-
ceiving the decay of Davison's business, in consequence of
his ambiguous practices, I resolved to seek the means of
existence in some other part of the kingdom. I could
have remained in my native town, had mere existence
been the limit of my desire; but I wished for something

beyond that. I felt that life was a serious thing, and I cherished the hope that there was something before me to be accomplished—something, somewhere in the wide world, to be done by me. Of wealth I thought not; but the idea of a life of dependence, when one has the power of doing something for the benefit of others, was intolerable. I was convinced that I should find my work, whatever it might be, elsewhere; and, with this conviction, I bade farewell to my aged parents, believing that I should never see them again in life.

It was a painful separation. That dear mother, who had, at the expense of her health, and almost of her life, watched through sad years over my feeble infancy; and that noble-minded father, whose cheerful and intelligent piety had breasted many a storm, and set me a lofty example—I see them yet, as they clung to me with tears in their eyes and blessings on their lips, at an early hour of a calm and beautiful summer morning. My heart trembled, and the parting scene would have shaken my resolution to leave home, but for the determination, which lay concealed in the depth of my soul, that, by the help of God, they should yet hear tidings of me which would make them glad, should their lives continue a few years longer. I might not be able to send them any substantial proof of gratitude for all they had done for me, but that I should not bring down their grey hairs with sorrow to the grave, and that, if possible, I should so act as to lead them to bless God on my account, were the settled purposes of my soul. True, I had only seen life on a very limited scale, and knew not the attractive temptations of a great city. The allurements and fascinations of the world had not been exhibited before me, and I was a comparative stranger to the wiles of avarice catering for the passions of the multitude in large populations, that it may fill its coffers at the expense of virtue; but the reader will remember that I was, in some degree, prepared for all this, by the terrible baptism of personal experience. Yet, as I subsequently found, direct contact with the agents of evil in the persons of living men, requires a degree of moral health and mental decision, for which even such a fiery ordeal is scarcely a sufficient preparation. To realise the presence of God as the omniscient witness of thought, language, and action, is essential to victory in such a struggle. Purposes are soon forgotten; resolutions slip from memory; but the thought of a *present* God is at once life and strength, before which the incarnations of iniquity are forced to quail. Were it in my power to reach the ear of the young man leaving home, even that of the young man who deems himself fortified against the assaults of temptation by the adoption of the highest principles, I would say, " Brother, be not deceived! Do not promise thyself too much. Be not over-liberal in enumerating thy moral qualities. There are serpent trailings on the surface of human society, which may prove like the slippery ice beneath thy feet. For thy soul's sake, walk humbly, lest thou fall. Place thy feeble hand in Christ's, and let Him lead thee. This will be better than falling back on previous convictions, and recalling resolutions formed amidst the tranquillity of home associations. Compass, chart, and helm are all good—without them thou wilt suffer shipwreck; but even with them, on an unknown sea, thou wilt be the better of a pilot. Engage, I pray thee, the services of Him who stilled the storm on the Galilean lake. Do this, dear young brother, and *conquer!*"

The mayor of Churchbank was a native of Edinburgh. He was pleased to put into my hand half-a-dozen letters of introduction to gentlemen in his native city, for which act of disinterested kindness I thank him, even at this distant date, as I believe he is still alive, and in the enjoyment of prosperity and of the deserved esteem of his friends and neighbours. Two other gentlemen, who had correspondents in the Scottish metropolis, also gave me letters of commendation, and my valued pastor volunteered important counsel, and wrote strongly on my behalf to two clergymen in Edinburgh, with whom he had some slight acquaintance.

Coach fare and " gratuities" paid, I stood on the High Street of Edinburgh, at eight o'clock on that *memorable* evening, with a small bundle in my hand, and five shillings in my pocket—an absolute stranger. I looked at the noble churches, at the lofty houses, and at the passing multitudes. I was faint and weary. A feeling of desolation overwhelmed me. I began to realise the fact that I was an utter stranger, without a friend, without a home, and almost without the means of support. Every thing was new and bewildering. No one seemed to see me. I was *alone!* There was something awful in this thought. I could not endure it longer. Looking down one of the narrow closes that lead from the High Street, and wishing to go somewhere, I asked a man if that was a thoroughfare. He did not at first understand me. I repeated the question.

" O, aye," said he, " ye'll win doon that way; but mind the stairs at the fit o't."

This friendly caution was necessary, for at the lower end of the passage there were some wofully irregular steps, flooded with a thick liquid, which would have been really useful on a piece of arable land, but which by no means improved the odours of the surrounding atmosphere. Having accomplished the descent in safety, I was startled by the question—" Whare ye gaun?" The speaker was the same who had advised me to " mind the stairs." He had followed me, for what reason was best known to himself; but I felt greatly relieved by the sound of a human voice addressed to me personally, although I could not answer his blunt question.

" I really do not know," I said.

" Dinna ken whare ye're gaun, mon ?"

" No."

" Hoot ! ye're either daft or jokan !"

" Neither, I assure you, friend," looking keenly on the man's eyes, in which I saw that he was neither rogue nor fool; " but I am an entire stranger, and if you will guide me to some place where I can obtain plain lodgings for the night, I shall feel greatly obliged."

" Oo, aye," said he, " I'll sune do that; bit what's ye're name? whare d'ye come frae? and what are ye gaun to do in Embro?"

This inquisitiveness somewhat annoyed me at first, but the thought occurring that the man might be of service, I answered his first and second questions correctly, and added, smiling, that the last was a poser. My new friend, for whom, in my desolate condition, I found a feeling of attachment springing up in my heart, asked me to accompany him. I did so; and, after two or three minutes' walk, he turned into a mean-looking public-house, and asked me to be seated.

" Ye'll gie us half a gill," he said. Feeling that refusal would be at once mean and impolitic, I complied with his request, at the same time ordering some coffee and bread and butter for myself. I found Peter Mc Donald as communicative, on receipt of the " half gill," as he had been inquisitive before. His history had some romance in it, sufficient to keep my thoughts from brooding over the profitless text of self for an hour, but nothing sufficiently remarkable to justify me in relating it to the reader.

At the close of our repast, Peter conducted me to the lodgings of a Mrs. McLaren, on the " seventh flat," in a house adjoining, where, with sad heart and weary frame, I passed the night. Peter had assured me that he had " no muckle" to do, and on the following day he called at Mrs. McLaren's, for the purpose of guiding me to the residences of the gentlemen to whom my epistles recommendatory were respectively addressed. My first insight into the oddities of human nature, on anything like an extensive scale, was afforded during the delivery of those introductions.

The first gentleman on whom I called was a W. S., or Writer to the Signet.* He received me very kindly, went into a long personal history of the mayor of Churchbank, said that he was sure that a young man recommended by Mr. Fraser must be worthy of patronage, regretted the dulness of business at that particular time, expressed an opinion that the lawyers in Edinburgh were like the locusts in Egypt, both as regarded their numbers and their destructive habits, smiled at his own similitude, and bade me good morning.

My next interview was with an estate agent. He was very busy at that moment; but, if I would call in the course of eight days, it would afford him great pleasure to serve me.

* The Signet, in Scotland, is the seal by which the Queen's letters and writs, for the purpose of justice, are authenticated. Hence the title of "writers to the signet," whose profession is nearly synonymous with that of attorneys in England. Their duty is to prepare the warrants of all charters of lands emanating from the Crown; to sign summonses, citing parties to appear in the Court of Session; and almost all diligences of the law for affecting the person or estate of a debtor, or for compelling the decrees of the Supreme Court. They have also the power of acting as agents or attorneys in conducting causes before the Court of Session.

Number three had indulged so freely in whisky, that he talked the most incoherent folly, mingling together disjointed remarks about the excellence of the Kirk of Scotland, the state of the weather, Islay whisky, the doctrine of election, the quality of herrings, English episcopacy, the novels of Sir Walter Scott, a dog-fight in the Grass Market, oysters, and the Reform Bill. I was glad to escape from the presence of this learned Athenian.

Four and five were both absent, but I left my letters for them, saying that I should call on the following day.

My sixth letter, the last of Mr. Fraser's donation, was addressed to "James J. Nichols, Esq., S.S.C."* I was given to understand that this gentleman possessed great influence, both with the members of his profession and the public in general. The non-success of my previous applications had increased my anxiety. I had engaged Mrs. McLaren's room for a week, at four shillings, and, as she was evidently very poor, I had paid that sum in advance, leaving me only a few pence on which to subsist during the time. I had some difficulty in dissuading Peter McDonald from accompanying me. I could not reward him, and I would not avail myself of gratuitous services from a poor man; so, thanking him for his kindness, and assuring him that I should find the addresses without difficulty, I dismissed him. I had partaken of a very moderate breakfast, and, as it was three o'clock in the afternoon when I called at the office of Mr. Nichols, I felt keenly the want of refreshment; but I wished to see the solicitor, if possible, before supplying this want. One of the clerks took the letter and went into an inner office with it. In a minute or two I was requested to enter. Mr. Nichols pointed to a chair. I

---

* Solicitors in Edinburgh who practise before the Supreme Court are members of the College of Justice.

bowed, and took the seat. My heart beat fast. Should this application fail, what was to be done? I had two or three letters besides, but they were only to small tradesmen, from whom, I thought, I had nothing to hope. Mr. Nichols scrutinised my features through a pair of gold-rimmed spectacles, and then asked my age, what I had been accustomed to do, what references besides Mr. Fraser's I could give him, and what I wished to do in Edinburgh. I satisfied him as far as I could on these points.

"Well," said he, "young man, there are more clerks in this city than there is any use for. Many young men, regularly brought up to the profession, are in want of employment, and, consequently, in want of bread. Not a few of them fall into loose habits. Intemperance and its accompanying vices follow. It is a dangerous place for a youth fresh from the country; and, as you know nothing about our profession, you really stand no chance whatever. I would therefore advise you to return at once to your native place, and to your friends."

"Thank you, Sir," I said, rising and taking my hat. As I did so, my hand trembled, and I staggered a little.

"Ah!" said he, "my advice is needed. You have been drinking to-day."

"Sir!" I exclaimed, emphatically, "you do me injustice."

"Oh, of course I do; but we shall not argue that point at present. It is my dinner hour."

I bowed, and retired. When I reached the street I laid hold on a lamp-post for support—mortification, anger, and disappointment, together with fatigue and hunger, having overcome me. I had been in this position, perhaps, five minutes, when some one touched my shoulder. An amiable-looking, well-dressed young man said, " I beg your pardon, Sir, but were you not in Mr. Nichols's office just now?"

" I was, Sir."

" I thought so. I am one of his clerks, and heard what passed between you and him. Have you dined?"

" I have not, Sir."

" Well, if you are not better engaged, I shall be happy if you will take a chop with me."

I thanked him, and began to frame some excuse. It was clear that he comprehended the state of matters, for he added, smiling,

" Nay, don't refuse. I have been out of employment myself, and know that finances are not generally over-abundant at such times. I want you to eat a chop at my expense to-day, and I shall eat one at yours, some fine day, soon. Here, take my arm."

Such unlooked-for kindness, under such circumstances, was like the discovery of a stream of water in the desert; and the contrast between the spirit of Mr. Nichols and that of his clerk, Frederick Sinclair, taught me a lesson of considerable importance.

I had made two closely-related subjects my study for some years—humanity and divinity. Everything which could cast light upon either, and upon their mutual relations, was valued. Sometimes painful, and sometimes agreeable circumstances yielded this light; but whatever the distinctive character of the medium might be, the information afforded was prized for its own sake. The secret wish that I might, and the secret hope that I should, some day be a preacher of the Gospel, lay at the centre of my heart, and animated and sustained me through years of struggle; and when events took place which seemed to affirm the impossibility of this, the depression of spirit was only of short continuance. With

God all things are possible. I opened my Bible that evening at the forty-second of Isaiah, and read, " I will bring the blind by a way that they knew not; I will lead them in paths that they have not known: I will make darkness light before them, and crooked things straight. These things will I do unto them, and not forsake them." I believed that the desire to which I have alluded was implanted by Him, for it sprang up simultaneously with the light and peace referred to in a former chapter; and if it came from God, I felt that He both could and would realise it. Still, occurrences which seemed to rebuke the desire, and to suggest the impropriety of cherishing it, led to self-examination and patience; and I am now prepared to advise all students of humanity to examine themselves faithfully, narrowly, repeatedly, if they wish to be successful students. I think all hearts have very much in common; and, if so, he who has traced the source of his own thoughts, emotions, feelings, passions, and desires, will generally succeed in forming a just estimate of his fellows. And I am certain that no man can understand the Christian system while he is ignorant of the peculiarities of the human heart. The science of moral anatomy is an indispensable auxiliary to the science of theology. They should be studied together; and whilst they mutually illustrate each other, the light of the latter should be made to fall upon the former. He who brings the light of the Gospel to his own heart will learn much concerning both. But the attempt to study man in the absence of this light will be labour in vain, so far as the grand purposes of intelligent existence are concerned.

I felt, at the time referred to, that I was at school. If I had no very definite object in view, except that sacred secret which lay hidden in my heart, still I could acquire knowledge daily, which might be of real service at some future period. I coveted education, and half-envied those who had the means of placing themselves at the feet of accomplished professors in the College—a building on which I gazed for nearly an hour of my first day in Edinburgh, with peculiar emotions. But the idea that one may learn much, and acquire profitable knowledge from the common events of life, in some measure consoled me in view of the impossibility of entering that building as a regular student. The cruelty of the solicitor's remarks gave me excessive pain at the time; but, on reflection, I felt thankful to him, and wished that I had more letters of introduction, that I might have additional opportunities of studying humanity in all its phases. Besides, it might be the man's manner—or some particular source of irritation, of which I could not know, might have caused him to speak as he did. He had the reputation of being a good man; and as only good men have shadows, because they only walk in the light, it might be that I called just at the moment when he was casting a shadow. The influence of pure air and fine scenery on one's charity is remarkable. It was during a visit to the Calton Hill on the following morning, that this charitable judgment on the S.S.C. presented itself. I had enjoyed calm and refreshing sleep during the night; and after breakfasting at a coffee-house on a roll and a cup of coffee, for the sum of twopence-halfpenny, I went to the Calton Hill, and felt myself lifted above all mundane cares for a time by the sublime view obtained from that deservedly famous eminence. Everything calculated to inspire thoughts at once serene and lofty was exhibited before me as on a living map. The foliage of the trees between the Hill and the shore was of the richest green. To the left, the town of Leith sent up its morning smoke, indicating the awakened life and activity of the inhabitants preparatory to the discharge of the duties of the new day. Passing the eye along the fine sandy shore, for some miles to the right, it falls upon the quiet little town of Portobello. Some large vessels lay at anchor opposite Leith. The vast expanse of sea was like a polished mirror reflecting the light poured from the sea through a cloudless firmament. The Bell-rock, recalling its tragic associations with the dark deeds of persecution, stood in the centre of the scene, and led my thoughts to the martyrs whom John saw in vision; and to the "sea of glass like unto crystal" that he beheld before the throne. Everything seemed pure and beautiful. The undulating scenery of Fifeshire, with its shores dotted with fishing villages, lay at the opposite side of this magnificent liquid mirror, giving a most beautiful skirting to the picture, and a pleasing relief to the eye.

I felt as much reluctance in leaving that mount of vision to pursue my worldly affairs as I do now to proceed with the narrative of that pursuit; but it was necessary that I should ascertain the fate of letters four and five. The gentleman with whom I had left the first spoke kindly, but regretted that I was too late, as he had engaged a clerk only two days before; and he was sorry for it, as he thought I would have answered his purpose better than the youth he had engaged. "But," he added, putting his hand in his pocket, "I may hear of something that will suit you. Call in, whenever you pass this way, and as seeking a situation is tiresome work, accept five shillings to help you on a little."

I need not say that I thanked this generous benefactor, and recognised the hand of a gracious Providence in the timely gift. Cheered by this occurrence I walked quickly to Greenside-street, to inquire after my other epistle. This was in the hands of a corpulent grocer, whose face was "red as a ruby," and whose small grey eyes twinkled so as to give you the idea of perpetual motion. I informed this comfortable-looking citizen who I was.

"Ah!" said he, "Tammus What's-yer-name? ye're lucky! I'm just wanting a light porter; but I'm thinking ye're ower wee; but ye can hae the place if ye like—on *trial*, ye ken. I gie my light porter a shilling-a-day, and find himsel."

"I am obliged to you, Sir," I said, trying to look very grave, "but I fear I should be too light, and lose instead of finding myself on the wages you offer."

"Hoot, toot, toot," cried the grocer, his grey eyes twinkling alarmingly, "ye're making fun o' me! Witty folk should no be seeking places, I'm thinking!"

Seeing that this man was a barrel of good humour, with a sprinkling of pepper by way of zest, I replied, smiling, "I don't know that, Sir. Those who are seeking situations have generally nothing to live on but their wits; and I don't think *you* would be so cruel as to deprive them of that poor living."

"Noo, really, that's gude! but I'se warrant ye're ower prood to tak' a porter's situation. Can ye sing?"

"Sing?"

"Aye, I'm an unworthy elder of Dr. Greekie's church"—at the adjective "unworthy" the rosy grocer looked supremely virtuous;—"and we are wanting a precentor. You are a churchman, I suppose?"

"I am sorry, Mr. Scales," I replied, "to say I cannot sing; and I am not a churchman."

"Eh? oh! that's a pity! Weel, weel, never mind. Look in some day as ye're passing. Farewell!"

My kind friend, Frederick Sinclair, had exacted a promise from me, that I should meet him at four o'clock that day at an eating-house near the Register-office. I was unwilling to trespass on such kindness; but as it was proper that I should keep the appointment, I went at the hour named, and found him there.

"I have been trying to find work for you," said he, "and I hope I have succeeded, to the extent, at least, of a temporary job. A friend of mine, in Pitt-street, has some documents to get ready in three days, and he wants an extra clerk. Will you go?"

"Certainly, and thank you too."

"Here's the address. Be sure to be there at ten to-morrow morning, and say to Mr. Spence that I sent you."

I amused Sinclair by relating what had passed between me and the Greenside-street grocer; and I told him, also, of the generosity of the gentleman on whom I had called in the morning.

"Quite so," moralised Sinclair; "this is the way of the world. What a mystery is man! Thompson, who acted like a Christian towards you, is no professor; and, to my certain knowledge, he is struggling with pecuniary difficulties. Scales, who has, at least, twenty thousand safe in the Linen Company's Bank, is a thorough-going professor, an elder of the kirk, a sand-the-sugar grocer, and a miser. Bah! it's disgusting!"

"It is," I said; "but, after all, the thing is not so mysterious as at first sight it appears; and I think I can explain the matter to your entire satisfaction."

"If you do I shall be under lasting obligation to you," said he.

"Well," I replied, "in the first place, let me clear Christianity of all participation in the affair. It is obvious that it rebukes and denounces faults, of which some of its professed adherents are guilty. No man of common understanding would blame it for the worldliness of Elder Scales; for it teaches that charity which seeketh not her own, is not easily provoked, and thinketh no evil. It instructs its disciples to look every man not on his own things, but on the things of others; and it commands men to bear one another's burdens, and so fulfil the law of Christ. The inference, therefore, is that Scales, though possibly a sincere, is not a well-instructed Christian. Instead of having too much, he has too little of the spirit of the Gospel; and if he knew his own creed better, he would be a very different man. His benevolence would be equal to his sincerity; and there would be harmony between his profession and his practice. As to Thompson, it is highly probable that, notwithstanding his non-profession, he has been indirectly benefited by the precepts of the New Testament. There are thousands in this country who have derived benefit from that book, although they do not know the fact, and, consequently, do not acknowledge it. But, secondly, setting aside all considerations of this kind, you know that there is great variety in the natural dispositions of men. Some are amiable, and others morose; some charitable, and others selfish; and some cheerful, and others sullen. Besides all this, circumstances, though they do not form character, as the disciples of fatalism absurdly teach, undoubtedly exercise a silent but powerful influence on many persons. Prosperity makes some men selfish. The increase of gold induces the desire for more, especially in minds that are so ill-instructed as to be unable to distinguish between enjoyment and the means of enjoyment. Scales, I have no doubt, would make as profound a bow as his fat-enclosed spine would permit, to the owner of a handsome carriage, and an elegant country mansion. He has sense enough to see in such things the result of money, and to see in money the power by which they were produced; but he has not sufficient refinement of taste to enjoy similar pleasures; and, therefore, he goes on adding to the gold-power by which the carriage and mansion were created, and probably will do so until apoplexy shall finish his career. Thompson, again, is struggling with the world, you say. Well, he knows the want of money, but not its value. He finds pleasure in relieving necessities such as, probably, he has himself experienced. The temporary pleasure of doing a good deed, which brings its own reward, is a greater thing with him than the slow accumulation of small sums, which would, in due time, amount to a fortune. He likes the good will, and derives pleasure from the good wishes of his fellow-men; but, depend upon it, his want of religion does not make him generous, no more than the orthodoxy of the grocer's creed makes *him* sand his sugar."

"Thank you," said Sinclair; "but I don't think Scales much of a Christian, and I believe Thompson is very near one of the right sort."

"Then, thank you," said I, "for you have strengthened my argument greatly."

My companion looked at me in silence for some time, as if something pressed for utterance which he did not like to say. I thought there was agitation from some cause in his breast. After a time he said—

"I have only known you, Sir, for some twenty-four hours, and the commencement of our acquaintance was somewhat singular. Yet I dreamed about you during the night, and I feel drawn towards you by some mysterious influence. I dreamed that you had something very important to tell me, and that it effected a strange change in my thoughts and habits. What can all this mean?"

"I do not know, Mr. Sinclair," I replied; "but if it is

in my power to do you any good, I shall be but too happy, as you have been very kind to me, an entire stranger."

"No," he said, "I believe I am, or soon shall be, the obliged party. My eyes were fixed on you as soon as you entered Nichols's office. I heard what he said to you, and had great difficulty in restraining myself from rushing into the room, and knocking him down. I saw your agitation, and followed you to the street, where I watched you until I thought you had recovered sufficient strength to be able to speak with me. From your manner and conversation, I conclude that you know far more than I do about something which greatly troubles me."

"What is it, my friend?"

"May I trust you?"

"Certainly."

"Will you not despise me?"

"No."

"Well," said he, lowering his voice to a whisper, and casting his eyes towards the ground, "I am very un-happy. I am not a Christian. I cannot believe the Bible, and yet I feel that I am a great sinner against God. What shall I do? Pity me!"

Tears filled the speaker's eyes as he spoke. I was deeply moved. I had longed to preach the Gospel. Here was an unlooked-for opportunity, and a ready ear. My heart was drawn towards the young man. He was evidently sincere, even to the extent of mental agony. To despair of doing good in this case, if the proper course were adopted, would have been folly and unbelief. I breathed a desire for aid into that ear which needs no human words. We spent the whole evening together, walking about the majestic sides of Arthur's Seat, and talking on subjects to which angels might have listened, and doubtless did listen, for "there is joy in heaven among the angels of God over one sinner that repenteth ;" and, three months afterwards, Frederick Sinclair was admitted a member of a Christian church. He is still a cheerful and consistent disciple of the great Saviour, and we have the mutual pleasure of occasionally exchanging letters.

* * * * *

To enter minutely into the experience of three years would be a wearisome task to the writer, and a cruel exaction on the patience of the reader. At the end of six months, during which I had occasional employment, sometimes as clerk, and sometimes as accountant, and frequent experience of dire poverty, I was seized with typhus fever, which was so severe for several days that the physician who attended me gave up the case as hopeless. I trace my recovery, under God's blessing, to the more than motherly care of the Christian woman with whom I then lodged, in Nicolson-street. This good lady, whose disinterested care I shall never forget, and which I traced to her genuine piety, for which she was remarkable, persevered in her attentions even after the medical adviser had assured her that death was certain. I was quite delirious for six days. On one occasion, Mrs. Golding had left the room in which I lay for a few minutes, and when she returned I was trying to open the window, not knowing what I did, but evidently with the intention of leaping out. The precaution of nailing it had been taken by the advice of the doctor, so that my madness failed to accomplish the fatal purpose. My head was twice shaved during the continuance of the fever. On the second occasion I was sufficiently collected to know what the barber was about, and I remember distinctly that he was an extremely garrulous person. I also recollect Mrs. Golding's kindness in reading to me soothing passages of Scripture and hymns, when the crisis had passed. But the first intelligence I received, after that event, was that my kind mother was no more. This painful news checked the progress of recovery for some time. Extreme debility and sleepless nights followed this severe attack for several weeks; and one fine afternoon I walked slowly to Arthur's Seat, in the hope that the exercise and the air would benefit me. Instead of keeping the winding footpath around the hill, I ventured on the rash experiment of climbing its precipitate side. My foot slipped, I fell, and rolled to the bottom. I was not injured, but severely shaken by the fall. I found my way back to my lodgings, and lay in a state of exhaustion for several days.

Mrs. Golding entered my room on one of those days, saying that a lady and gentleman from Leith had called to see me. My memory had been weakened by the fever, and it was some minutes before I could make out from the name who they were. Mr. and Mrs. Langfield, at whose house I had been an occasional visitor, had heard of my illness, and had come up to Edinburgh to inquire after my health; but, more than that, Mr. Langfield had also heard of a situation which he thought I could fill with advantage both to myself and the firm. This agreeable intelligence had a very beneficial effect on my health, and my strength rapidly returned. In another week I was able to remove and enter on my new duties; but I was pale, and, as my head had been shaved, I wore a little cap, so that I looked ten years older than I really was at the time. On examining the state of my affairs, which was easily done, I found, to my dismay, that I was several pounds in debt. Doctor's bill, nurse's charge, and lodgings, looked in my face, and, if possible, I became paler than before. The situation on which I had entered, however, was the only permanent one that had yet presented itself; and as the salary, fifty pounds for the first year, with the promise of an annual addition, was quite a fortune in my estimation, I resolved that the debt should be quickly liquidated. No very long time elapsed before I was enabled to carry this resolution into effect. Would that I had been as faithful to other good resolutions! It would have saved me some heart-aches, and more rapidly advanced my highest interests.

Previous to my illness, I had united myself with a Christian Church in Edinburgh, which enjoyed then, as it does still, the ministration of an eminent scholar and theologian. I had become a Sunday-school teacher—had been brought into contact with several earnest-minded men—had frequently addressed the children—and had twice or thrice spoken at public meetings. At this time the celebrated "Voluntary Church Controversy" was agitating all Scotland. Dissent on the one hand, and Churchism on the other, were engaged, like two powerful armies, in a pitched battle. The thing became a mental epidemic. High and low, rich and poor, the divine with half-a-dozen diplomas, and the bricklayer's labourer, were all hot with the conflict. Cities and villages wafted the war-cry, and mountains and valleys prolonged its echo. Public meetings, with their "resolutions;" soirées, with their after-tea witticisms; and discussions, with their exhibitions of intellectual gladiatorship, were held. Newspapers were filled with correspondence; pamphlets, good, bad, and indifferent, fell upon the country like showers of snow-flakes; large volumes issued from the press, much to the advantage of paper-makers and printers; regular periodicals, such as "The Voluntary," and "The Churchman," made their appearance, with their varied contents of argument, exposition, denunciation,

G

attack, defence, and drollery; the pulpit, so far from escaping the contagion, helped to diffuse it; and perhaps it is no exaggeration to say that there were few families, over the length and breadth of Scotland, in which it was not the every-day topic of discussion for a long period. That there were numerous personal alienations, separations between friends, fomentations of dislike, heart-burnings, and evil surmisings, in consequence of this famous agitation, need not surprise any one who is acquainted with the workings of human hearts, and the limited and partial view which the multitude generally take, even of questions of world-wide interest. To keep a great question within its proper province, and to discuss it on its own merits, require a degree of perspicacity and of self-command to which very few men can lay claim. That there were some, on both sides of this question, who really did this, is matter of history—and the fact is honourable to them; but neither " voluntaries" nor " compulsories," considered in the aggregate, could be expected to reach such a lofty position in the severe and protracted battle.

I was, neither by disposition nor conviction, likely to stand by as a mere spectator; nor did I. I found time, first, to write to the newspapers, and then to publish a pamphlet, containing my views of the matter at issue. What those views were will be inferred, when I state that my maiden publication was warmly praised in Dr. Marshall's " Voluntary Church Magazine," and referred to, in terms of high commendation, in a public meeting by one of the champions of the Nonconformist argument. This pamphlet was followed in a few months by another, of larger size and greater pretensions, which met with similar approbation, and I was chosen corresponding secretary to a " Young Man's Association," formed for the purpose of diffusing information on the whole subject. I confess that my heart was never in my proper business. I endeavoured conscientiously to discharge the duties of my office, but I am bound to acknowledge that I did so rather mechanically than with the whole heart. Journal, day-book and ledger had no attractions for me ; goods and £ s. d. were burdens. In reading and solitary musings I found pleasure; public meetings, especially when the speakers were men of ability, gratified me; and a successful argument in controversy—that is to say, on *my own side* of the question—by which the antagonist was floored, was a treat most highly valued. I spent more than I should have done in purchasing the ephemeral tractates and sermons by which the war was conducted, and, as a matter of course, my own publications, instead of realising a profit, " gained a loss." Still, to " see one's self in print," and to have the complacent conviction that one's own views were certainly correct, were sources of gratification which amply compensated for the trifling pecuniary loss! So I doubtless thought at the time, and if I think differently now, that is no reason why I should fail to record the weakness of former years.

Let it not be imagined, however, that I consider that famous controversy to have been either a mistake in theory, or a loss of time in fact. It was neither. A fierce storm passed over the country, and, in its course, some of the beautiful flowers that grow in the soil of brotherly kindness and charity were blighted, or torn up by the roots; but as an offset against this minor loss, the dead sea of Kirk formalism was troubled, and the pestilential mildew of moderatism was driven from the ecclesiastical field. The eyes of multitudes were opened, and a state of things was discovered, of which they had not dreamed. A great principle was involved in the ques-

tion under discussion—a principle of vital importance both
to Church and State; both to religion and civil politics;
both to Christian and national liberty. It was not imagined, at the time, that the result of the conflict would be,
at no very distant day, that remarkable community of
energetic and practical Nonconformists, the " Free Church
of Scotland." Such, nevertheless, is the fact.

The historical details connected with this great secession from the endowed Church of Scotland are too well
known to need relating here. They have become an
essential part of the ecclesiastical history of the nineteenth
century. My intention, in a single paragraph, is merely
to extract the kernel; to look at the soul of that memorable movement, which issued in the organisation of the
Free Church. I do not consider it a libel to suggest that
neither party realised, during the earlier stages of the
discussion, the full importance of the principle involved.
There was, undoubtedly, a great principle at stake in the
" Veto;" and as the stream of agitation proceeded, year
after year, it assumed the form of two watchwords of intense importance—"the rights of the Christian people," and
" the crown rights of the Redeemer." Separately, these
phrases are very significant; unitedly, they express the
entire idea upon which the controversy hinged: the idea,
namely, of Christ, the sole lawgiver in His Church, and
of that Church enjoying its privileges, and discharging its
duties, exclusively with reference to Him. It was, in
other words, a battle for liberty to attend to the dictates
of *conviction*. It was believed that Truth would be a
gainer, if those who were committed to her interests were
at liberty to give practical shape to their desires respecting
her. Such was, substantially, the position taken by those
who ultimately seceded. Failing in their efforts to obtain
a concurring government, and resolved—a resolution for

which posterity will thank them—not to surrender conviction as the price of a retained Establishment *status*, they " forsook Egypt,"—to borrow one of their own favourite metaphors,—and built the temple according to the pattern which they believed they had seen in the mount. The day which saw them in possession of their liberty—a liberty which they have permanently memorialised in the name given to the new body, the *Free* Church—also saw, not the death of Truth, nor even an omen of its mortality, but the triumphant vindication of one of its essential characteristics. " Rights" is the suggestive term used in each of the watchwords : the " rights" of the people, the " rights" of the Redeemer. Upon this significant word the controversy turned, and the intimation that these two classes of rights were, in the case under notice, inseparably united, gave an impetus to the agitation which no power on earth could have stopped. The idea was electric. The established Kirk was agitated to its centre. Other Christian Churches in Scotland, which had, in the eighteenth century, acquired their liberty, looked on the tumult with feelings alternately of hope and doubt. The result is known. The non-intrusionists gained their point, by abandoning the unsuccessful attempt to reconcile law with conviction, and by surrendering themselves to the pleasing authority of the latter. They gained their point, not as they had originally hoped, by conquering opposition, but by yielding themselves as the conquered to a great and vital principle, older than human law, and nobler than imperial governments.

This is the way that Truth usually deals with her friends ; she conducts them farther than they thought she would. Her revelations are gradual. She does not say all during her first interview, but she calls again and again, unfolding slowly, but certainly, that this or that principle to which you have committed yourself must be carried out, though it conduct you far beyond what you considered the limit of the journey. This is precisely the case with the Free Church. When she was in non-intrusionist embryo, she had no intention of going so far " from Egypt " as we find her at this moment, but having committed herself to a principle, she has travelled thus far; and, as I look upon her as a witness to the truth, and love her for the truth's sake, I affectionately tell her that she must go a little farther yet. She must not look back. Let her " remember Lot's wife." Let her speak to the people, and they will go forward; so shall her practical voluntaryism be the result of a scriptural faith, and a scriptural faith the spring of energetic practical voluntaryism.

Having said thus much on the general question, I feel it proper, in deference to my own convictions—whether they be correct or erroneous—to guard against the inference that I think ecclesiastical establishments wrong under every conceivable state of society. I certainly do not. Under the present dispensation I believe it is literally impossible to organise a *just* national religious establishment. Whilst the principles of Christianity have to contend against the hereditary opposition of an ungodly world, to ask the sanction and support of that world to those principles is a suicidal prayer. Experience too fully justifies the soundness of this position. But, experience apart, the obvious character and design of the Christian system involve the duty of jealous separation from secular influences, and, above all, from secular control. I think the separation of the Church from the State as clear a duty, as the separation of the individual Christian from the world. But I also think there is a time approaching when there will be an establishment in our world, as much superior to any that priests and kings have fashioned as the noonday of June is to the midnight of December. I, of course, refer to the days of the final kingdom—the times of the predicted theocracy, when "the Lord shall be King over all the earth," and "when the mountain of the Lord's house shall be established in the top of the mountains, and shall be exalted above the hills; and all nations shall flow unto it." Nonconformity in relation to that glorious economy will be a sin; as nonconformity in relation to the existing ecclesiastical establishments of Europe is, in my judgment, a duty. I am not ignorant of the circumstantial evils of dissent, as the reader will shortly find; but I think them comparatively light, when placed in the balance opposite the essential evils of establishments.

But to resume my personal narrative. The gentlemen in whose office I held a situation were strongly attached members of the Kirk of Scotland; the knowledge, therefore, that one of their clerks was actively siding with the advocates of voluntaryism, was not likely to raise that person in their esteem. This fact reached their ears through the parasitism of a junior. I blame him not; but, as he was one of those youths who seem born with a propensity to seek the smiles of the affluent by the use of gentle whispers and significant gestures, why should he not make the best of his time, and be diligent in his chosen vocation? My employers were kind and generous men, and never expressed any fault with the manner in which I discharged my duties, and, as I was always remarkably punctual, there was no ground of complaint; nevertheless, the head of the firm expressed the charitable opinion, when the junior informed him of my literary and speech-making tendencies, that " he was convinced that no person who sought the destruction of the Establishment could be a Christian, because its removal would inevitably cover the land with infidelity." This piece of information which was actually communicated to me by the young man himself, redoubled my vigilance, so far as the performance of my stipulated duties was concerned; and—shall I confess it?—increased my zeal for the prosperity of voluntaryism. I resolved, on the one hand, that what I considered " a good" should not be evil spoken of by reason of any negligence on my part; and, on the other, that no worldly advantages should keep me silent respecting the claims of a principle which I thought scriptural and Divine. I would not willingly offend my employers, but neither would I have my liberty curtailed; and, as the office hours were only from nine till five, I could serve the former and maintain the latter without much inconvenience.

Whether I acted wisely or otherwise in this matter, the reader can determine for himself. I relate the facts without comment. Only I must say, that were it possible for me to begin life again, with the benefit of personal experience, I would do many things which I omitted, and leave undone much that I did. My views, as respects public discussions and agitations, especially if they involve approaches to sectarian peculiarities, have undergone considerable modification. Whether this mental change be the result of greater wisdom, or of the deep waters through which I have gone, or of both united, I shall not venture to say; but the fact is as I have stated. I think my love to truth is stronger than ever, but I do not express the attachment in exactly the same way that I did, fifteen years ago; and I believe that my regard to principle has suffered no deterioration, but my esteem for good men everywhere has so far increased that I would shrink from offending them, if it could be possibly avoided. Alas! the knowledge of one's own infirmities is a painful lesson to learn; but when it teaches patience with the infirmities of others it is worth learning.

As I was returning from Church one afternoon, about this time, one of my fellow-teachers in the school came up to me and said,

"The very man I want."

" Well, what is it?" I asked.

"I want you to preach this evening," he replied.

"To *preach?*"

"Yes; and you *must* comply. Mr. Grierson was engaged to preach to the poor people at the village of A——, and something has occurred to prevent him. We have fixed upon you as his substitute; and as there is no time to lose, you must be off at once."

"Nonsense! my friend. You are in jest."

"Jest? on such a subject? I am in earnest."

" Well, so am I. I can't preach. I never attempted it."

" Don't say you can't, after the speeches we have all heard you deliver. Some of us think it is high time you had begun."

" I—I am not prepared."

" A—— is three miles off; get a cup of tea at the house of our friend Alfred, and then study as you go. You will find only a few poor labourers, in a cottage, and they will listen to you thankfully. There—now no more about it; will you go?"

" Yes," I answered, musingly, " I will."

"Well, good bye—God go with you!"

I need not attempt to describe the agitation created by this sudden summons. I went to the village, found the house, where about thirty poor persons were assembled, conducted the preliminary devotional services, and then gave out, by way of text, the words on which I had fixed as I walked to the place, namely, John i. 29, "Behold the Lamb of God, which taketh away the sin of the world." What I said I do not recollect; and certainly, if I did, I should spare the reader the trouble of reading my *first sermon*. I remember well, however, an old German clock ticking in the corner of the cottage. I kept staring at it, rather than face my audience, and I wondered that its hands were so slow in moving; from which I infer, that I was either short of matter, or agitated by this new scene in my history. Nevertheless, the clock managed to announce the usual hour of departure at last, and I returned to my lodgings—*thinking*.

I did not sleep much that night. What had I been about? What right had I to preach the Gospel to my fellow-men? Who authorised me? Besides, I was too sinful to presume to take upon me such an office, even occasionally. The responsibility was so great, that even the holiest of men might well tremble under it. Such thoughts followed each other with incredible rapidity. I tried to meet them by considering the destitute condition of those poor people, who had not the opportunity of religious instruction unless it were thus brought to their very houses by Christian kindness. I was wet with a profuse perspiration, and shortly after midnight was beginning to slumber, when a deep groan from an inner room aroused me. My landlady had two bed-rooms for lodgers. When she had a tenant for the other, he had to go through mine; and as she had had no lodger but myself for some weeks, I at once concluded that she had obtained another that day, and had forgotten to state the fact. If so, he must have gone to bed early. I listened eagerly. The groan was repeated.

" Who is there?" I asked, rising in bed.

"Are you awake, Sir? O! if there is any bread in the house, rise and give me some, for I am faint!"

I sprang to my feet, cut a piece of bread from a loaf in the cupboard, and, by the help of a little light from the street-lamp, I handed it to the person, whoever he might be. I was considerably agitated when, apparently, a very tall man sat up in the bed, and stretched out a long arm, snatching the bread from me, and putting it into his mouth with voracity. His hair was white, and his face very pale.

"Who are you?" I asked.

"O, never mind, Sir, I will tell you in the morning. I am hungry and tired now. Many thanks."

I lay down again; but sleep had departed. I confess, I felt uneasy. I had scarcely been in bed five minutes when he called again, in a voice of agony that made me tremble,

"More bread, dear Sir, for the love of heaven! and water! I am famishing!"

This was terrible. I sprang up again, and said, "Shall I get a light?"

"O no, no! only bread and water, and be quick if you please!"

This time I did not cut from the loaf, but handed it to him, just as it was, together with a tumbler of water. I cannot describe the avidity with which he seized both. I passed the remainder of the night in great uneasiness. Was he a lunatic? How came he there? Would he cry out again? All was still after he had eaten the loaf— for there was none of it left in the morning—and towards dawn I had the satisfaction of hearing him in a heavy sleep, frequently interrupted by moaning, as if he had a troubled dream. I now began to reflect on the incident, and to connect it with the event of the previous evening.

" If people are famishing for bread," I reasoned, " every man who has it is bound to bestow it on them. And is not this true, also, with respect to the bread of life? Who shall forbid the humblest Christian to instruct his fellow-men, according to the ability which God giveth, in the things pertaining to eternal life?" This view of the case met the objections which had been suggested in relation to my first attempt " to teach and to preach Jesus Christ."

I called to the mysterious inhabitant of the next room, about seven o'clock in the morning, and asked if he would rise and breakfast with me. He was soon in my room—a gaunt, wasted figure, about six feet tall, with an unnatural brilliance in his eyes, and very meanly clad; though his clothes had been of fine texture, and evidently so made as to fit his person. He apologised for the annoyance he had given me—stated that he had at one time been a commercial traveller — that he had suffered serious reverses—that he had tasted nothing for three days but some whiskey which had been given him at a public-house—that he had travelled thirty miles on foot on the previous day—and that he had not the means of paying for his lodging. Whether all this was true or not I had no means of ascertaining; but his sad condition, about which there could not be two opinions, and his intelligent conversation, induced me to keep him for a week, to pay for his lodgings, and to give him a few shillings when he departed. He said his name was White, and expressed great gratitude for my conduct. I have never seen him since, and can scarcely believe that he is alive. Poor fellow!-- Misconduct *may* have been at the root of his sufferings; but let the sinless cast the first stone at him !

When I had been two years and a half in my situation I began to think seriously about sending for her, between whom and myself a tender correspondence had been kept up, and whom I had known and loved for nearly seven years. My employers seemed to have a flourishing business. My salary had been increased; and I thought that to furnish a couple of rooms and to marry would greatly increase my comfort, and not involve much more expense than lodging. Perhaps the heart had more to do with this than the judgment; but that is an old tale, and need not be enlarged upon. The decision was taken. My loved one was sent for. We were married.

My chief anxiety after marriage sprang from the impression that possibly the plans of my youth, and the purpose of riper years, might be frustrated. Nevertheless, the deed was done, and I bless God for it, as that which I thought a barrier proved an unexpected and mysterious facility. We were happy in each other's company. Our wants were moderate. I had married a gentle and economical wife, and my evenings were times of home-peace. I had less to do with public meetings, and more with the pleasures of domestic quiet. For a long time I had attended a Sabbath-morning prayer-meeting, in the fellowship of several young men, who employed themselves on that day in various spheres of Christian usefulness. In addition to my Sunday-school labours I frequently preached in rooms in the town, and in villages around. I heard of instances of good done, which greatly cheered me, and I felt that I must persevere. Business, as I said before, was discharged rather as a duty than a pleasure. Every spare shilling was laid out in books. I purchased a Greek grammar and lexicon, and resolved to study that language. To read the New Testament in the original I felt to be desirable, not that it is at all essential to the correct understanding of the Gospel, or to clear and consistent exposition; but it affords facilities, both in reading and study, which none but those who understand the language can appreciate. I persevered and succeeded; and I found myself amply rewarded for the labour by the pleasure I derived from first reading a verse in the Greek Testament correctly.

By frequent correspondence with the newspapers on ecclesiastical and literary subjects, I acquired considerable facility in composition. On one occasion, about three months after my marriage, among the " Notices to Correspondents" in a certain newspaper, was a request that the writer of some articles which had appeared anonymously in its columns would favour the editor with a call, at his private residence. What this foreshadowed I knew not, and conjecture was useless, especially as the editor had the notoriety of being a learned eccentric. I went, as requested, and found him sitting in bed, with a small writing-desk on his knees, a pen in his hand, a curious, aristocratic-looking night-cap mounted on his head, and the bed and the table at its side covered with newspapers, books, slips, and proofs, in admirable disorder.

" Good morning, Sir," exclaimed the learned editor, " you find me in a regular pickle! It is a case of ' pie,' to use a professionalism. Perhaps you will ask, with the immortal Will, ' How cam'st thou in this pickle?' The fact is, I have got a villanous headache! The cause of ' the people,' most of them scoundrelly ingrates, threatens to put ' Finis' to my career! Did you read my last article on our magnificent ministry? What do you think of it?"

This was the first time we had met; and as the circumstances, together with these pithy sayings, were sufficiently ridiculous, I laughed, and replied,

" It is well written, but *somewhat* severe."

"Severe—yes! Ah, ha! Spice is up in the market! Nothing else will go down with the mad Rads. Besides, the imbeciles who disgrace office at present must be held up to richly-deserved contempt. I am greatly obliged by your able contributions; but I wish you would turn your pen to politics. I want some first-class articles on the present state of parties. There is a conspiracy against my paper. It must be exposed, braved, trampled under foot! By-and-by we shall be able to pay handsomely for your services. What d'ye say?"

Here was a revelation which suggested caution; and I replied, briefly, that though sincerely attached to the cause of the people, and anxious for the prosperity of the country, I had no taste for political excitement.

"Ah! Here are the sheets of a pamphlet on the corn laws, which I mean to get out next week. I wish you would look over them, and suggest such alterations as may strike you, as I wrote in violent haste."

I complimented his ability—and with great sincerity—on that subject, as greatly superior to mine; and said that I entertained no doubt the pamphlet would do without revision.

Finally, he intimated that his paper would speedily become valuable property; and asked whether I would invest some money in it, for which I might calculate on six *per cent.* at least, and enter into literary partnership with him.

The affectation of wealth, in the case of a poor man, is one of the most despicable exhibitions of human pride. As I have always felt this, I at once undeceived the worthy editor, and said that whatever I might have thought of his proposition—for which I was obliged—under other circumstances, it was out of my power to advance money for any purpose whatever. After some further conversation we separated; and thus ended my interview with a man of singular intellectual ability, which, had it been balanced and controlled by something still nobler, would probably have raised him to eminence, and given him a name among the literary nobles of his fatherland. His career has ended. His dust lies in a quiet, country churchyard. Peace to his memory!

One morning, shortly after this, we were all startled by the mournful intelligence that the head of the firm had died very suddenly. Not long subsequently, in consequence of losses in India and other misfortunes, the house stopped payment, bankruptcy followed, the clerks were discharged, the premises were closed, and I was—both metaphorically and literally—at sea. The causes of this movement will be found in another chapter.

CHAPTER VI.

CLOUDS AND SUNSHINE.

"God moves in a mysterious way
    His wonders to perform :
He plants His footsteps in the sea,
    And rides upon the storm.

"Deep in unfathomable mines
    Of never-failing skill,
He treasures up His bright designs,
    And works His sovereign will.

"Blind unbelief is sure to err,
    And scan His work in vain;
God is His own interpreter,
    And He will make it plain."—*Cowper*.

APOSTROPHE TO COWPER'S SHADE—DOTH GOD LEAD MEN?—POSITIVE TRUTH—ADDISON—FAITH AND FATALISM—DISAPPOINTED PLANS AND REALISED HOPES—THE MISSIONARY DEPUTATION—I THINK OF EMIGRATING—BREAKING-UP HOUSE—A BRIGHT LIGHT—MORE DISAPPOINTMENTS—THE BROOMIELAW—STARTLING INTERVIEW—FEARFUL HURRICANE AT SEA—LIVERPOOL—LODGINGS FOR A NIGHT—A TALKATIVE LADY—AMERICAN "SHIN-PLASTERS"—GRIEF AND POVERTY—BIRTH OF MY FIRST CHILD—A DARK PERIOD—BENEVOLENT CLERGYMAN—THE TEMPTATION—OUTLINES OF A SERMON—THE BLESSED SABBATH—THE "NEWS ROOM"—EXCITING ADVERTISEMENT—I AM EXAMINED AND APPOINTED—THE WORLD IN TRANSITION—THE JOURNEY OF HUMANITY—THE HUMAN SIDE OF THE QUESTION—THE DIVINE SIDE—REVOLUTIONS—THE STAKE AT ISSUE—CHRISTIAN PARADOXES—COMMENCEMENT OF MY PUBLIC MINISTRY—MANY CALLS TO PREACH—NOTICES OF TWO OR THREE MINISTERS—EXPECTATIONS OF THE WORLD—EDUCATIONAL AND CHRISTIAN AGENCY—TRIUMPH OF GOOD.

SHADE of "the stricken deer that left the herd," if, in these days of spirit-journeying, thy calm felicity is ever interrupted by a transitory visit to England, and if thou art capable of hearing the words of mortal lips, accept my thanks for these pathetic lines, whose poetry is equal to the sentiment it clothes, and whose sentiment is strength to the faith of men led by God!

"Led by God?" Doth GOD lead *men?* Sad is the history of humanity, gloomy the retrospect of six thousand years; but the one were sadder, and the other far more gloomy, if He did *not!* In that case, if war, pestilence, and famine, and the myriad inferior scourges of the world, had not long ago exterminated the race, the cloud that envelopes the story of man would be infinitely darker than it is. In Divine condescension, and with Fatherly care, God leads men. There is not the pillar of cloud by day, and of fire by night, as there was in the case of the wilderness wanderers, but the absence of a visible symbol of the Divine Leader's presence does not involve the absence of the Invisible Guide. Strangely, mysteriously, but safely, are Christian men conducted. Their personal experience is a record of, and a commentary upon, the fidelity of Him who is bringing "many sons unto glory." There is surprising diversity in the circumstances of that experience, but there is essential unity in the fact, that all its modifications are under the control of a Hand that never committed an error, or omitted to do the best thing at the best time. Doubtless, there are times when even the eye of Faith is so dim with tears that it cannot see that Hand; and there are seasons when the heart is so cold by the frosty fogs of the wilderness that it feels not the warmth of the Elder Brother's love; but these things affect not the "Yea" and "Amen" of the Unchangeable Promiser. The "blind" are as safely led as are those who journey through a clear horizon to the land of rest. That the word of the Immutable is ample security for *ultimate* safety, Faith will allow, even when her words come in broken sobs, and when salt tears are on her cheeks; but the intermediate steps are all ordered, as well as the issue of the last one; and every stage in the progress is arranged as surely as its glorious end. A *positive* system of redemption, which admits no vacillating " yea and nay" to impede its actions, includes a positive providence. If the Christian Gospel be complete as a whole, it is complete in all its parts; if *you* predicate the symmetry of the system, *we* affirm perfection of each of its constituent elements; and if you declare its adaptation to man's spiritual nature, and teach that it furnishes life to the soul, we plead that this, its supreme characteristic, includes the subordinate, and involves the guardianship and protection of the body in which that living soul is enshrined. In other words, men who have committed their souls to the Saviour of the world are warranted to expect direction during the journey of life. Nor is this warranty merely inferential, or deduced from arguments such as have been suggested. It is matter of clear revelation. There are assurances and promises in relation to this very thing. He who " takes care for oxen," and feeds the raven and the sparrow, hath not overlooked men. The stages of being are noted, and the wants that characterise each are supplied. The infant, the child, the strong man, and the feeble by reason of age, are entered upon God's " book of remembrance." " Thy providence," wrote Addison—and if the hymn had been the sole contribution of his pen, his name would still have been well known to his countrymen—

" Thy providence my life sustained,
   And all my wants redressed :
When in the silent womb I lay,
   And hung upon the breast.

> "Unnumbered comforts on my soul
> 　Thy tender care bestowed,
> Before my infant heart conceived
> 　From whom those comforts flowed.
>
> "When in the slippery paths of youth
> 　With heedless steps I ran,
> Thine arm, unseen, conveyed me safe,
> 　And led me up to man.
>
> "When worn with sickness, oft hast thou
> 　With health renewed my face ;
> And when in sins and sorrows sunk,
> 　Revived my soul with grace."

I adopt this song. I cannot do otherwise. And that, not because I think it religiously true, but because I know it is a matter of fact; not an opinion, or a general conviction, but a reality. If, after a review of my experience, I failed to recognise evidences that I was led by an Invisible Hand, I should be inexcusably blind; and if, after such recognition, I hesitated to declare the fact, I should be criminally ungrateful. Not because I think this personal retrospect discovers anything essentially different from what other men would find in a review of their lives—for where differences exist they are only circumstantial, not essential—but because I am persuaded that whilst multitudes have expressed the same sentiment, there are multitudes more who have felt its emotions kindling gratitude in their hearts, and inducing them

> "To let expressive silence muse His praise ;"

and such men are pleased to see their sentiments clothed in words.

But there is nothing in all this calculated to lead to the doctrine of fatalism, or necessity. The duty of personal action is proclaimed by the very fact of life. Being, with its rational faculties, must manifest itself. Life has a sphere in which it must work. Its powers of thinking, planning, deciding, acting, choosing, and refusing, cannot lie dormant without guilt. Diligence in business is as much a duty as fervour of spirit. We must "go forward;" yet in the full recognition of the truth that "the steps of a good man are ordered by the Lord." We must "put our hand to the plough;" although conscious that "God giveth the increase." Necessity would paralyse action, and make human purposes vain. It is *action*, not indolence, that is controlled by the unseen hand of the Father; and it is the purpose of the mind, not indecision, that is realised or defeated by Him who only knows what is best for the recipients of His kindness. We may even resolve on a *good* thing without being permitted to carry our resolution into effect, but the providential hindrance will be no proof of providential displeasure. The son of Jesse intended to build a temple for the service of God. He was not allowed to carry the intention into practical effect, yet he was assured that he "did well that it was in his heart."

Faith in Divine Providence is not fatalism. The belief that actions are controlled is not the same thing as necessity; but there are many who, when they recall the scenes through which they have gone, and remember that they considered them at the time opposed both to their interests and plans, gratefully confess *now* that they were neither. The goal has been reached, but not by the self-elected road. The end has been realised, but not by the process originally intended.

My narrative illustrates these remarks, and if it tend to encourage

"A forlorn and shipwrecked brother,"

the labour of writing it will be recompensed. I coveted knowledge, and wished for that systematic instruction which colleges are supposed to afford. I acquired the limited information I possess without system, except that which experience created, and without any facility except personal application. I thought of the importance of wealth as subsidiary to the purposes of life, but had the mortification of knowing that the wealth of my parents had vanished before it could be of any service to me; yet the purpose of my life has been thus far realised without parental gold and silver. I imagined the happiness of those who, by virtue of social position, are able to command those results upon which their purposes are centered, but discovered, that though my father was the representative of a very influential family, he was entangled in the net of affliction and poverty; yet the honour of teaching, though on a limited scale, and in connexion with the social impediments of nonconformity, those truths which shall outlive the splendour of empires, is at once my happiness and honour. And I wished to instruct idolaters in foreign lands respecting the unity of God and the redemption by Jesus Christ, but my plans failed, and my hopes were disappointed; yet it is my valued privilege to unfold the everlasting Gospel in my native language and in my native land. Thus, essentially, all the cherished designs of early life have been realised, whilst, circumstantially, every plan which contemplated these ends has been set aside! Is not this the finger of God? Alas! for the piety, and shame on the intelligence, that can say " No!"

Shortly before the change briefly alluded to at the close of last chapter, I had meditated on several schemes, and dismissed most of them as impracticable. A deputation from London, representing a Missionary Society, visited the north. I attended the meetings; heard what the reverend representatives said; felt excited by their pictures of the moral condition of heathendom; regretted the scarcity of funds, upon which they pathetically enlarged, and especially the want of suitable missionaries, willing to encounter the trials and privations of this sublime "foreign service." At the close of one of the meetings I went, with beating heart, to the chief man of the deputation, and offered myself as a missionary. The reverend doctor heard my statement with evident satisfaction, and advised me to write to the secretaries of the Society. I lost no time; the next day's post carried my letter to London, and eight days subsequently I received a reply. This document was, in some respects, necessarily formal; nevertheless, it was evidently written by a man of warm heart and generous feelings, who felt at once the responsibility and the greatness of the cause with which he was officially connected. Several questions were proposed in this letter, which I fully answered, and the answer was despatched without delay. I waited the result with deep anxiety, pondering the probabilities and possibilities of the future, until patience was exhausted by long disappointment, and the non-arrival of a letter convinced me that the correspondence was at an end.

The idea now occurred that emigration to America, with whose romantic history I was well acquainted—whose pilgrim origin captivated my heart—with whose national constitution I felt considerable sympathy, and whose progress among the nations of the world I foresaw as certain—would be the wisest step, under all the circumstances of the case, which I could possibly take. I accordingly procured books on America, made inquiry concerning the expenses of a transatlantic voyage, and resolved—should circumstances favour the design—to go to the land of the Pilgrim Fathers. My dear wife, though willing to leave the matter to my judgment, evidently shrunk from the contemplation of a sea voyage, especially as we had not the means of paying our passage, and no certainty, even if that difficulty were overcome, of obtaining a situation there, should we ever reach the shores of America. I could not, of course, promise exemption from the unceremonious tossings of the Atlantic, but an ingenious mode of conquering the second and third difficulties presented itself to my imagination. I would go to Liverpool, in the first instance; obtain letters to mercantile houses there which had branches in America, and thus secure a situation in the latter country—my travelling expenses being, as a matter of course, paid by the English firm, which, I had little doubt, would avail itself of my proffered services. The sale of our little furniture would surely bring as much as would pay our way to Liverpool, by steamer from Glasgow; and, once at Liverpool, the future was clear. You smile, respected reader, at my simplicity; or, perhaps, amidst the enjoyments of your comfortable room, you call it folly. Well, I shall not dispute the point. I shall even admit that I was inexcusably foolish, although I would very respectfully ask, just by way of information, what *you* would have done, had you been placed exactly in my circumstances, and with exactly my feelings? But as you do not please to answer, I must unfold the sequel.

I named my purpose to several gentlemen, who, whilst they regretted the occasion of my resolution, prepared highly satisfactory letters of introduction to friends in Liverpool. I called on a broker about the disposal of my furniture, who examined it, and named the sum it would bring. I thought he had made a mistake in the calculation, or that I had not heard him correctly. But no; such gentlemen never make mistakes, and the sense of hearing of persons in my condition is generally too acute.

I was appalled. The loss was fearful. And the books—those precious books—those household idols—must *they* go for *that* sum? Alas! the "broker" had a peculiar mode of estimating my cherished volumes, which I understood not, but which I heartily detested as abominable heresy.

Pending the delivery of my chattels, out of which I had only had some seven months' service, to this disinterested stranger, an event occurred, which sent my thoughts into an entirely new channel, threw a bright light across my dark path, and pointed to the speedy realisation of my long-cherished hopes. An advertisement appeared in the newspapers for two or three young men of character, talent, and piety, to proceed, under the auspices of a certain Society, as missionary schoolmasters to one of our colonies. I was excited with pleasure and gratitude, and felt as confident that I should be elected as if my name had appeared in the advertisement as having been already chosen. I went directly to the address, and found the gentleman who had been deputed to arrange this business. He examined me on several points—doctrinal, educational, and ecclesiastical; said that he was highly satisfied, felt thankful that he had met with me, and entertained no doubt that, on his report, the committee for whom he acted would forthwith engage me. He was going elsewhere, however, for eight days, and at the close of that period I should hear from him, when the thing would be satisfactorily closed; and he hoped it would prove a source of pleasure both to myself and to the Society of which he was agent. In this hope I most cordially concurred. Here was the silver lining of the cloud growing rapidly broader! My heart was filled to overflowing with joy! I went home, and told my beloved young wife that all was right yet—

H

we had not been precipitate—we were in the path of duty—we should be blessed, and made blessings. We parted with our furniture, made things as square as possible, and waited with mingled patience and anxiety for the important letter of my reverend friend. The stipulated time slowly elapsed. The letter came not. I waited two days longer. No letter. I called at the address, where the examinator had his temporary lodgings. He had not returned, and the occupant of the house could give no information concerning his movements. I waited two days more. Still no reply. What was to be done? I could not wait. We were living in an almost empty house, and with more than economy, as we had just as much as would pay our passage to Liverpool, and scarcely ten shillings over! The engagement alluded to, if completed, would remove all anxiety about the present, as it was to take effect immediately. There was a vessel to sail in a few days, in which the missionary schoolmasters were to embark. But I could wait no longer. Besides, the time had much more than expired, and I had received no intelligence, neither did I know where to address a letter of inquiry, except at the house already referred to, whose inhabitants were as ignorant of the reverend gentleman's movements as myself. That there was a mistake somewhere was too evident; but I could not, and would not believe that the agent had deceived me, or that he was insincere in his expressed belief that the engagement would be confirmed. I saw *that* in his countenance which precluded any suspicion of this kind.

It was about three o'clock, in a December afternoon, when we reached the Broomielaw, Glasgow. I placed my wife in the steam-ship, and went into the city to make a small purchase. The ship was to leave in an hour. As I crossed one of the streets hastily on my return a carriage stopped, and at the same moment I heard my name called. The speaker was the agent of the Society. We were mutually surprised.

"We have been daily expecting to hear from you," he said.

"From me, Sir?"

"Yes. I wrote to you, a few days after I had the pleasure of seeing you, stating that you were appointed."

"I never received the letter."

"Indeed; strange! but that accounts for your silence. Well, what do you intend?"

The reader will be kind enough to imagine my perturbation. There was not a moment even for explanation. I muttered something concerning uncertainty, which I suppose was unintelligible to him; and I fear, in my agitation and haste to reach the ship, I left the impression upon his mind that I would call.

It was getting dark when the noble vessel began to steam down the noble Clyde—dark, cold, and wet; and, therefore, an appropriate time for a dialogue on "mystery!" My dear travelling companion concurred with me in the sage conclusion that the whole matter, as well as the sudden and unexpected meeting just mentioned, was strange! There we had to leave it. Time might shed some light upon the mystery; but it was certain enough that to the colony, fixed on by the committee as the scene of my labours, it was determined by the Great Disposer of events that I should not go. To return was out of the question after going so far; but, indeed, my mind was in such confusion from the events of the preceding days, as well as from the occurrence of that afternoon, that I was incapable of acting otherwise than I did.

The evening was dull and wet when we left the

Broomielaw, but there was not much wind.   There was a heavy cargo on board, and there were many passengers. The scenery on the banks of the Clyde, which tourists describe as grand, varied, and imposing, was, of course, shrouded in darkness after we had passed Greenock, so that I had not the pleasure of seeing it.   Towards midnight, the ship began to roll heavily; most of the passengers suffered from that intolerable visitant, sea-sickness; the wind moaned and howled dismally, and, from the rapid movements of the sailors on deck, it became evident that a storm was feared.   That fear was speedily and too fully justified.   It arose, and increased till it reached one of the most violent hurricanes ever remembered on the coast of England.   The morning and noon of next day came, but they brought neither abatement of its fury, nor even the consolation of light, except just as much as made the darkness visible, and exhibited the uproar of mountainous waves as they danced around us, and dashed over us.   Every thing that could be swept from the deck was carried in their liquid arms.   The terrified passengers, especially the female portion of them, presented a picture of absolute helplessness, in most cases amounting to despair.   A veteran pilot, who had weathered many a storm on different parts of the great ocean, happened to be on board—I say happened, for he was on that occasion the substitute of the usual pilot, the latter being unwell—and I was arrested by the earnestness, energy, decision, and coolness of the fine old man, as he peered through the thick spray, gave orders right and left, and threw the line to ascertain whether we were in danger from the sunken banks of the Mersey.   Our vessel rushed on under the terrible impetus of the power of that apparently feeble thing steam.   Yet, with all her giant force, the careering winds and boiling ocean compelled her to labour fearfully, the paddle-wheels being alternately submerged, and driven furiously in the air; and thus, rolling from side to side, we proceeded many miles, until two anchors were thrown out opposite the town of Liverpool. We passed several vessels in distress, and that day became memorable for its shipwrecks. So furious was the sea, even in the comparative calm opposite the harbour, that the small steamers did not venture to put off for the passengers for several hours. At last, however, the storm abated sufficiently to make this practicable; and about seven or eight o'clock that evening, we stood upon St. George's Pier, as miserable-looking objects as fasting, sea-sickness, pouring rain, fatigue, and fear, could make us. But over all now came the rush of joy, that the peril was past, and of unfeigned gratitude to God, that we stood on the solid stones once more. We crept towards the town, the streets of which were rushing with water, whilst, at the distance of every two or three yards, might be seen pieces of chimney pots and tiles, which the wind had torn from the houses.

But we were on *terra firma,* that was much!

> " The eye that watches o'er wild ocean's dead,
>   Each in his coral cave,
> Fondly as if the green turf wrapped his head,
>   Fast by his father's grave,"

had watched over us; and though we knew not where to go, or what should "be on the morrow," our hearts were cheered by that beautiful angel, HOPE, which God sends to sing to his human children, as they travel across the storm-swept wilderness. Blessed and beautiful Hope! how she smiles at the storm, and sings a sweet lullaby in the ear of the sad; how she whispers her consolations in words of the richest poetry; how she lifts her gentle finger to the place where the Sun *is*, though His light be eclipsed by thick, intervening darkness; and how she lays one hand on a happy future, and the other on the heart of her eagerly listening ward, saying, " I will bring you together yet!" Kind, generous, celestial Hope! blessed be God for Hope!

By the kindness of a policeman we were directed to " comfortable" lodgings for the night. The good woman, who saw our sorrowful plight, and who had peculiar affection for travellers by sea, her husband being a sailor, prepared some capital tea with the usual accompaniments, with extraordinary celerity. It is true, that we had much need of refreshment, but it is likewise true, that our exhibition at the tea-board was not very remarkable. Unhappily, the house was at sea, playing at pitch-and-toss with the drenched strangers. We were more than satisfied with the amount of exercise of this kind we had already experienced, but our opinion was not consulted; the house rolled from side to side, and everything kept up the motion with very disagreeable perseverance. To add to our " unrest,"—as our Germanic neighbours, or, rather, their would-be-thought-original copyists, phrase it,—Mrs. Roberts was as expert in the use of the " little member," as she was in the preparation of tea. In the course of half an hour, she inflicted upon our swimming heads a detailed, but remarkably parenthetical, history of her whole life, including that of her husband, and those of the parents and parents' parents on both sides, interspersing the extempore memoir with vivid descriptions of storms at sea, and accidents by field and flood.

" But, why don't you eat, ma'am ?" was introduced at the end of every two or three rapid sentences, when she saw that my poor tired wife was only looking on vacancy. " Why don't you eat? You must be hungry. Here's a nicely done toast. Try a slice of ham. How d'ye like it? Sick? Yes, it's a nasty sensation! But, la! it's nothing when it's over, you know. I remember—let me help you to a little milk—once being at sea in a storm— a bit of sugar, Sir?—far worse than this. *This!* Its nothing! Our ship was often quite under the water— do try this cup, ma'am—and once she was lifted clean out of the sea, and carried several yards by the wind— are you warm enough, ma'am?—some more coals?— there!—I was dreadful sick; but when I got on shore, la! *wasn't* I hungry? Roberts ordered a fowl for me— and it wasn't a small one, I assure you—and I ate it up, every bit of it, bones and all!"

"Bones and all?" I inquired by way of relief, that I might have a polite opportunity of smiling.

"Fact, Sir, I assure you! La! there—it's no use pretending to a thing, you know. I was never so hungry in my life! We must eat, you know. I'm very sorry— what *shall* I get for you?"

"A comfortable bed, Mrs. Roberts, as soon as you can," I suggested.

"Yes—I'm sure you're very fatigued. You want to be quiet, don't you? Well, you have just come to the house for that! You might hear a mouse walking across the floor all day, I assure you, Sir; it's the quietest street in all Liverpool; every body says it is; but I'm *so* sorry!—this dear lady will get no sleep—people can't sleep, you know, on an empty stomach—la!"

The following morning presented as entire a contrast to the day which preceded as it is possible to imagine. The sun was most brilliant. There was not the vestige of a cloud on the horizon. The storm had effectually cleared the atmosphere. Perfect calmness looked down on the wreck of the previous day, on sea and shore, as if enjoying the result of the wild hurricane. The streets were thoroughly washed; and it was difficult to realise the suddenness of the transition, during one short night, from terror to repose.

I paid Mrs. Roberts, and found myself in a strange place, not knowing a single individual in the town, and with the large sum of six shillings and threepence-half-penny in my pocket! I left my wife in the company of our talkative hostess, and went in search of the gentlemen to whom I had letters of introduction. I naturally thought of my former experience in this line, and wondered what the result would be this time. "Messrs. Wetley, Brothers," near the Exchange. Well, I shall try my fortune here first.

"Is Mr. Wetley at home?"

"Which?"

"The senior."

"Yes. Walk in, Sir. Name, if you please."

I presented my important epistle, upon the issue of which so much depended.

Mr. Wetley, an intelligent-looking, bald-headed, pleasant man, who had seen about sixty winters, read the letter, looked at "the bearer," and said,

"Look here, Sir. Do you know what these are?" at the same time spreading on his desk a number of small, dirty-looking scraps of paper, with apparently something printed and something written on them.

"Can you tell me what *these* mean?" he asked, in a serio-comic voice, looking disdainfully at the bits of paper, and inquisitively at me.

"I cannot, Sir."

"I thought not. If you had foreseen *these*—the gifts of Brother Jonathan!—you would not have come to Liverpool with the view of going to America!"

"Indeed! But what are they, Sir?"

"What are they? why, *shin-plasters* to be sure."

"Shin-plasters," I repeated. "I have heard of such things, but I never had the pleasure of seeing them before."

"The *pleasure!*" shouted the worthy merchant, with bitter emphasis; "the pleasure, indeed! Why, that is all I have for twelve hundred pounds' worth of first-rate goods. Its abominable, maddening! The dirty trash! There's not a bit big enough to light one's cigar! You've come at the wrong time, young man. Banneman should have known better than to send you here at such a time. We have nothing but ruin before us."

"Coming to Liverpool was my own deed, Sir," I said; "Mr. Banneman kindly complied with my wish to be introduced to your influential house."

"Ah! very well. But it's no use, you see. Just look at these shin-plasters—look at them! But, where do you lodge? It will be as well to leave your address, though I don't think things will get better. Worse, worse! Good morning!"

"Good morning, Sir."

So saying, I left the office of Messrs. Wetley, Brothers, never to return.

Where next? "Mr. B. G. Robertson, Jun."

This gentleman was also at home.

"Terrible storm yesterday!" said he, after reading the note; "severe losses at sea, I fear. How are things in Scotland?"

"Much as usual, Sir."

"Would you like to go to India?"

"I am not particular as to place."

"Well, look in, any day. I am not sure, but perhaps I may hear of an opening in India."

"When, Sir, do you expect it?"

"Can't say positively. Last I heard, a clerk there, in the office of a friend of mine, was very ill—expected to die, from the climate. Very trying to European constitutions. Perhaps, in about three months, should poor Brown die, my friend will want another."

Thus terminated my interview with "Mr. B. G. Robertson, Jun."

I returned to my temporary lodgings, saying with Dryden,

> "That present joys are more to flesh and blood
> Than a dull prospect of a distant good."

My prospect was dull enough. I had no particular anxiety to hear that "poor Brown" had departed this life. But something had to be done forthwith. What should it be? An easy question for those in easy circumstances; but rather tantalizing to a man in my critical position.

I would fain draw a veil over four months of terrible anxiety, much mental conflict, many disappointments, and many fruitless schemes; but the goodness of that Providence which hath so remarkably held me up cannot be omitted. I was four days in one place writing circulars for a person who was commencing business on the puffing principle, for which service I got ten shillings; and I spent a fortnight in another place, balancing the books of a tradesman who was retiring to enjoy a green old age, which brought me the remuneration of two pounds ten shillings. We had lived, or rather existed, at the lowest point; but all would not do; we were behind-hand with the rent of our lodgings—not the same where the first night was spent—the good woman was clamorous; and we must pay, or leave! Against the propriety of this intimation we had, of course, nothing to advance. And—O how it wrung my heart!—certain little presents, which had been handed to my wife at the time of our marriage, were given to the landlady instead of money. She was satisfied. We left and went to strange lodgings, absolutely penniless; and *that very night* my beloved wife was seized with the pains of childbirth!

I shudder at the remembrance of that dark period, and hasten to pass it over; but I must record two significant facts, illustrative at once of the watchful care of God, and of the different dispositions of men. On the following day, my wife having given birth to a son—shall I add, "and heir," in imitation of the miserable vanity of certain newspaper announcements?—I saw an advertisement for a clerk. I obtained a scrap of paper from our landlady, a warm-hearted Irishwoman, whose thoughtful kindness I shall not forget, and applied for the situation, and then went direct to the minister whose chapel I attended. He gave me a letter to a clergyman residing some distance off. I went to his house, but he was absent. The servant asked whether I would wait. I said I should return in an hour, by which time she expected her master. The fact is, my heart was breaking, and I wished to be alone with God. I had noticed a field or common in the neighbourhood, and resolved to go there. There was no " closet" into which to enter, and no " temple made with hands;" but I knew that the Refuge was there, and I thought of the words of Isaac Watts,

" Amidst temptations sharp and long,
   My soul to this dear refuge flies:
Hope is my anchor, firm and strong,
   While tempests blow and billows rise."

If ever I prayed it was in that open field; but my words were few. It was a sacred season, a holy hour. I returned to the house of the clergyman—a man of high intelligence, crowned with piety, and rendered attractive by genuine benevolence.

"My brother speaks highly of you in his letter," he said; "and I wish it were in my power to introduce you to some suitable situation. I understand you preach occasionally?"

"I have attempted to do so, sometimes, Sir."

"That is well, if you have reason to think you have been called to that honourable service. Persevere. Christ trains His servants in various ways; and if He has chosen you for the ministry He will open the door. Wait His time."

Thus speaking, he held out his hand to bid me farewell, leaving a small parcel in my hand, which, on opening, I found to contain five sovereigns. I could scarcely thank him, because of the depth of my emotions. He saw this, and said, in tones of tenderness which he had learned at his Master's feet,

"Never mind, brother; hasten home to your poor wife and child. She will be glad to see you. God bless you!"

I did hasten home—but not until I had revisited the common, and offered up thanks where I had presented petition—and my wife, now, if possible, doubly dear as a mother, *was* glad to see me, and happy, weak as she was, to point to the babe in her bosom.

"Mother!" holy and gentle name! Blush, young man, blush, weep, and pray for pardon, if ever thou hast wronged thy *mother*. It was a sin of saddest kind! Little knowest thou about a mother's heart, its unfathomable love, its tender yearnings, its warm life-cells, its holy solicitudes. To thee it is a sacred mystery, and ever will remain. Cast no shadow over it, I beseech thee; cause it not to shrink and tremble; impose no painful weight upon it by thy folly; but make it glad by thy filial reverence and unostentatious piety!

The other fact to which I have referred, was the result of my answer to the advertisement. A reply came in the course of two or three days, and I went, as intimated, to the office of —— Brothers, merchants. The duty required was that of making out invoices; wages, thirty shillings a week. I was immediately engaged. Sunshine once more being thrown on my path, I resolved to discharge my duty with earnestness and energy; but I had scarcely been an hour at the desk, when I discovered that the " Brothers" were men of the most ungovernable temper. I heard them cursing and swearing fearfully, and saw the clerks looking alarmed when either of them went past. I was also told that they were perpetually changing their clerks, and that, in fact, no young man could live with them. I was extremely sorry for all this; nevertheless, as I knew I could perform my allotted task, I saw no reason for apprehension on my own account: nay, I went so far as to cherish the Utopian hope, that, in some way, I should be the means of checking the wicked habit of my employers. The week passed on, and every day, from ten till four, my ears rang with the bitter curses of those men, addressed to one or other of their clerks, or to the poor labourers and porters engaged on the premises. Saturday evening came; one of the partners, addressing me, said,

" Be here at ten to-morrow morning."

" *To-morrow* morning, Sir?" I asked, very respectfully, thinking he had forgotten the day.

" Yes, d—— you! How dare you repeat the words after me?"

" I beg your pardon, Sir; I thought you meant Monday. To-morrow is Sunday."

" What of that? blockhead! fool! Are you a saint? There are some invoices to be done, and you must make them up, and then go to Church, or wherever else you please; but come you must, d—— you!"

Here was a trial. I suddenly remembered days when we had almost wanted bread. The picture of my wife and child rose before me. Here was a tolerably good situation, so far as wages were concerned. What was to be done? Done? I am ashamed that I hesitated for a moment, but it was only a moment. The " Brother" was looking at me with fury in his face. I said,

" Mr. ————, I will gladly serve you to the extent of my ability, and come earlier and remain later than usual every day of the week, but I cannot attend your office on the Sabbath."

" D——! Here, cashier, pay this canting hypocrite for his week's work, or blundering more likely; we want no whining saints here. You are discharged, Sir."

I went to my lowly lodgings, where my earthly treasures were, with thirty shillings in my possession, and—an approving conscience. I placed the money in the hand of her I loved, and thanked God that I had been kept from complying with the voice of the tempter. Still there were not wanting whisperings in my bosom—whence came they, ye mental anatomists?—that evening, that I had acted unwisely; that I had decided rashly; and that there could not have been much harm in complying with my employer's request for once. It might have soothed him. Possibly he might not have asked me again. Probably it might be long before another situation occurred, and so forth. I replied to all these fine-sounding suggestions by saying, " But the deed is done, and shall not be undone; and I will wait the consequences." One thing troubled me; how should I mention it to my wife, especially after witnessing the pleasure with which she looked on me when I placed my week's earnings in her hand? I told her the whole history, and waited her reply. She looked up in my face, and said,

"My dear, you have done right."

It was enough; I was satisfied. The next day I went to my usual place of worship. The able pastor announced his text, Psalm xxxvii. 3, "*Trust in the Lord, and do good: so shalt thou dwell in the land, and verily thou shalt be fed.*" The announcement of this Scripture struck me as peculiarly appropriate both to my state of mind and circumstances, and its analysis by the preacher deepened the soothing impression. He described the text, generally, as a command and a promise: the command including two things, faith and obedience; faith—"*trust* in the Lord;" obedience—"*do good:*" and the promise including two things, local residence, "so shalt thou dwell in the land;" and suitable nourishment, "verily, thou shalt be fed." He then named and illustrated the following particulars, as involved in the passage :—

1. That the dispositions and conduct of all men are noticed by the all-seeing God.

2. That He regards all human actions in the light of the motives from which they spring.

3. That the bounds of our habitation are fixed without interfering with our free agency; and

4. That the supply of the obedient believer's wants, both spiritual and temporal, springs from the grace of God in Christ, and is therefore certain.

My enjoyment of this hallowed Sabbath was great. I felt it better to have heard this discourse than to have made out "invoices;" and better to trust in the Lord for a lodge in the wilderness, and necessary food, than to purchase both at the terrible price of violated convictions.

Apart, in the meantime, from its religious significance, the prophecy of immortality which it unfolds, and the glorious deeds of which it is the standing memorial, what a blessed day is the Sabbath!   It is, indeed, the

"Day of the Lord, and lord of all the days !"

It soothes the mind amidst the storms of life, and checks the torrent of worldly passions; brings consolation to the sad, and animates the failing hopes of the doubting; exorcises the evil spirit as if with the harp of David, and invigorates the toil-worn for the labours of a new week. It stands by the side of the sentence, "In the sweat of thy face shalt thou eat bread," and modifies it with the assurance of periodical repose.

> "Approaching softly with the flag of truce,
>   Its words are gracious, and its presence mild;
> Like a pure angel, with a heart of love,
>   Smoothing the pillow of a suffering child !"

It is the sanitary day of the seven, being, when observed as it was intended, most beneficial to health, both mental and bodily; and those, consequently, who make it a day of labour, whether in the service of Mammon, or in that of the exacting tyrant, Pleasure, adopt a course which is most injurious to the mind, and most exhausting to the body.

On the Monday morning following I was disappointed and sorry that the regular employment, on which I had entered eight days before, had so suddenly and unexpectedly terminated; not sorry that I had refused to comply with a demand which my late employer had neither legal nor moral right to make; but sorry to be again idle.   Hating idleness, even on its own account, as an essential evil, and, in most cases, the source of moral injury, it being "a personal habit of Satan," to quote Mrs. Stowe's application of Watts, "to find some mischief still for idle hands to do!" Nevertheless, I was not melancholy. One of those mysterious influences, which float invisibly through the universe—perhaps they are the result of angelic ministrations—and which often cheer men with the thought of coming good, had visited my heart. Whence it came I knew not; but I felt like a man in possession of an "earnest" of something pleasurable. The kindness of the Christian minister, mentioned in a previous page, had cheered me, and his generous gift had enabled me to pay the expenses attendant on the birth of my child; but the mental influence to which I allude seemed to be entirely of an anticipatory character.

I went out after breakfast that morning, "not knowing whither," but saying that I should be absent about an hour. After strolling along two or three streets I noticed a "news room," and the thought occurring that I might have a glance at the doings of the great world, and cast my eye over the advertisements—although from repeated disappointments I was nearly sick of the latter—I entered. I read a powerfully-reasoned leader in the *Times*, and another, not a shade inferior, in the *Morning Advertiser*. Both were on the same subject—one of the principal political topics of the day; but the respective writers viewed the matter under discussion from entirely different points; and, consequently, reached entirely different conclusions. I felt little interest in the thing beyond the exhibition of logic to which it had given birth, which led me to muse for a few minutes on the educational influence of the newspaper press. I glanced at the local papers, and then mechanically took up one, published in a large town in one of the northern counties,

when my attention was arrested by the following advertisement :—

"WANTED A CHRISTIAN GENTLEMAN, to superintend the ——— Instruction Society. An ordained minister is not essential, but he must
be an acceptable preacher. Salary, £75 a year. Apply, naming references, to ——— Secretary."

I need not say that a verbatim copy of this "want"
was transferred in pencil to my note-book very quickly;
and my application was written and posted that day. I
felt confident of success, and I succeeded!

Three days afterwards a reply arrived, in which it was
intimated that the claims of the different applicants were
being examined—that the committee, feeling the responsibility of their position, required more time—that they
intended to reduce the number to two, or, at most, three
persons—that they would require a personal interview
with these—and that, so far as they could judge, it would
be well for me to hold myself in readiness lest they should
send for me.

This was satisfactory, business-like, and to the point.
I concluded that such men were "up to the mark," and
that, though I should be rejected, the Society, on whose
behalf they acted, would obtain the services of an efficient
man.

Ten days after this I sat in the presence of the
examining committee, and answered a series of questions,
personal, doctrinal, and ecclesiastical, to the entire satisfaction of the judges, of whom there were seven, and
who were all unpretending, earnest-minded, Christian men,
belonging to several religious denominations, and caring
more for the triumph of principle than that of party, and
more for the happiness of the people than the supremacy
of sect. Such men are the sinews and marrow of England. May their number be increased, and may every

nation soon possess men like-minded, and regard them more highly than either ecclesiastical sectarianism, or political parties.

"Such an aspiration," some reader may say, "is theoretically sound, and I can have no objection to its utterance; but it is not likely to be soon realised."

Esteemed objector! Wait a little. The crisis is nearer than you imagine. Time, seemingly slow in its evolutions, really hurries onward. Its motion increases as it approaches the destined goal. The speed is accelerated in proportion to the distance reached, for the power at work is "perpetual motion." Events of slow growth develop rapidly at last. Right principles, true men, just laws, and a healthy commonwealth are in the pathway of our old planet, and she will overtake them. Let patience have her perfect work; keep hope with her telegraph on the outlook; and have the ear ready for every note of the watchman. It is hard to say what his next communication may disclose. We are, at present, like the inhabitants of old Athens, waiting for some "new thing." And what is more, however its arrival may surprise us, we shall not be disappointed. There *are* tidings on the wing. They will come, surely, speedily, suddenly!

The fact is, the world is in a transition state. The past is old, the present evanescent, the future big with meaning. Sometimes a great thought enters the minds of many persons at the same time, though they may be separated from each other by seas and continents, living under different laws, surrounded by diverse circumstances, and influenced by contradictory religions. Whence came that thought? What mysterious power is it that reaches the soul of humanity unbidden and at will? Is there not a world of reality, intangible and unseen, enveloped in the world of common things? If the human eye were not so gross and earthly, so shut in by shadows, and circumscribed in its range of vision by clouds, would it not perceive spiritual legions ever at work, impelling, controlling, ruling the actors on the busy platform of this earth? Which is most piercing and powerful—the bodily eye, or the mental? Undoubtedly the latter. Hence it is that ideas, and the intercommunion of ideas, are greater things than obvious facts, and their reciprocal action upon each other. The idea which has come from some of those unseen regions, which embrace the visible in their invisible grasp, and settled upon many minds in several countries at the present time is, that the world has reached a certain point in its eventful history—a turning point, from which all things shall undergo great changes. The thought partakes of the nature of prophecy; and, changing like a summer cloud charged with electricity, now luminous, now black, sometimes the prophetic picture is sublimely beautiful, and at other times terribly dark; but always ominous of a new era for the dwellers upon the earth. Hope and Despair, the old warriors, alternate. Visions of glory interweave with pictures of gloom. Much, doubtless, depends upon the position of the seer. One man hears shouts of triumph and songs of joy, anticipates milder heavens and a more fruitful globe; and taking his brethren of the nations in his hand, says, "Come on, make haste, fear not; a very little longer and all things will be made new!" Another listens to muttering thunders, sees the atmosphere charged with threatening storms, and gazes gloomily on a rapidly-approaching catastrophe, which will carry disaster in its course and leave ruin in its train. It may be that a calm will succeed the storm, and beauty spring from the wrecks left by the hurricane; but who shall live to witness the ultimate issue, and to enjoy the repose when the din of battle shall have ceased? But whether meridian or midnight fill the eye, whether hope or despair tenant the breast, all men feel—that is to say, all who can feel — that we have come to a point upon the great pathway of eternity upon which humanity journeys, that will introduce us amidst scenes and circumstances which, if not essentially different from all that have preceded, will, at all events, be circumstantially different from those which have hitherto affected the experience of man. It is felt that these changes are at once imminent and inevitable. We cannot go back. We cannot stand still. To retrace our steps is impossible; to remain where we are, equally so. "Fate" urges us on. It is so decreed. A master Will commands. A strong Hand impels. We need not remonstrate—we ought not; and, if we knew all, we would not. Is not that Will friendly? Is not that Hand favourable? On, then, and let us see; for compliance with the former is the sure way to obtain help from the latter. On, then! and we shall speedily ascertain whether this widely-diffused thought be a great delusion, or the herald of a still greater reality.

In truth, this transition period might have been foreseen. It is but—speaking from the human side of the question—the legitimate growth of the world's deeds; or, admitting " development" in its rational sense, suppose we say that the growth of the world demands additional room? Is not a race analogous to an individual? Is not the child, the boy, the man, representative of the infancy, youth, and maturity of the race? There are those who deny the analogy; but a sufficient number of facts to oppose the denial might be collected both from the nature of the case and the history of the past.   Probably, so far as individual cases of moral goodness and mental power are concerned, one might fix on any given age, even far back in the past, near the original spring of the great family, and produce men in every respect equal to any found in modern times, or in the living generation; but this is too limited and partial to be admitted in evidence of the non-development of the species.   Besides, this view involves the improbable doctrine of limitation, and gives the humbling idea of an endless circle-journey, every generation in its wearying round longing and sighing for something that never comes, and transmitting the ungratified wish as a sad legacy to its successor, and so on for ever!   But it is to nations rather than individuals, and to ideas rather than nations, that I refer in proof of the growth that has necessitated transition.   The progress of nations is a fact too obvious to make doubt possible.   They may have fallen into decay after a long career, but not until they had transmitted to others the ideas which made them great.   Thus they were reproduced in a higher type, or rather, those ideas found new fields, and exhibited their power and their presence under new and still-advancing circumstances.   Now, it is this fact, the development of the world's ideas, as these are embodied in its social and religious systems, that constitutes the growth of the race, and that has brought it to the verge of a great crisis.   It has tried every plan, has become wearied of them all, and now it requires something higher and better.   This is its desideratum, and it is passing over all ancient boundary lines to enter upon an untrodden path.

Where is the nation that has not, at some period of its history, passed through the agonising throes of revolution?   Or, if such a nation can be found, does not all the rest of the world look upon it as lagging behind in the destined career of humanity? What is this, if it be not declaratory of the fact under notice? Some nations, France for example, have drunk this bitter cup repeatedly; but, upon the whole, those tumultuous heavings have tended to advancement rather than retrogression. There is a "good" for which nations labour, often blindly it is true, but not the less eagerly on that account. Mistaking the means for the end, they have sought the unknown good in forms and systems. The reality is yet in the future.

But these staggering steps, after all, may turn out to have been in advance. National agitations are in harmony with individual experience and natural phenomena. The individual is the type of the nation. Constant mental quiescence is inconsistent with the state of an imperfect being who is under training for another world. There is much to learn, and much to unlearn. There is good to embrace, and evil to shun. Hence, in the experience of individuals, there are periods of repose followed by periods of excitement—times of deep thought succeeded by times of frivolity—and seasons of patient endurance introductory to seasons of restless passion. Exactly so is it with communities. The nation is but the individual on a great scale. The body politic is congregated men. The multitude is the man multiplied. This accounts, also, for those popular heavings in neighbouring States which frequently follow a great commotion in any given nation. They are the utterance of the great heart of humanity—the actings of social sympathy or dislike—the declarations of approval or reprehension—the upheaving of the hidden fires—the aspirations of intelligence, or passion if you will, after something better, or something which is supposed to be better. For it is of no consequence to the argument whether the revolution be wise or foolish, just or unjust, or whether the change effected be for the better or the worse. The solution of this question is not needed. Either way, it is clear, there was discontent with the pre-existing order of things, and a conviction that something new was required to displace it; and that those changes have always uttered predictions, subordinate to those of the Bible, respecting the decay of the mutable and the introduction of that which cannot be moved, is, I think, at once a reasonable and Christian conclusion.

For the conflicts of peoples are not between thrones and republics. They are the battle-shouts of invisible principles. They are the cries which agitate the nations when right and wrong, truth and error, struggle with each other for supremacy. The stake at issue, though men may be ignorant of the fact, is neither the symbol of royalty nor that of republicanism, but the triumph or defeat of principles older than the world and immortal as mind. Man acts in the great drama with all the freedom of an intelligent agent, but he is unconscious of the dignity of his mission, and of the part which he is playing in the history of glorious principles. He is free, yet under constraint; an accountable agent, yet the creature of necessity; a self-prompted worker, yet God's hand. Hence, the world has reached its present position, and must proceed with still accelerated velocity, either to wear its laurels or to suffer its disgrace. It has both prepared itself and has been prepared by an unseen Power for a great change. It is both active and passive; it has laboured in pain; it is near the time for the solution of the mystery; it cannot recede; it cannot repose; and, strange! it *wills* neither.

But there is another element. From the human side of the question pass over to the Divine. Take divinity manifested in Christianity, and see what this has to do with the matter. The finest, most beautiful, and most potent thing on the earth at present—all who really understand it being judges—is Christianity. Now, it is not a little remarkable that this is at once the solace and the stimulant of man. It dries his tears, and makes them fall. It satisfies his wants, and creates them; for, no sooner has it prescribed for his moral diseases, than it excites in his mind an irrepressible desire for something greater still. He grasps it eagerly as soon as he sees its value, and then, by its aid, and in conformity with its conditions, he "reaches forward" to a distant "prize." It gives him peace, and clothes him with the armour of a warrior; it sanctifies his experience, and urges him towards the end of the discipline. It creates in him the confidence that all is right, and yet, without contradiction, convinces him that all is wrong. It banishes his fear by the same influence by which it fills him with hope; for that which it bestows now is but earnest, first-fruits, pledge. Hence it is, that Christianity the peace-preacher, is also Christianity the herald of a kingdom whose approach must be signalised by war, revolution, and wide-spread change. The Giver of rest says, this is not our rest. It is also note-worthy, that the degree in which men are influenced by Christianity is the measure of their preparation for the transition state; in other words, and in paradox still, the measure of their content is the measure of their dissatisfaction. They rejoice and groan. At the same moment they are filled with the seemingly opposite emotions of deep gratitude and earnest expectation, of calm resignation and the sublime covetousness of something yet unseen. This may account for the fact, that the world's benefactors are its "troublers;" and for the fact—for it *is* a fact—that some men, who are

I

deeply penetrated with a sense of the divinity and glory of Christianity, are accused of indifference to its claims. It has taught them to press forward, and they are charged with forsaking *it;* it has filled them with faith in its promises, and they are suspected of infidelity respecting its realities; it has convinced them that it is the herald of another dispensation, and they are branded with the guilt of treating it as a failure; and they have devoutly received it as a whole, accepting what it gives, and crediting what it promises, whilst their accusers, who have fallen into the not uncommon error of deeming a part equal to the whole, bring against them the indictment of a desire to be wise above that which is written!

Now, it is easy to perceive that the idea of the transition state, if not created, must have been powerfully fostered by these impressions. It seems to grow out of them; they give shape and form to it, constituting at once its aliment and its guide, its shower and sunshine. In the light of this sunshine it basks, looks forward, anticipates, longs, hopes. And why repel it? Is it injurious to the world? Is its voice anarchical? Does it preach discord? Is it inimical to the common weal? Does it paralyse benevolent exertion, and seal the springs of human sympathy? Does it despise means, and underrate agency, and resign itself to a morbid fatalism? On the contrary, its tongue is musical with hope, its spirit energises what it touches, and it takes poor suffering humanity by the hand, shouting, "Never despair!" It looks for improvement, is active in promoting knowledge, truth, and love, and proceeds with firm step to hail the advent of better days for man. Its faith is not shadow, but substance; not a wish but a verity. It would not put back the hands of the world's time-piece, but neither would it force their motion, to gratify the vision of party;

for it is satisfied that the past and the present belong to a series of preparations, of which the future will furnish the sublime development; and, consequently, while it can calmly wait the " time of the end," it sows its seed, morning and evening, in the full assurance that not one grain will be lost.

Unwilling to speak directly of the feelings and state of mind with which I entered on my new and exceedingly pleasant duties in the prosperous town of ——, these remarks will give the reader some information concerning both. Here I found enough to do; all my time was fully occupied, every day in the week, by the special duties of the Society, and very soon every Lord's day likewise. Here, in fact, my public ministry began. There were several chapels in the town, in all of which I preached occasionally, and in some repeatedly. The good men with whom I was officially associated were, as already intimated, Catholic Christians in the proper sense of that term. Justice to myself requires me to say, that I considered this no small recommendation. I regarded them for it, and look back with almost unqualified satisfaction to the year I spent in the town. With its ministers I had, of course, much to do, and found them all courteous, kind, and friendly. It would not be correct to say, that there were no peculiarities of disposition, and no sources of temporary disquiet; such an assertion would be out of keeping with the characteristic frailties and imperfections of men at their best estate; but upon the whole, and all things considered, I deeply respect those of them who survive, and cherish the memory of the departed. One of them, the minister with whose church I became connected, was a man of vigorous understanding, great talent, and considerable literary fame. His style was peculiar, and his mode of illustrating a subject such as no man, who was afraid of being thought singular, would have ventured to adopt. With a certain class of minds in the place he was popular; but he frequently said things so much out of the way, that he was charged by some, most unjustly I am certain,—for I spent many hours with him in his study, and, consequently, knew him well,—with affecting an originality to which he had not sufficient claim.

Another, poor warm-hearted E——, was the orator of the town, but a cloud came over him. May the blessing of Heaven rest upon his widow and children!

A third was a plain, humble, unassuming Christian pastor, to whom the great truths of the Gospel were unspeakably precious,—perhaps the more so from the trials of his lot. He needed, personally, those consolations which he was in the habit of administering to his flock. He struggled many years with domestic affliction and deep poverty; and now, good K——! his struggles are for ever ended.

For one or other of these ministers, when not engaged in the surrounding villages, I was frequently called to supply; the first, however, was not only my pastor, but my special friend and adviser; and it was by his advice that I was induced to accept a call to the pastorate, which, before the close of the year, was presented to me by a village congregation.

Details, as well as the results of five years' experience of the rural pastorate, must be left for another chapter. Meantime, I conclude this with a brief recurrence to the subject of the era at which we live; for there never was a period in the world's history when it was more necessary than at present that Christian men should be fully alive to the signs and seasons.

The world—whether or not it be a delusion remains

to be seen—has caught the echo of the strain to which I have referred, and has struck for itself the key-note of a new song respecting the good time. Men lift up their eyes, and labour in hope. The wearied traveller rejoices that his journey will come to an end. The burden becomes lighter when the thought enters that it will fall off some day. The night of terror gropes its way to the anticipated dawn. Vernal suns will rend the thick-ribbed ice. The iron gate will open, and the prisoner will go free. The eyes of the blind shall be opened, and the lame man will leap as a hart; and the groaning creation will laugh in the exuberant enjoyment of glorious liberty.

And why should not these things be so? Is the idea of the progress of humanity inadmissible? Are all the seeds of education lost? Have all the days of light been absorbed by the thick darkness? Are schools, colleges, and pulpits—the press and the platform—the home, city, and foreign missionary fruitless? Not so. They have all prepared, directly or indirectly, for the impending change; they have created a thirst which must be satisfied, and excited desires which demand gratification. They have not done all that they intended, but, perhaps, more than they meant. It is so far well. The impulse given to mind is likely to be permanent; let it, therefore, feel the attraction of that which lies beyond, and its course will be " straightforward."

Meantime, existing agency should be employed with increased vigour. Educate, educate! It is light that makes manifest. Theology, philosophy, science, art, and song—come all! There is for each a niche in the great temple, if it will but clothe itself in the love-wrought robes of Christianity. There need be no mutual collision; there is room enough; and if ye understood each other better, there is need for you all. A friendly conference might exhibit unity in diversity, without a particle of discord. At any rate, whatever lightens the burden and cheers the heart of man, asking him to look upward and onward, has a hearty hail from the believer in the new age. Nations are tiring of ignorance, slavery, and war; they covet light, liberty, and peace. Preparatory elements for the ultimate gratification of their wishes are rapidly accumulating, gathering shape and form, and will shortly receive vitality. China has sprung from a sleep of incredible length. India looks with an eye of incredulity on her gods. The gates of the world are open to the heralds of Christ's everlasting kingdom. The continent of Europe waits for a purer type of the truth. The people of the Jews are everywhere moved by mysterious expectations. And thinkers are everywhere, without mutual consultation, impressed with the thought that the world has not been abandoned by its Redeemer; and that the dark problem of humanity is about to be solved—and that very soon—amidst transcendent light, to the utter confusion of EVIL, and the measureless joy of GOOD!

CHAPTER VII.

EXPERIENCE OF A VILLAGE PASTOR.

"Whether in crowds or solitudes, in streets
Or shady groves, dwells Happiness, it seems
In vain to ask—her nature makes it vain;
Though poets much, and hermits, talked and sang
Of brooks, and crystal founts, and weeping dews,
And myrtle bowers, and solitary vales,
And with the nymph made assignations there,
And wooed her with a love-sick oaten reed;
And sages too, although less positive,
Advised their sons to court her in the shade.
Delicious babble all! Was Happiness,
Was self-approving, God-approving joy
In drops of dew, however pure? in gales,
However sweet? in wells, however clear?
Or groves, however thick with verdant shade?"

Pollok.

THE RURAL PASTORATE — POETRY AND SOBER TRUTH — HOME AND FOREIGN BENEVOLENCE—GORGEOUS CHAPELS—A DIALOGUE—THE THREE ANSWERS—A COLD DAY AND A NEGATIVE CREED—THE COACHMAN'S OPINION — NATURE AND ART IN WILLOWFIELD— EPITAPHS—SABBATH SONGS—THE FIRST CALL—ORDINATION—MR. ARDPHIST — MY DEACONS—INCREASE OF THE CONGREGATION— CROSS FIRES—CLERICAL ZEAL AWAKENED—ADVENT OF THE CURATE —A SCENE—THE CURATE AND MRS. PRIESTLY — "NO PRAYER FOR A CASE OF THAT KIND"—CLOSING OF PUBLIC-HOUSES, AND THE MOTIVE THEREOF — CHAPEL DEBT — I GO A BEGGING—CHARITY AND ITS COUNTERFEITS—FIRST IMPRESSIONS OF LONDON—A BAD SYSTEM—A PLEA FOR HOME.

"THE rural pastorate." How pleasant the association of ideas which these words suggest! Innocence, primitive simplicity, beautiful natural scenery, the Gospel, the Sabbath, and the village Chapel, are all brought before the mind. The train of humble worshippers, in plain but clean attire, going to and returning from the lowly house of prayer, appears before the eye. There they have often heard words of peace, which have fallen on their hearts like the dew of Hermon, diffusing holy joy, and imparting that hope which maketh not ashamed. You hear in the distance the sound of the morning hymn rising from grateful souls. The music might offend a scientific ear, but the psalm goes direct to Heaven, for it speaks the language of the heart. The toil-tired peasantry, feeling that the Sabbath is a gift from the Father in heaven, hail the day as a blessing both to body and soul. They listen with noiseless attention to the reading of the inspired lesson from the sacred pages, some of them, with the open Bible in their hands, keeping their eye on the words. They unite, silently, but with spiritual earnestness, in the pastor's petitions, offered in the well-known name of his Master and theirs, and love him for the fervour with which he asks good things for them all. Unused to the critic's profession, they seek not the charms of poetry, logic, and eloquence in the discourse from the pulpit, but the higher attributes of fidelity, earnestness, and truth. Strangers to the theological disputes which have shaken the world concerning the meaning of certain words and phrases, they receive with confidence the instruction of their teacher, and return to their cottages wiser and better men.

> " One man there was, and many such you might
> Have met, who never had a dozen thoughts
> In all his life, and never changed their course ;
> But told them o'er, each in its customed place,
> From morn till night, from youth to hoary age.
> The word philosophy he never heard,

Or science; never heard of liberty,
Necessity, or laws of gravitation;
And never had an unbelieving doubt.
     He lived—
Lived where his father lived, died where he died—
Lived happy and died happy, and was saved.
Be not surprised, he loved and served his God."

Yes, the rural pastorate is a fine theme for the imagination of the tale-writer and the poet. Goldsmith, Cowper, Crabb, Pollok, Longfellow, and a host of others have sketched it, sung it, praised it, and it remains an attraction still, especially to those who see it *from a distance.*

But from the pen of the historian people expect facts, rather than fancy pictures, and grave truth rather than romantic sketches. I am an ardent lover of the beautiful in nature, and of the poetry of life, even to the verge of idolatry; but, in the present instance, as I am about to record five years' experience as a village pastor, and as the profession of a Christian teacher involves relations of the most sacred kind, I should consider it a positive crime either to colour the attractions or to exaggerate the privations, difficulties, and sorrows of the rural pastorate. Besides, this chapter should have been very brief, but for the hope that it may help to secure increased attention, on the part of wealthy Christians and influential churches, to the religious condition of the agricultural population—to lighten somewhat the burden that presses the hearts of many worthy pastors to the earth—to raise the question whether, with our world-wide benevolence, we have weighed in a just balance the claims of Home—and to draw the scattered influences of the Christian brotherhood into closer union, and therefore more powerful action. The chief religious denominations of this country are numerically strong; but numerical strength, without harmonious co-operation, is practically useless in the day of conflict.   And whilst, on the part of the feeble, there is jealousy of the encroachment of centralisation, with its impudent offspring—dictation, and, on the part of the strong, comparative indifference to claims which roll not across deserts and seas from the lands of demon-worship, the hope of overtaking, with thoroughly evangelical influence, the half-civilised masses of our peasantry, is vain.   I speak advisedly, having stood on both sides of the hedge, and examined the field narrowly.   From the very heart of Heathendom springs up the cry of agony, " Come over and help us !"   It is perilous to shut our ears to that cry.   Spiritual dearth, blight, and ruin will visit us if we do.   But is there no voice that asks, " *Where is the flock that was given thee; thy beautiful flock?*"   Is a claim urgent in the ratio of its distance? Surely, home-fields " white to the harvest" should be gathered before the storms of winter come upon them, especially seeing that the elasticity of Christian benevolence can do this without diminishing the number of labourers on foreign shores.   High-churchism, Popery, and Mormonism, each zealous in its work, are diligently imbuing the ill-taught multitude with their respective forms of fanaticism, while Evangelism lifts up a protest in words without corresponding action ; and, alas ! when it does act, the preposterous mutual jealousy of Churches that are really teaching the same essential truths, comes in to nullify its exertions.   The poor village pastor, except he be a man of uncommon faith and strong mind, has his energies exhausted by the incessant action of corroding care.   He reads of the glories of " voluntaryism," and is expected to echo its praises, while his wife and children are ill clothed and worse fed,—like a debtor in the Queen's Bench admiring the exploits of a " fortunate" gold-digger.   He hears of princely donations to projects whose utility remains to be tested by experience, whilst he, who is engaged in a work to which the Lord of Heaven has set the seal of approbation, cannot afford to send his eldest boy to a humble school. He peruses, in a *borrowed* newspaper, eloquent speeches from the lips of the Reverends A.M., LL.D., and D.D., delivered at the opening of the loudly-lauded Brother Successful's new " Church," and finds that the building is a marvellous exhibition of architectural skill—that the painted windows are the admiration of all—that the twelve Apostles are faultless—that the pulpit is a gem rarely equalled—that the lofty spire can be seen for many miles —that the bells are the sweetest-toned that ever welcomed wanderer to the fold of Christ—that the noble organ is the most superb instrument ever built by the celebrated firm of Harmony and Sons—that the completed structure cost the " really moderate" sum of seven thousand pounds —and that, in consequence of the fabulous power of the "voluntary principle," the whole is out of debt; a peroration which is applauded by sundry " Hear! hears! and prolonged cheering." I say, the village pastor reads all this, whilst at the same moment he is trembling lest a rap at the door should announce the arrival of the poor-rate collector, whom he cannot face, or the village grocer, whose bill has reached the appalling figure of five pounds, being exactly the tenth of the good man's annual income.

Mr. Successful is an able and true man, of high standing and unstained character, and the village pastor unfeignedly rejoices in the facts relating to him; but it is impossible, for all that, to prevent the intrusion of reflections of a painful kind, on the continuance of struggles in the service of the Gospel, which that same vaunted voluntaryism might have terminated long ago, without weakening its powerful spring.

" But there is no reason in the world," said one, " why wealthy Christians should not erect costly places of worship. The money is their own; they exercise no compulsion on their neighbours; and the result is, after all, an illustration of voluntaryism."

" You are right, Sir," I replied; " there is no reason in the *world* why they should not. On the contrary, the world is just the authority likely to patronise the thing by an approving smile. The multiplication of ornate edifices, even though they are consecrated to the service of religion, is one of the things that the world will most surely applaud; for they add to the appearance and importance of cities, and proclaim the wealth and taste of the citizens; and, in the end, they will injure the very object they seem to facilitate, by fostering a worldly and a selfish spirit. But if there be no reason in the world why the surplus gold of the prosperous should not build for itself monumental towers, is there none in the true idea of Christian benevolence; none in the solemn fact of Christian stewardship; and none in the wants and woes of neglected human souls?"

" Well, there may be something in that," said my friend; " but you will allow that those buildings illustrate the power of voluntaryism very clearly."

" Undoubtedly," I replied, " of *voluntaryism*, inasmuch as the parties who built them were willing to do so, otherwise they could not have been built; but voluntaryism is a term of wide import, and it is frequently illustrated on a still grander scale by mercantile companies in their gorgeous warehouses, and by mere men of the world in the pursuit of short-lived pleasures. But I speak of *Christian* voluntaryism—a principle, which gives its gifts and does its deeds for the sake of Christ, and disinterestedly; but that the glory of Christ, or the good of human souls, is advanced by the cloud-wreathed spire, or the 'dim religious light' of the stained window, no rational being will pretend; and instead of the idea of disinterestedness being suggested by those imposing temples, they suggest the painful thought of religious pride, shrinking from the simplicity of the puritanic sanctuary, and trying to rival the architectural extravagance of a system which derives its funds from the national wealth."

" O! come, be charitable."

" Want of charity is not a fault with which I am usually charged; but it is a matter of fact, that passers-by and disinterested persons make the remark to which I have alluded."

" That may be; but our modern chapels add to the respectability of dissent, and give it a social status which it never had before."

" The power of Nonconformity," I replied, " lies in its scriptural simplicity, and its evangelic pulpit. Remove these, and its glory has departed. Obscure these by the symbols of worldly pomp, and a cloud eclipses its ancient light; or attempt to buttress these by material grandeur, and you may retain the body, but the soul will depart."

" Why, you are getting serious," said my friend, smiling; " you would really do for a Quaker, so far as plain meeting-houses are concerned."

" I am serious. Meeting-houses need not be plain— that is, in the sense of studied plainness; but they should not be extravagant, until the poor of the land have the Gospel preached to them, and, especially, when the claims of the rural population suffer in consequence of those costly erections."

" But I see no possible connexion between the two things."

" I do, though, and I will illustrate it by a fact.   I know an excellent and laborious country pastor, who has toiled long, and been greatly blessed in his labours. Wishing to erect a school-room for the neglected children of the village, he went to London, a year or two since, to seek assistance, his flock being utterly unable to raise the trifling sum which was required.   His case was well authenticated by names not unknown in London circles. He received the following answers from three gentlemen, on whom he successively called; three gentlemen, who had hitherto been known for their liberality.   The first said, ' I cannot help you, for I have just given five hundred pounds to our new Church.'   The second said, ' I am unable to assist in this case, for we purpose building a new place, and it will cost a great deal.'   The third, pointing to a cathedral-looking building in the opposite street, said, ' Do you see *that?*   If Dissenters go on in that fashion, I will never again give a shilling to Chapel or School.' "

At this point I resume my personal narrative, which will exhibit, incidentally, the claims and wants, the virtues and vices of the rural population, if the village in which I lived may be taken, as I think it may, as a specimen of most others.

Having received an invitation to spend a month in Willowfield, and to preach on probation during that time, I left —— by the stage-coach, early on a cold frosty morning, in the month of February.   I had nearly two hundred miles to travel, which could not be accomplished in one day.   The prospect was, therefore, a cold one, especially on the outside of the old " Velocity," which, as is generally the case, did not literally justify its name.   I had, during the early part of the first day, a solitary companion on the front seat, a young man about five-and-twenty, well-dressed, but rather over-adorned with seals, rings, and chains, which might have been of the precious metals, and might have contained real gems for aught I could tell. He exhibited these valuables freely at first; but as the biting easterly wind began to take effect, he found it expedient to hide them all under a rough overcoat. For some time we sat in silence, excepting the original information we had imparted to each other that it was "a cold morning;" or, to speak correctly, I had first ventured on that opinion, which he politely corroborated. Before we had travelled fifty miles together, however, I found that this was the *only* sentiment in which we were agreed. A discussion, warm and earnest on both sides, soon sprang up; and if it had no other effect, it tended to the circulation of the blood—no small comfort in such weather. I believe the movement of the " Velocity" was somewhat accelerated by it too; for the rubicund coachman, who sat before us, overheard every word of the debate, and became so far excited by it as to telegraph the horses to that effect. I do not intend to report our controversy. It is enough to say that my jewelled companion in travel had a remarkably negative creed, with here and there a positive principle by way of cement, to keep the detached negatives from rolling in all directions. He did *not* believe the doctrines of the Bible; he did *not* think its writers inspired; nay, they were *not* even possessed of common sense, for they did *not* understand geography, nor astronomy, nor mathematics, nor the laws of mind. He did *not* believe there ever was such a person as Jesus of Nazareth; or, if there was, he did *not* believe He was the Saviour of the world, for the world did *not* need a Saviour, seeing it was *not* guilty or sinful, as parsons taught; the only object of the aforesaid parsons being, *not* to save souls, but to feed their own precious persons. He did *not* believe that Deity took any notice of men; and he was sure there was *no* heaven, *no* hell, *no* day of judgment, *no* hereafter, *no* immortality! The few positives which held these wayward negatives together were these: he believed the world was eternal, man the result of development, chemical laws the cause of the seasons, human reason the effect of electricity, and the size of the brain the standard of intelligence! What I said to all this, any intelligent man may easily imagine. At last, my neighbour, having reached his destination, left us; and I was gratified by the spontaneous proof that the coachman had taken some interest in the discussion. After changing horses, and starting for another stage, he glanced towards me, and said,

"Look'ee here, Sir! I've been on this here road, off and on, for the matter of twenty years, and I've heard many strange talks, but anything like that *never* afore." So saying, he administered a gentle cut to the leader. "Sir, you floored that there gemman, you *did!*"

"Well, coachman," said I, "that was not a difficult matter. When common sense and religion pull one way, you know, like your leaders there, one gets on."

"Ah, jes so!" he replied, evidently satisfied with this illustration, "that's where it is. My poor old father said, jest when he were a-going off—he drove the 'Cantrip' for more'n twenty year—'Tom,' said he, 'my boy, religion's the best thing *arter all*,' he did, poor old man!"

"Your father was right, Thomas; and I hope you have not forgotten the remark."

Night was now setting in. I was nearly benumbed with cold. Snow was falling fast; and when we reached the town, where I had resolved to remain during the night, the warmth of a room in the "Greyhound," with a blazing fire in the grate, and smoking refreshments on the table, was very agreeable. On the following morning I resumed my journey. The face of the country was covered with snow, so that I could form but an inadequate judgment of its general appearance. The monotony of the drive, however, was relieved by conversation with an intelligent clergyman, who was proceeding some thirty miles in the same direction as myself. We talked about the Ministry and the Opposition, corn-laws and free-trade, Cobden and Bright, Oxford and Puseyism, Cambridge and mathematics, socialism, chartism, and sundry other isms, and, with an occasional difference of opinion, we managed to have a very agreeable chat. This gentleman would have been considered an adherent of the "low" school by certain dignitaries of the episcopacy, a circumstance which did not lower him in my judgment. He was excessively indulgent to all classes, expressed contempt respecting the folly and crime of petty persecutions, thought that all dictation in religious matters sprang from ignorance of the genius of truth, and the wants and yearnings of the human heart, and held the opinion that the signs of the times pointed to a supernatural intervention at no distant day.

Towards evening I reached long-looked-for Willowfield, the scene of my first pastoral labours—of many pleasant and many sad hours—of births and deaths in my family, and among my flock—of successes in the ministry, and reverses from local causes—of high enjoyment from exquisitely beautiful natural scenery—and of bitter sorrow from being compelled to witness among the peasantry poverty which I could not remove, and privations which I could not alleviate. Willowfield holds a

tender place in my heart. With my recollections it is
fondly associated. Its simple-minded and loving-hearted
people I cannot forget, and those among them who were
brought from darkness to light during my pastorate will
not forget me. Strong and sacred is the tie formed
under such circumstances. It exists during life, notwithstanding its vicissitudes; it continues through the
" valley," notwithstanding its " shadow;" and it will
remain in the future world, notwithstanding its higher
glories. This I gather from an exulting statement of
Paul, which is both a doctrine and a joyful anticipation.
" For what is our hope, or joy, or crown of rejoicing?
Are not even ye in the presence of our Lord Jesus Christ
at his coming? For ye are our glory and joy."

The population of Willowfield, at the time of my first
visit, was about seven hundred. Poverty, emigration,
and death have sadly thinned it since. The village
stands upon a gentle elevation, and skirts the sides of the
old turnpike road, over which the London coach, with
its cheerful herald-horn, used to run, before the iron
rails had disfigured the country with their innovations.
The view is most extensive, diversified, and interesting.
A little crystal stream forms the boundary line between
the village and the neighbouring parish of Rowly. Beyond this, pasture and arable land, orchards, gardens,
and thickly-wooded spots, are romantically scattered,
while a lofty hill in the distance bounds the view in that
direction. On the other side, the eye sweeps over the
greater part of two counties, undulating, richly wooded,
fertile, and beautiful in the extreme, and rests on an
eminence thirty miles distant. Immediately around the
village the gentle willows bend by the brooks, like so
many patient anglers with their rods. The larch, the
fir-tree, the poplar, the oak, and hawthorn abound; and

over the fields myriads of flowers of beautiful hue and pleasant odour cast their beauty and mingle their perfume. Such are the features of the spot, so far as nature is concerned. But the works of *art (!)* seem to have been executed with a settled purpose to show the effect of contrast. There is a main road, and two or three branch roads, or lanes, in Willowfield, and they are made in the most uneven places that the village site affords. The houses are built, some of stone, others of brick, and a few of mud; two or three are roofed with slate, most are thatched, and several are innocent of any covering, except the skeleton rafters. As to colour, they are quite picturesque; white, grey, brown, and red, may all be seen. Respecting position, the same interesting variety prevails. Some front the road, others show a corner, and several have coldly turned their backs upon it In some cases a pig-sty forms the frontal ornament; but the porcine portico, like many other relics of primitivism, is falling before the Vandals of reform, and the hog tribe are ruthlessly driven to the rear. The parish Church is three miles distant, otherwise I should have described it before the Chapel; but, as it is practically useless to the villagers there, so it would be practically useless to the reader to sketch its architectural peculiarities *here*. There is, three quarters of a mile distant, however, the parish Church of Rowly, a rather handsome gothic edifice, around which the dust of generations of parishioners has gathered a little table-land, with the usual stones of memorial, and an over-plentiful supply of almost ludicrous epitaphs, as if the genius of absurdity had resolved to defeat the solemnising influence of the scene. Every person of taste, when visiting a grave-yard, feels offended by such inscriptions. Some of them are totally destitute of meaning; others are ridiculously absurd; frequently they defy all grammar, although this is a trifling offence when the sentiment is appropriate; but the greatest evil of all is, when you find elaborate and studied eulogy, attributing to the dead virtues and excellences so remarkably conspicuous that you deem it a serious loss to the world that such a man should have left it! As to the theology of some of these records, the revelation which it gives of the religious knowledge of those who commanded them to be made, cannot fail to touch the heart with a pang of grief. We pity the ignorance that dictates the request,

"PRAY FOR THE SOUL OF PATRICK O'BRIAN."

But what feeling should be stimulated by *this*, from the pen of a Protestant?

"Sacred to the Memory
OF
SAMUEL STELLAR, ESQ.
HE WAS POSSESSED OF EVERY QUALITY THAT COULD ADORN
HUMANITY;
HE NEVER INJURED ANY OF HIS FELLOW-CREATURES;
HIS VIRTUES RECOMMENDED HIM TO THE FAVOUR OF GOD;
AND HE HAS GONE TO HEAVEN TO
OBTAIN HIS REWARD."

If the one presupposes an unfinished redemption, and points to an imaginary purgatory, the other makes redemption, either complete or partial, altogether unnecessary, entirely ignores the work of the Saviour, and proudly talks of the virtues of a poor fallen man attracting the notice of GOD, and obtaining a reward in heaven! "If my survivors," the scripturally educated reader will say, "think it right to mark the place of my sepulture, and if there be no other alternative, let me have the helpless cry of O'Brian, rather than the arrogant falsehoods of Stellar!"

Our modern cemeteries are, in this respect, as in others, a great improvement on the old church-yards, although, in some of them, I regret to see the introduction of inscriptions fitted to offend the man of taste, to make the giddy smile, and to wound the heart of the devout. This is a matter of greater importance than to some it may seem. Where is the family which has not lost a relative by death? and where, consequently, is the man or woman who has not had to pay a sorrowing visit to the place of the dead? Is it not, therefore, important that the writings on stone, upon which the eye of the visitor is sure to fall, should be in keeping with the solemn character of the place? Moreover, public cemeteries are becoming favourite promenades; they are laid out so as to please the eye, to divest the associations of mortality of some of their gloom, and to give the idea of peaceful repose; it would be well, therefore, that the living, who walk among the memorials of the departed, should meet with thoughts calculated to rebuke indifference, to encourage faith, to purify the heart, to elevate the mind, and to lead to Him who is the Resurrection and the Life.

There is one building in Willowfield which I have not yet named. To me, as well as to many of the villagers, it was the most important in the place; of course I mean the Chapel. Architectural beauties it had none! External attractions, none! The passenger, indeed, could not avoid seeing it, for it stood in the most conspicuous part of the village, on a little elevation adjoining the main road, and all who saw it must have known its use. But it had attractions of another kind, which some felt and admired; and to *them*, in consequence, it had external attractions too. It was the house of God; it was the place of holy instruction; it was the gate of heaven; it was set upon a hill. Poor, very poor, were most of the worshippers within its walls, but they thought not so on the first day of the week. It was a high day; and several earnest believing ones now stand before the eyes of memory, each of whom, had he been acquainted with the racy Herbert, would have sung—

> " Thou art a day of mirth :
> And where the week-days trail on ground,
> Thy flight is higher, as thy birth.
> O let me take thee at the bound,
> Leaping with thee from seven to seven,
> Till that we both, being toss'd from earth,
> Fly hand in hand to heaven !"

Of the incumbent of Bemerton, probably, they had not heard; but with the writings of Isaac Watts they were familiar, as the repeated and earnest singing of the following lines testified : —

> " How did my heart rejoice to hear
> My friends devoutly say,
> In Zion let us all appear,
> And keep the solemn day !
> I love her gates, I love the road;
> The Church, adorned with grace,
> Stands, like a palace, built for God,
> To show His milder face."

Or these :—

> " Great is the Lord our God,
> And let His praise be great ;
> He makes His churches His abode,
> His most delightful seat.
> These temples of His grace,
> How beautiful they stand ;
> The honours of our native place,
> And bulwarks of our land."

Or these :—

> " Great God, attend while Zion sings,
> The joy that from thy presence springs ;
> To spend one day with thee on earth,
> Exceeds a thousand days of mirth.

> Might I enjoy the meanest place
> Within thine house, O God of grace!
> Not tents of ease, nor thrones of power,
> Should tempt my feet to leave the door."

Or these :—

> " When I can read my title clear
>   To mansions in the skies,
> I bid farewell to every fear,
>   And wipe my weeping eyes."

In short, their feeling respecting the humble place of worship was,

> " I have been there and still would go,
> 'Tis like a little heaven below !"

But, alas! I speak not of them all. There were men of different habits, and very different tastes. Every variety of human depravity could be found in that little community. Iniquity in its most repulsive forms had its votaries in that finely-situated village ; and such, in a word, was the place where I preached four Lord's days, on " probation."

Three weeks after my return to ———, I received an earnest and unanimous invitation to become the settled pastor of the church at Willowfield. This document was signed by all the members, and expressed, in terms of warm friendship, their sentiments respecting my late visit, and temporary services.

Here, then, was another landmark in my life, another of those points around which thought rolls, and which involuntarily lead to serious reflection. What my thoughts and feelings were, on the occasion, I shall not say; but a *first* call to discharge the duties and sustain the responsibilities of the Christian pastorate is no trivial matter to the man who calmly views the position in which that call places him, in relation to the particular Church which has elected him—to other Churches which surround

it—to the inhabitants of the place where it is situated—
to the mental, moral, and religious interests of the congregation—to the authority and Gospel of Christ—and to
the bearing of his doctrines and practices on eternity.
Heart-chords are touched by that first call which were
never moved before, and never will be so moved again.
Recollections of the past flash vividly before the eye of
memory; the intermediate stages of life's journey up to
that particular period are seen; again they are all rapidly
run over; and again those incidents, which had made
deep impressions at the time of their occurrence, are
suddenly aroused from their slumbers, and exhibit themselves as so many spokes in the mystic wheel of Divine
Providence.   The future, too, tries to paint itself on the
eye, but, happily for man, without success.   Probabilities
are weighed, and possibilities are guessed; hope and fear
alternately predominate; good resolutions come with
liberal influx; and purposes are formed whose realisation
would make a noble man.   Would that the pastor in
action always fulfilled what the pastor-elect promised in
his heart on receipt of the first call!

But let me neither hint at the short-comings of others,
nor seem to covet praise for humility by parading my
own.   Every man of Christian sensibility knows his own
failings best.   I have mine—a greater share than I relish,
and I would not wish them transferred to another.   There
is a voluntary confession of personal infirmity for which
the confessor gets little credit; and if He, whom good
George Herbert always called "My Master," has borne
with me, surely my fellow-servants may.   He put me
into the ministry, and He has kept me there for nearly
fourteen years; and never, since the day on which I
accepted that *first* call, have I been detached for an
hour from official connexion with the laborious, trying,

responsible, and much-loved work of the Christian pastorate.

In the month of May, I and my family—for I had now two children—were settled in Willowfield. The ordination was attended by neighbouring ministers, and by some from a distance. The charge was delivered by the highly-esteemed tutor of one of the colleges belonging to the Denomination. The services of the day were instructive to all, but particularly solemn and impressive to me; a solemnity and impression of which I am always reminded, when I witness or take part in the ordination of others. And now, preliminaries satisfactorily settled, and the harness girded on, it is proper that I give the reader a condensed narrative of the events which followed.

The Chapel was capable of seating two hundred and fifty persons. The congregation, at the time of my settlement, was about one hundred and twenty; the number of church-members between fifty and sixty, two of whom were deacons, and who, of course, managed the temporalities of the body. There was a Sunday school of some seventy children, instructed by five or six teachers, with their superintendent. There were two services during the week, and two and three, alternately, on the Lord's day. There were two hamlets in the neighbourhood where I occasionally preached; in one of them, in a small school-room—in the other, in a dwelling-house. My annual income was sixty pounds. The majority of the congregation, as I have already said, were poor, composed of small tradesmen, shop-keepers, and farm-labourers. There were two substantial farmers who, with their families, occupied the best pews, and paid for the accommodation at the ordinary rate. There was one person, a kind of village gentleman, who, according to report, was

K

possessed of considerable wealth. His occupation consisted, during the week, in visiting the blacksmith's, the barber's, and the public-houses, in search of scandal and strong drink, and on Sundays in blowing a villanous flute in the front seat of the gallery. While engaged in the last-named capacity, the contortions of his beer-coloured face, aided by a suspicious habit of voluntary squinting, were to me unutterably annoying. This gentleman was a thorough-going voluntary. He hated all State-church establishments with a perfect hatred; church-rates, tithes, and Easter-offerings were special objects of his abhorrence, and, I fear, he had not much charity even for the clergy. Whenever we had a collection in the Chapel for incidental expenses, or for foreign missions—for, poor as we were, these were not forgotten—my voluntary was absent. It was an "unfortunate" coincidence, but it so happened that on these occasions poor Mr. Ardphist always had either bilious headache, or a slight cold, or an attack of the gout. His services on the flute he considered more than an equivalent for his sitting, and those of his two grown-up daughters. I was assured, by one who had the means of knowing, that he had attended the Chapel for nearly thirty years, without giving a single penny for any benevolent or religious object whatever. To him, the Gospel was without heart-power; it had not reached his spirit with its transforming and benevolent influence. With its theory he was acquainted; to its power he was an entire stranger. Its call to repentance and faith he had heard and neglected; but, at last, there came a call from God which he obeyed—the only call which such men obey. He was called to die, and he died.

With the deacons, James Hedger and William Small, and the school-superintendent, Daniel Hayall, I was, of course, frequently brought into contact. James Hedger was a market-gardener, William Small a tailor, and Daniel Hayall a farmer. They were sincerely religious men, but of very limited information, and, unhappily, of dispositions which could not well harmonise with each other. The consequence was, occasional little disputes which I was required to settle, and differences of opinion on matters so paltry that when I acted the part of umpire I could with difficulty retain the necessary gravity. Hedger was a remarkably devout man, in whose prayers the most accomplished scholar of the age, if possessed of reverence towards God, would have heartily joined, forgetting, in the holy unction of his feelings, the petitioner's ignorance of the rules of language. That man seemed to wrestle with God. He grasped the promises with an earnestness seldom equalled, and, perhaps, never surpassed. He had been in his youth notoriously wicked. Intemperance, impurity, Sabbath-breaking, and profanity, had been his habitual practices. At the age of thirty he had been arrested, convicted, humbled, and saved; and his subsequent life was a vivid illustration of the Divine power of Christianity. He was a Bunyan on a limited scale; and the mothers of the village, who had formerly held him up to their sons as a warning, now pointed to him as an example for imitation. His humility and tenderness of conscience were remarkable. Everything approaching to profanity or thoughtlessness in word or look filled him with sorrow, and his efforts to promote truth and piety exhibited the depth of his religious convictions, and the genuineness of his piety.

William Small justified his cognomen. His ideas revolved in a circle, and that a very narrow one. To express an opinion different from his, was as painful as if you had punctured him with one of his own needles.

The best suggestion was ill-timed and impracticable, or quite out of the question, if it did not originate in Small's mind. Nothing moved properly if he were not the motive-power. He was fond of praise, and would draw his bony fingers over his thin cheeks with obvious complacency, if a slight compliment entered his ear; but he was by no means liberal in praising others. Among his other qualifications he was singularly addicted to the practice of writing long epistles to his neighbours, and even to persons at a distance, who were reported to have said or done anything which he thought wrong. I got into ill-favour with the worthy man on one occasion, and was honoured with a long and very serious letter in consequence. My offence consisted in pleading the cause of missions to the heathen, and asking the congregation to contribute as liberally as their circumstances would permit. The affair was rather caustic in its way, and substantially urged the following points :—that he had no objection to the Gospel being sent abroad—although, if the heathen were not among God's elect, it was no use; but he thought the rich men in London, and elsewhere, should do it, and not send their begging-letters to poor country people who scarcely had bread to eat;—that the foreign missionaries were kept like gentlemen, and did little but send home letters to be printed;—that all that was done was not worth the hundredth part of the expense incurred in doing it;—that the Directors were haughty gentlemen, who would not condescend to speak to a poor body, except when they visit the country as deputations, and then they are all kindness and humility in the hope of obtaining funds;—that we have too many heathen at home, and to send the money out of the country while they were neglected was a very wicked thing;—that the poor people had not a penny to spare;—

and that I must not beg in that way again! I smiled at the epistle and threw it in the fire. Honest William does not know to this day whether it ever reached my hands.

Daniel Hayall was a singular being, afflicted with constitutional melancholy, which caused him to follow his business like a man half asleep. Occasionally, however, there were spasms of energy, in connection chiefly with school and chapel matters, when he threatened to carry everything before him; and when, as a matter of course, Mr. Small's official dignity was wounded, and Mr. Hedger's solicitude for the peace of the Church was awakened.

Such were the men with whom I had to act, in my efforts to accomplish the work to which I had been set apart. But how to harmonise these singular materials was a problem requiring some thought. Happily, it was soon solved. I noted their individual peculiarities, and sought some common bond of union—something common to them all—which I could make the basis of an effort to promote united action. I found this in their piety. They were all good men, consequently they were sincerely anxious for the prosperity of the Church; and even William Small, notwithstanding his notions about the heathen, rejoiced as sincerely as the rest in the conversion of transgressors to the obedience of faith. I appealed to their *hearts*, therefore, whenever united action was necessary, and invariably succeeded. I also felt the importance of avoiding anything like partiality. Men of limited information are jealous of preferences shown to their equals by their common pastor. I laid down the rule, therefore, that the three brethren should be called to engage in the prayer meeting in rotation. This answered well; and, after a little patient training, I found them not only useful, but anxious mutually to carry out my suggestions for the good of the people.

The congregation soon increased, and several persons were brought under the influence of truth, and gave evidence of its power in a new life. During the first year of my ministry, thirty names were added to the list of church-members. By an examination of the church-book I found that, during the twelve years of my predecessor's pastorate, only ten persons altogether had been enrolled. This revival and these proofs of prosperity supplied matter both for gratitude and vigilance. Let it not be thought, however, that I was allowed to proceed quietly all this time. Such events in a rural population seldom take place without exciting opposition of some sort. My own people were united, happy, and grateful; but as soon as the rumour of an increased congregation and church circulated, I was exposed to a cross-fire from quarters which certainly had very little sympathy with each other. There was a small Chapel in the village, occupied by a very select society of persons, who were more remarkable for their attachment to the doctrine of election than to that of charity. My soundness in the faith was doubted by those worthy persons, and the suspicion was zealously circulated. It is true, they did not come to *me* with the generous purpose of instructing an erring brother; perhaps *this* idea did not occur to them; but they did the next best thing—urged the villagers to hear their teacher, and warned them against hearing me. It was certain that I was an "Arminian," and it was not at all impossible that I was a Jesuit; for in these days of pretence, Popery, and false doctrine, no man could trust another; and, in fact, no man could be safe except he went to Mr. Height's Chapel. I may remark, by the way, that this was an alarming climax, as Mr. Height's

Chapel could hold only one hundred and fifty persons. On the other hand, the slumbering zeal of my neighbour, the vicar of Rowly, was suddenly awakened. He noticed, to his dismay, that several members of his congregation were more than usually irregular in their attendance. Although, geographically, he had no right to superintend Willowfield, yet the Church-going portion of the villagers had practically given him that right by attending his ministry. The repeated absence of some of them was, therefore, a subject for inquiry. And, to make the matter worse, several of his own parishioners, over whom he had a legal right to watch, had been seen wending their way to Willowfield on a Sunday. What was to be done? To denounce the schismatic from the parish pulpit was an easy thing; but what good would that do, if the wandering sheep were not present to hear the denunciation? Besides, the Rev. Godfrey Patristic was too wise for that. It would have acted like the intimation of spring-guns upon thieves—or an auctioneer's placard, on the pump opposite the " Wounded Hare," upon idlers and tipplers— the next Sunday the Chapel would have been crowded with gaping and eager listeners. And as to the petition in the Litany,—

> " From all false doctrine, heresy, and schism :
> Good Lord, deliver us!"—

why, it had been so often presented that unhappily it had come to mean—nothing. The sixty or seventy Rowly petitioners, who said " Amen," through the lips of the worthy Mr. Parrot, would never have thought of me, or any other schism teacher in particular, but of all sorts of bad things in general—that is to say, if they thought at all. Mr. Patristic was too well acquainted with the peculiarities of human nature to give me the benefit of a gratuitous advertisement of this kind. Hence he adopted the not very original, but generally successful plan of trying to countervail nonconformist teaching by those substantial gifts which appeal to the senses. Shoes, stockings, flannel, coals, tea, sugar, and medicine found their way into the houses of the poor, the aged, and the sick, as if some good genii had reported the domestic circumstances of the people to the benevolent dwellers in the vicarage; and the bearers of these useful articles were instructed to insinuate that the recipients were expected to show their faces at Church. These donations were followed, in most cases, by a visit from the reverend vicar himself, who admonished his parishioners respecting the evils of carelessness in general, and the sin of dissent in particular, with a zeal which was both edifying and new. I could not find fault with all this. Why should I? On the contrary—it gave me real pleasure. The poor people stood in need of these bodily comforts, and I was as willing as the vicar to bestow them; but I had not the means. There was only one thing with which I could reasonably quarrel, namely, the condition upon which a repetition of these gifts was suspended. This, however, was only the thin edge of the wedge. The zealous clergyman came again and again,—and when his efforts failed to accomplish all that was intended, the inhabitants were surprised, one fine day, by the advent of the curate of Willowfield, in *propria persona*. Never before had he visited this distant corner of his extensive parish. Indeed, the poor people did not know who or what he was. But this ignorance was speedily removed. He went from house to house, as a successor of the apostles should; but whether he carried the apostolic message, or visited in the apostolic spirit, let the following scene between him and Mrs. Brown, a labourer's wife, and a member of my Church, testify :—

Curate—" Good morning, Mrs. Brown. I hope you are quite well, and your husband and the children."

Mrs. Brown—" Thank you, Sir, we are all pretty well at present, through mercy. Will you please be seated? But you have the advantage of me, Sir."

C.—" I am the curate of Willowfield—the curate of this parish, and I have come to visit my parishioners."

B.—" Indeed, Sir. Thank you. I'm pleased to see you. I'm sorry my husband's not in."

C.—"Oh! no matter. Do you attend Church? I don't remember seeing you at Church."

B.—" No, Sir; the parish Church is too far off for us poor folks that have families to see after."

C.—" That makes no difference, Mrs. Brown. You see, *I* don't think it too far to come here to visit you; and you ought to 'go, once a day at least, on Sundays, to your parish Church. What will become of you if you don't ?"

B.—" Sir, I never had the pleasure of seeing you before, and—and I hope you will excuse me, Sir—but we have the Gospel faithfully preached in the vill—"

C.—" The Gospel? what do you mean by that, Mrs. Brown? No one knows anything about the Gospel but your clergyman, nor has any one a legal right to pretend to—"

B.—" Sir, I beg your pardon for interrupting you, but our minister—"

C.—" Your minister? *I* am your minister."

B.—" Perhaps you are, Sir; but I never saw you before."

C.—" Your own fault, ma'am."

B.—" Be it so, Sir; but our minister preaches the Gospel, and we are very thankful for his—"

C.—" He has no right, ma'am; knows nothing about

it; was never ordained; is leading you all to hell, and—"

B.—" Sir, you are a clergyman, you say, and a gentleman, I suppose; but you are bearing false witness against your neighbour!"

C.—" Tush! foolish woman! Eh, allow me to ask, is that child yours?"

B.—" Yes, Sir."

C.—" Baptised?"

B.—" Yes, Sir."

C.—" By whom?"

B.—" My pastor, Sir, of course."

C.—" You mean that layman schismatic, who has set up for a teacher in the village?"

B.—" Sir," said the poor woman, deeply agitated, "my religion teaches me to be courteous; but you will greatly oblige me by not speaking in that way of my beloved pastor. *He* would not speak so of you. I know that!"

C.—" Well, well," said the curate, changing his tactics, " I wish you to bring this child to Church to be baptised, and I will overlook the past."

B.—" The child is baptised, Sir, I have told you."

C.—" It really is not, Mrs. Brown, no more than if you had wickedly attempted to do it yourself! If the child die, it will be lost for ever!"

In an agony of maternal love, the grieved mother snatched her child, and pressed it to her bosom, exclaiming, with tear-filled eyes, " Blessed Saviour, forbid! *Thou* wilt not cast out this little one, that has been prayerfully dedicated to thee."

This was too much, even for the curate. When the weeping mother looked around, he was gone. He visited immediately afterwards a middle-aged lady, of the name of Priestly, in whom he found rather more than he expected. Mrs. Priestly was a widow, living on a small annuity, and, as she was the daughter of parents rather above the middle class of society, she was well educated. Moreover, she was fond of reading, took in some of the monthly periodicals, and felt particularly interested in all the ecclesiastical intelligence of the day. In early life she had been an adherent of the Episcopal Church, which she had left from conscientious motives; and she had a brother, a clergyman, still living, in a distant part of the country. This brief notice of Mrs. Priestly will account for the substance of her remarks to "our curate." I should add, that she was considered somewhat eccentric by her neighbours.

"I am visiting my parishioners, ma'am," said the clergyman, in his blandest tone, "and I shall be happy to have a little conversation with you, if you please."

"With much pleasure, Sir," replied Mrs. Priestly; "a pastoral visit from the clergyman of this parish is *such* a treat!"

Curate—"Ahem! Why, ma'am, we have such a pressure of official engagements, and our parish is so extensive, that we cannot see all our flock so often as would be desirable."

P.—"True, Sir; the parish is very large, including a large town, and five or six villages, for which the State has provided one *Church*. What do you think would become of us all, but for the Dissenters?"

C.—"The evil will be remedied soon. It is in contemplation to build one or two Churches. You know the population has increased greatly since the parish Church was erected."

P.—"It is scarcely necessary, Sir; for there are five or six Chapels in the parish, some of them large and well filled, and you owe it to the exertions of the good men who preach the Gospel so faithfully in them, that your parishioners are not all heathen. May I presume to ask to what we owe the honour of this visit to-day? I have been in this place some fifteen years, but this is the first time, I believe, that we have had such a visit."

C.—"I regret it much, ma'am; but these days require increased activity, and we must try to check growing evils."

P.—" So far as we are concerned in Willowfield, it is no matter, Sir. We have a faithful and successful pastor—"

C.—You mean the clergyman of Rowly, of course? Your parish Church being so distant."

P.—" Did you really *think* I meant him, Sir ?"

C. (Colouring slightly.)—" I—I know of no other; that is to say, I recognise no other in this neighbourhood, and even he is not in your parish, but his Church is near."

P.—" But the pastor to whom I allude *is in* our parish, and, though you do not recognise him, he is recognised both by God and men. But I rejoice that you are alive to the evils of the times, and intend to check them. I wish you great success; more labourers are wanted all the world over."

C.—" Schism is a fearful sin, Mrs. Priestly."

P.—" Indeed it is, Sir. I'm pleased you made that remark, for it shows you and I were thinking of the same thing—Puseyism."

I remember, many years ago, a mischievous schoolboy blowing a pea through a tube with such exactness that it hit the nose of a fair young lady, who was sitting at an open window. The suddenness of the curate's start from this stroke of sarcasm was similar to hers, at least I was reminded of it when Mrs. Priestly related the circumstance to me. He sprang from his chair, seized his hat and walking stick, and made for the door.

" Don't be in a hurry, Sir," said Mrs. P.; " your visit is very short. Pray sit down again. I was about to ask you one or two questions, if you please."

" Well," said the clergyman, " certainly; what are they? My time is precious; I must visit others."

P.—" I should be sorry to deprive them of the pleasure, Sir; but what do you think of these?" taking from a sideboard, and placing before him, several of the " Tracts for the Times."

C. (After a pause, and a look of surprise.)—" There are several opinions in our Church respecting these publications."

P.—" I am sorry to hear it, Sir; but pray, if I may make bold to ask, what is *your* opinion?"

C.—" I do not visit my parishioners to answer questions, but to propose them, and to receive answers."

P.—" O, I beg your pardon, Sir, very sincerely; but it is, if I am not mistaken, a clergyman's duty to guide his flock, and surely you will tell me whether I ought to receive the teachings of these tracts or not?"

C.—" Yes, ma'am; but there are different opinions in our Church."

P.—" Then what becomes of its unity, Sir?"

C.—" Do you ever attend Church, ma'am?"

P.—" I have the privilege of being a member of the Church, Sir, and my place is never empty when I am in health."

C.—" I am very sorry, madam, to find a lady of your intelligence encouraging and aiding schismatics; and I must faithfully warn you of your sin and danger, and entreat you to return to the Church of your fathers. You would then duly attend to its sacraments, and hear the apostolic ministry, which alone can lead you safely through life and to heaven."

P.—" I am obliged, Sir, for your compliment and advice, but I beg to assure you that there is no schism among us. We are perfectly united. We have also an apostolic ministry—as of course you mean, by that, the preaching of apostolic doctrine—the sacraments are duly administered, and we are looking for everlasting life through the merits of the great High Priest and Saviour, Jesus Christ."

C.—" Good morning, madam."

P.—" Before you go, Sir, will you have the kindness to step into the next cottage, and pray with a poor man ? He is very ill, and would be thankful for a visit."

C.—" What is the matter with him ?"

P.—" He has had some of his ribs broken by a fall from a building."

" Ah ! indeed," said the curate, pulling a book out of his pocket, and turning over the leaves. " No, I must decline at present. I find there is no prayer here for a case of that kind ; no prayer for broken ribs. Think of what I have said to you, Mrs. Priestly. Good morning."

P.—" I will, Sir, *often.* Good morning, Sir."

There were three or four public-houses and beer-shops in the village, and intemperance was the great sin of many, with its ever-attendant evils, especially on the Lord's day ; for these haunts of temptation were all open on that day, as on others. Shortly after these clerical movements, which unquestionably had their origin in the growing prosperity of the congregation under my care, I was gratified by the intelligence that the churchwardens had ordered the public-houses to be shut during the morning and afternoon of the Sabbath. Here, at least, was a step in the right direction ; but, alas ! how many seemingly good deeds have their beauty soiled, when the motives from which they sprang are revealed. It was not long concealed, that the object of this movement was to enable the wardens to detect those of their farm servants who were guilty of going to Chapel. The argument was briefly this: they cannot be at the public-houses, and if they are not at Church they must be at Chapel. One of the wardens, by no means remarkable either for morality or temperance, threatened his labourers with a discharge from his service if they attended the Dissenting Meeting; and if he missed them at Rowly Church on Sunday, he questioned them on Monday morning where they had been the day before. This paltry and abominable persecution continued for some considerable time. The poor men, several of whom had to keep large families on nine or ten shillings a week, could ill afford to lose that wretched sum; and these threats, together with the influence of the vicar's gifts, increased the attendance at the parish Church for some time. But the ringleader in this sorry crusade against religious liberty, the farmer to whom I have alluded, died suddenly of an apoplectic stroke, some three months afterwards, and the spasmodic zeal of Mr. Patristic gradually evaporated; so that the Chapel retained its average congregation during the time, and the three last years of my ministry witnessed a religious prosperity which Willowfield had never seen before.

There was no increase to my salary; for the people were poor, and the sum offered by the Church at first was greater than had been given to any of my predecessors, and was calculated on the assumption of an increased congregation. If the reader will deduct twelve pounds for house-rent and taxes, he will see that I had not overmuch left for all the necessary expenses of a household, including, before I left, the parents, three children, and a servant. But I do not intend to enter into particulars of this kind. My second child died at two years of age. The pang of grief occasioned to the parents by this first domestic bereavement, those who have drunk a similar cup will be able to understand. About the same time I received intelligence of the death of my good and venerable father, who had lived to know that the providence of God had realised the hopes of his youngest son, and who died full of that quiet confidence in his Saviour which had been the tenant of his breast for many years, and of that hope which maketh not ashamed in the valley of the shadow of death.

There was a debt of about £150 on the Chapel. To have this removed was most desirable; but we were utterly unable to accomplish it without help from a distance. The collection of the annual interest was all that could be effected by my people, in addition to the minister's salary, a trifle to the Missionary Society once a year, incidentals, and Sunday-school expenses. There were several large towns in the neighbourhood, in all of which I had repeatedly preached; and having reason to believe that I was esteemed in them all, I hoped that Christian friends in those towns would aid us in the reduction of this old debt. The " case" was prepared, and when I had been two years and a half in Willow-field, I set out on that perilous and justly unpopular project, begging for a chapel debt. The appeal being readily authenticated by their pastors, the good people in these towns reduced the debt to £100. Though footsore and weary with this circuit, the pleasure of having lessened the burden by one third prompted me to try to throw it off altogether. After resting a few days, I resolved to go to London, the city of gold, greatness, and unequalled philanthropy. *There,* of course, I should speedily receive this paltry sum. What was £100 to the merchant princes of the greatest city in the world? But, query, what if the smallness of the amount should prove an obstacle? To me and my village flock it was a burden; but to the people of London it was nothing. Well, I shall try. Perhaps some benevolent gentleman may hand me a cheque at once for the whole amount, rather than see a Christian minister wandering about the streets like a guilty thing, reading names at office-doors, interrupting people by asking the way, or poring over a tattered map of " the great metropolis."

The result, at all events, would show which of these possibilities, or whether any of them, was near the truth. I had never seen London, and, of course, I had a strong desire to visit a place so long celebrated over the whole world. Providing suitable pulpit supplies for my intended absence of a month, I undertook the journey, and partly by coach, and partly by rail, I reached it in safety. By correspondence I had a slight acquaintance with two or three gentlemen in the metropolis, but personally with none, except one or two ministers whom I had seen in the country as missionary deputations. I took my place on the top of an omnibus at the railway terminus, that I might get a view of the route as we went to the "Bank." Everything from that point of vision was new, strange, and exciting. The contrast between my village home and the streets of London was complete. In the former there was quietness, and a feeling of repose, with the open canopy of heaven overhead. In the latter there was unceasing din, like the roar of old ocean as it groans along the shores of the world, and a feeling of never-sleeping restlessness, with a canopy of smoke overhead. Signs of poverty, humility, and age marked the village; wealth,

luxury, pride, and perpetual youth were the visible
features of the city. Poverty was a thing out of sight,
driven to, or attracted by, those wretched and unex-
plored regions where the millionaire and the noble, the
jewelled lady and the man of business never go; and on
the chief thoroughfares there is no room for age. Youth
and manhood keep the great heart of the empire in perpetual motion. And the humble village was my home,
the scene of my pastoral labours, where were the fruits
of my ministry, and where I had property in the grave
of my departed child; but in London I was a stranger,
and, as I began to fear, by no means a welcome one, for I
was about to knock at the door of charity on behalf of a
few poor country people, of whose existence on the face
of the earth London knew not. True charity is a lady of
exquisite beauty, of noble mien, and perfect form. The
light of benevolence plays on her countenance, and there
is a mingled expression of holy sadness and joy in her
eye, which assures the poor and the fallen that she weeps
in secret over their afflictions and sins, and that her heaven
upon earth arises from efforts to relieve and restore them.
Her eye affecteth her heart, and the sympathies of her
tender soul are drawn out by the pale cheek of hunger,
and the trembling steps of age. In the feeble wail of the
little orphan, and the furrowed brow of the widow, she
hears and sees that unwritten monody whose pathos stirs
her spirit. The chief characteristic of her nature, and
that which gives beauty and glory to all the rest, is the
love of man as the wandering child of God. She loves
angels with calm complacency, because, good herself, she
cannot but delight in goodness; but she loves men with
benevolent compassion, because, taught of God herself,
she would lead them back to the Father. The supply of
bread to the hungry, and of clothes to the naked, are, in

her hand, religious acts, because her motive is regard to Him who, though He was rich, yet for our sakes became poor, that we through His poverty might be rich ; and whilst she ministers of her substance to the body, she ministers with still greater earnestness to that mysterious life within, of which the body is but the frail casket ; and, in a word, she needs not, like those who, coveting her fame, imitate her voice and manner, the repeated strokes of skilful argument or cunning flattery, to elicit the warm spark from her heart, for the living flame is already there, and the sacrifice is accepted, because it is offered willingly as to the Lord, and not to men.

But has charity counterfeits? What more likely? There have been many false Christs, and why not many false charities? The true gospel creates the true charity; but there are many gospels, and each of them, in imitation of the true, has its accompanying charity. There is the gospel of counsel, which, like the drug vendor, gives " advice gratis ;"—its charity consists of words, which tell you how to proceed, but it neither puts shoes on your feet nor a staff in your hand. There is the gospel of sentiment, which pathetically describes the wants of the poor;—its charity is employed in calling upon *others* to remember the children of woe ; but it sells its appeals at so much per sheet. There is the gospel of the ball room and the public dinner, which proclaims its message by the dance and the wine cup;—its charity hands the " surplus" to the refugee and the society ; but without the dance and the wine her heart would have felt no warmth. There is the gospel of imitation, which makes the list of subscribers the standard of duty ;—its charity has no particular reference to the merits of the case, but thinks it would be mean to refuse when so many neighbours have given. There is the gospel of ease, whose charity opens her hand that she may get rid of a troublesome applicant.   And there is the gospel of popular fame, whose charity gives one thousand pounds, with the well-understood condition, that the name of the " princely donor" shall appear in the newspapers, be loudly cheered at the public meeting, and surrounded with a cloud of incense in the annual report.   This charity does things only on a magnificent scale.   The minute and the obscure are beneath her notice.   She comprehends a whole, but sees not the use of parts.   She will build churches, endow a bishopric, found a college, glorify a sect, colonise a wilderness, or emancipate a nation of slaves; but a sovereign to a village pastor, whose soul is wrung between the fear of debt and the fact of poverty, or a cast-off coat to a brother shivering in the cold, or any other trifling gift which would attract no notice, except the warm thanks of the recipient, and a place in his prayers to God, is foreign to the practice of that magniloquent charity that is born of the gospel of fame.

Each of these charities has its work to do in the many-sided world, and each of them has its reward; but, though bearing the name, neither of them· is, in the remotest degree, related to the greatest sister of the heaven-born three.   It was clear, therefore, that if I failed in the discovery of *her* address, my visit to London would be in vain.   As the monks live in the cloister, and the clergy in the Cathedral-close, I concluded that I should find charity in the precincts of the Church.   Where should she live, if not near her generous mother's side?   If the gospel of love, to drop metaphor, do not open the hearts and hands of those who sit under its influence to feelings and deeds of benevolence, nothing else will, nothing else can; for though the other gospels create their characteristic charities, and do deeds of real service to humanity, yet the disinterested motive which sanctifies the action is found only in hearts which beat in sympathy with the holy and loving heart of Jesus the Lord.

I spent a month in London—a month well remembered! during which I discovered that I was wofully ignorant of the sublime science of begging. Many a weary mile I walked; many odd excuses, instead of odd shillings, I received; many brows were contracted, and shoulders shrugged, at the sight of my little book; and many remarks were made in reply to my humble request, some witty, some wise, some withering. I shall give a short list by way of specimen:—

No. 1.—" How did you come to call on me first? I never head a list."

No. 3.—" With whom have you left those few sheep in the wilderness? I should say, make haste back to your village, and tell your people to raise the money themselves."

No. 5.—" Can't do anything for you. Good morning."

No. 6.—" Perfectly absurd! Country people think we are made of money. Not a day passes without some begging case. It's really *too* bad! Pray excuse me."

No. 9.—" Humph! I should not like to hurt your feelings, my friend, but only just think, only think, and let your own good sense determine whether this is wise. You have travelled—how far do you say? One hundred and fifty miles? Exactly, one hundred and fifty miles, and mean to spend—how long?—one month in London, in the hope of collecting one hundred pounds. Why, Sir, it's preposterous! Who advised you? You seem a man of sense. But you cannot have calculated. All that you can possibly get will be short of your expenses. I cannot encourage this sort of thing."

No. 12.—" Oh! a Chapel case! It is with me a principle, Sir, never to give to Chapel cases. If it were for a school, or a clothing society, or foreign missions, I might give a trifle, but not to a case of this kind."

No. 16.—" Ha! ha! Well, this is exactly the seventh begging case I have had to-day already, and it's not yet two o'clock! It's downright persecution! I must change my name and address, or go to the workhouse!"

No. 21.—" Ah! Sir, I am *very* sorry! There is no class of men I esteem, or rather, I should say, love so much as ministers of the Gospel; and if I make any difference among them it is in favour of those faithful and laborious village pastors who are doing so much good to the souls of the agricultural poor. What a pleasant and happy life yours must be! You know nothing of the cares of a London merchant. I sincerely hope you will get the little debt wiped off. Had you called at *any other* time I should have had so much pleasure in helping you; but, will you take a cup of tea with me to-night? Ah! now I remember, you would scarcely be comfortable, for they are all busy packing up, as we are going to the Continent to-morrow. I and my family visit Switzerland this year. Good day, good day; I hope you will be quite successful!"

No. 22.—" Willowfield? Where's that? Never heard of it! I am very busy at present. Call again this day week. No; stop! I am going to Brighton—yes, I fear, Sir, I can't help you."

No. 25.—" Churches should be self-supporting, and pay their own debts. We cannot be responsible for every little knot of people that gather together in out-of-the-way places. Our hands are full at home; but I'll make you a present of a valuable book. Here's a copy of Baxter's 'Saints' Rest.' Tell your people what *I* said."

No. 28.—" Our own place is desperately in debt!"

No. 30.—" There are so many begging impostors that I have determined to give to no more cases. You do not look like one, or I should have you taken up on suspicion! How should I know whether these alleged names of ministers are genuine? My time is valuable. 'Morning!"

I made it a point to copy down the exact answers I received from all on whom I called; and I studied them in the evening, by way of improvement in the knowledge of humanity. It would be a foul libel on the Christian people of London, however, to let the above worthy twelve go forth to the world as fairly representing all the answers I received. I found the dwelling of true charity, as well as that of her unrelated namesake; and I shall also quote a dozen of her replies.

No. 2.—" With much pleasure, Sir, will I give you a guinea, regretting that it is not more."

No. 4.—" I don't care for paying old Chapel debts. The system is bad, and should be discouraged; but I feel deeply for the servants of Christ, who are toiling amidst many discouragements in our rural districts. Put this couple of guineas in your pocket. Don't enter it on the book. It's for yourself. God bless you!"

No. 11.—" I am not a Dissenter, you know; but I love all who love our Lord Jesus Christ. Preach His Gospel faithfully, my brother. Live near to God—*very* near, if you would save souls. In this case only can you look for the Holy Spirit's influences. Accept five pounds, with my prayers for your spiritual usefulness."

No. 14.—" I wish something could be done to increase the income and comfort of country pastors. We talk about it; but I wish our leading men would act as well as talk. I think there should be a common fund for this purpose, and most gladly would I contribute to it. For *this* case accept a sovereign."

No. 23.—" Dear Sir, I cannot spare a moment at present, or I should like to have a little chat with you. Will you forgive me, and enter my name for a guinea-and-a-half."

No. 26.—My circumstances are not equal to my will, Sir; but you will not refuse five shillings, with a poor man's blessing. Don't enter it; lest others who are able to do more should follow my bad example."

No. 29.—" There are three gentlemen waiting for me. I dine at four. Here's my address. Be sure you come at the moment, and after dinner you shall have my mite."

No. 33.—" Certainly. With all my heart. I never refuse really deserving cases. Take a sovereign. Good bye!"

No. 39.—" I have heard of you, Sir, and am very glad you have called. If half-a-guinea be worth your acceptance, you are most welcome; but don't measure my good-will by the amount."

No. 42.—" A sovereign. I wish I could make it more."

No. 44.—A similar answer.

No. 45.—" What family have you? How many in congregation? May I also ask, not from any wrong motive I assure you, how much your people raise for you?" I answered these questions. The good man's lips quivered for a moment. He looked at me again, put pen to paper, and wrote a short note, which he sealed, and placed in my hand, saying, " Now, my dear Sir, don't be offended, and don't misunderstand me. Take this note to the address. You will be measured for a suit of clothes. Get them of good quality. Let me hear from you sometimes. Farewell!"

Reader! Have you ever felt a hard substance, causing a choking sensation? It is a curious compound, and I tried to analyse it after I had left the office of good charity, No. 45. It almost baffled my chemical skill; but, as nearly as I could resolve it, I found that it consisted of four elements in about equal proportions—pride, humility, vexation, and gratitude! But I read Matthew vi. 30, and sent a letter of thanks to my generous brother, by whose hand the Great Father had, in this instance, fulfilled His promise.

The whole amount collected was £45 15s. In many respects, the month spent in town was a pleasant one. I had the happiness of becoming acquainted with some excellent men, and of forming friendships which have continued ever since. I heard some of the most popular preachers, and was called upon twice to preach before London audiences. No. 45 had been one of my hearers on the Lord's day preceding the interview recorded above.

But I intended to say something respecting my first impressions of the Great City.

London has been described by many writers of ability, and by multitudes of very little ability. Historians, topographers, poets, novelists, literary limners, magazine contributors, and penny-a-liners, have all done something,—each in his peculiar fashion,—to transmit to posterity the whereabouts and whatabouts of the British metropolis. But I withdraw the statement. London has never been described. The achievement is impossible! The thing cannot be done! London is indescribable. A bird's-eye view by the aeronaut, a traveller's view by the tourist, a painter's view by the panoramist, a politician's view by the statesman, a chronological view by the annalist, a philosophical view by the thinker, and a fancy view by the novelist, are all well, each in its place, and I should be sorry to trespass on the territory of either of these useful members of society. I cannot improve, and will not disparage any of their views. The extent of my ambition on this subject is only to transcribe the impressions made on my own mind, on the occasion of my first visit to the metropolis.

I thought, first, of the patience and forbearance of God. Let any one with a correct, though by no means adequate, view of the purity and extent of the Divine law—that law which is essential to the being of man, and the well-being of the universe—walk the streets of London for a few days and a few evenings, and he will assuredly concur in the opinion which forced itself on my mind, that "the Lord God is merciful and gracious, long-suffering, and abundant in goodness and truth." The multiform aspects of sin, the many-shaded transgressions, the words, deeds, and signs of iniquity that force themselves upon the eye and ear of the spectator, compel him to admire the long-suffering of that sleepless Being who sees and hears all, without rending the heavens in wrath over the heads, or causing the earth to open in vengeance beneath the feet of the rebels.

I thought, secondly, of the wisdom and goodness of Divine Providence. The population of the world, variously estimated, but at the lowest figure of enormous amount, is too great for any mind to comprehend. The vast aggregate of a city of two millions and a half, however, though even that can only be very partially conceived, gives an impression of awe and wonder respecting the goodness and wisdom that *can* provide for them all. The world, in all its regions, commerce with all its appliances, industry with all its resources, atmosphere, ocean, and fruitful field, with all their products, seem to be laid under contribution to supply London with the necessaries and luxuries of life! How do they all, how can they all live? I involuntarily asked, as I gazed upon thronged streets, crowded courts, omnibuses, steam-boats churches, hotels, lodging-houses, pleasure-gardens, promenades, and market-places. By what wonderful means is food provided for all these? Whence come bread, water, raiment, and the other essentials of existence to this living, moving, agitated ocean of human beings, not to speak of the many myriads of inferior creatures that must live too, if they are to be of any service to their human masters? Who but a superintending Being of infinite resources, and of goodness equal to His resources, could care for, and supply the daily wants of all these? And yet, perhaps, not one in ten recognises His hand, asks His protection, or adores His glorious majesty; whilst a lamentably great proportion defies His authority, neglects His mercy, despises His gospel, curses His law, and blasphemes His sacred name.

I thought, thirdly, of the vast machinery created by the conjoint efforts of the State and of private benevolence to do good—social, intellectual, moral, and religious—to the inhabitants of the overgrown, and yet ever-growing city. A mere list of the establishments, institutions, societies, charities, endowments, associations, churches and chapels, which professedly seek to accomplish this object, would fill a volume. The field covered by the several sections of the Christian Church must be very great. The number of schools of all kinds, from the infant class to the university, is enormous. The charities which seek only the physical well-being of the citizens are exceedingly numerous; and yet, with all this, the amount of suffering, ignorance, immorality, and impiety is awful to contemplate. It seems as if in the fearful race good cannot overtake evil, nor benevolence want, nor Christianity sin. Yet, with all these melancholy facts, it is perhaps true, at all events I think it cannot be fairly questioned, that, in proportion to the population, there is more genuine benevolence, more high-toned morality, and more vital religion in London than in any other city in the world. Yet one must speak very generally, as this is a subject in connexion with which statistics are not available, nor could they be received as authentic were the effort made to furnish them.

And I thought, lastly, of the inimitable beauty, the moral splendour of the greatest and most wealthy city on the face of the earth, if all its inhabitants were entirely under the influence of the Christian Scriptures. If all were pure, moral, and devout—all upright, loving, and religious—all believers in and lovers of those divine and soul-ennobling truths which fell from the lips of Jesus and his apostles—how incomparably beautiful were London! How attractive to the good of all lands, to the angels of heaven, and to the Lord of angels and men! And how speedily it would accomplish the high mission of the Church, to preach the Gospel to every creature under heaven! But, alas! this is but a picture of the imagination, a dream of the fancy! Shall it ever be realised in fact? Will that day ever dawn that shall shed its glad light on a thoroughly evangelised London? and shall the intelligence ever circulate around the globe, that all the dwellers in the British metropolis are walking with God?

My opinion on this great question would scarcely be in place here, nor could I do it justice without the introduction of an argument that would materially change the character of this book.

    *   *   *   *   *

Returning home with the result of my begging tour, I placed it in the hands of the treasurer. Finding all, happily, in peace, and seeing many eyes brightening with pleasure, I valued the welcome, and resolved to resume work with increased earnestness—a resolution which I kept to the injury of my health. My month's experience, however, had convinced me that the whole system—or rather practice, for there is no system in the thing—of chapel-begging is bad, incurably bad, and should be forthwith abolished by the universal consent of good men. I determined that, under no circumstances, would I ever act the eleemosynary again. "To beg I am ashamed." It is a degradation, from whatever point of the compass you view it. Places of Christian worship must be built, and what is more, they must be greatly multiplied both in towns and the country. They are the glory of the land, the conservators of peace and civilisation, the best kind of training establishments for the mind of the community, scenes of unspeakable consolation to myriads of sorrowing hearts, memorials of the greatest love of which humanity hath ever heard, evidences of the progress of truth, and lights to guide the traveller to a happy immortality! Let them, therefore, be multiplied; and may He whose right it is to choose His own servants, send the proper men! In many cases, the Christian voluntaryism of private individuals, whom the owner of the silver and the gold has constituted His stewards, can erect them. An individual lady or gentleman cannot do a thing more likely to promote the best interests of the people than to fix upon a destitute locality, and say, "I will build a chapel and school-room *there!*" In other cases, the united contributions of several persons whom the Lord hath prospered can accomplish the desired object. In a third class of cases, the funds entrusted to

Chapel-building Societies can do it. And in a fourth class of cases, congregations can enlarge or build for themselves, and for the good of the locality in which they meet. But, in *every* case, the architect's receipt should be in the hands of the building committee before the house is thrown open for public worship; and in *no* case should ministers of "the glorious Gospel" be sent over the country, like mendicant friars, to endure the scorn of some, the snappish remarks of others, and—what is more intolerable than either to a man of fine feeling—the *pity* of a third class. And, above all things, let not the eye of Christian benevolence, as it sweeps across the moral wilderness of an apostate world, forget a glance of compassion towards the villages and hamlets of the British islands. Let that charity which is born of faith do good on the most extensive scale that her power can embrace, but, oh! let her not forget to *show piety* AT HOME!

CHAPTER VIII.

THE INNER LIFE.

" *   *   *   What a fearful crowd
Of wild emotions, passions, fears, and hopes,
Rush like a fierce tornado on the heart,
Burning and madd'ning by their demon dance,
And leaving desolation in their train !·
Wars, hot as ever rocked a continent,
Or made a planet stagger in its path,
Are daily fought within the bleeding soul
Of many a child of Adam.   Never yet
Hath the full portrait of a man appeared ;
And never yet hath dearest bosom friend
Known all that passed in his companion's soul."—*Leask.*

THE INNER LIFE—SELF-STUDY—DISTRESSING NERVOUS SENSIBILITY—
DR. SCOTT—THE PEACE MEETING—THE SOCIETY OF FRIENDS—
MR. CORESOUND'S LETTER—HOW TO PERFORM AN ACT OF KINDNESS
—HASTINGS—EXAMINATION OF MOTIVES—HELPLESSNESS OF MAN
—PECULIAR DANGER OF MINISTERS — PAINFUL FEELINGS — THE
TRAINING PROCESS—FAITH—HOME AND THE TEA-PARTY—FAULTS
FOUND WITH THE PULPIT SUPPLIES—ARMINIANISM—MEASURING
THE STARS—BURYING THE PRAYER BOOK—MRS. HOBLE'S QUESTION
—HOW TO PREACH EXPERIENCE—A PLEASANT CLOSE.

How comparatively insignificant the external events of
life appear, when a man retires within himself, and
honestly and earnestly examines the processes going on
there.   The noise of petty rivals at a parish contest ; the
conflict of parties at a local or general election ; the fear
of one political sect, and the exultation of another, when

one ministry falls and another rises; the commotions consequent upon war or revolution, and the thousand other occurrences which claim the attention of men; how their magnitude sinks into minuteness, when the spirit realises the fact of its immortality, and examines beneath the light of Scripture the interests which that fact involves. The external, with all its seeming importance, yields to the internal, and the visible retires before the unseen. The health of the inner life may not be neglected with impunity; and he who devotes himself to the benefit of others will not succeed to any great extent if he neglects his own. If religion consisted solely of an intellectual perception of certain doctrines, and an ability to propound and illustrate them, to understand and to speak would be the necessary qualifications of the religious teacher. If sound in doctrine, and apt to teach, he would be a fully qualified man. But, happily for humanity, religion is more than this. It is power, life, health. It creates motives for word and deed; it animates and regulates the intellectual life with a new moral life, and it restores health to the diseased spirit. If it come short in relation to any of these things, in the case of a man who thinks that he is under its influence, that man has reason for deep solicitude.

An autobiography, destitute of any revelation of the writer's inner life, would have little interest for those who wish to study mind rather than visible phenomena, and men rather than things. This may be thought a subject more appropriate for another pen, and, in some respects, it is; yet the on-looker, though he be also the intimate friend, is never so fully qualified as the individual himself to give that revelation. " For what man knoweth the things of a man, save the spirit of man which is in him ?" Frequent incidental glances at the state of my mind under different circumstances have been already given, but the successive stages of one's progress in life either bring out feelings, or impart impressions, previously unnoticed, or unknown. We are not made by circumstances, in the sense of circumstances being the originating cause; but they modify feelings, and give tone to thought and character, in the sense of their being secondary or mediate causes under Divine Providence. A number of circumstances arose during the fourth year of my ministry, which led to frequent self-study. Domestic cares, repeated inability to meet growing pecuniary demands, incessant labour, in addition to pastoral and pulpit duties, by speaking and lecturing in the villages and towns for many miles around—for which my remuneration was always a " vote of thanks," with, occasionally, travelling expenses—and deep mental anxiety, all acting on a delicate constitution, brought on a nervous debility and prostration which made life a burden, and threatened to bring it to a speedy close. I became most wretchedly sensitive. Every thing was wrong. A rap at the door made me start. A cloud passing over head was the bearer of doom. The whistling of the wind among the branches was the sighing of invisible spirits. If a gig passed at a brisk pace, I was sure that an accident must happen. If any of my people called, I was convinced there was some heavy charge against me. My sleep, when I did sleep, was a succession of wild dreams. When closely shut up in my study I found relief, and in the pulpit I was happy; albeit I knew well that these remedies were only adding to the disease. I took drugs, but in vain. I would not consult a physician, because I could not afford a fee; and I should add, that I wrote at this time a work extending to three hundred pages of manuscript, and which, by the way, is in manuscript still.

At last I was persuaded to consult an eminent physician, residing in a large town twenty miles distant. I managed to preserve, notwithstanding my constant difficulties, a guinea from going in another direction, put it in my pocket, and walked to the town. Happily, the skilful doctor was at home. He looked at my tongue, felt my pulse, and sounded my chest carefully. Dr. Scott, who was a fine healthy-looking man, about sixty-five years of age, with grey hair, and a countenance in which energy of purpose, decision of character, and benevolence of spirit were attractively blended, then said :—

" What have you been about, Sir ?"

This blunt question might refer to so many things, that the only answer I could give was to act the echo, which I did to perfection, by saying,

" About, Sir ?"

" Yes," said he ; " I am acquainted with your name and your goings on; and, seeing you have come to me for advice, I tell you it won't do ! You must turn over a new leaf!"

Worse and worse. What could these words mean? I believe, had the doctor tried my pulse again, he would have found a rapid circulation. Seeing my confusion, he smiled and added,

" You are perfectly sound, but exhausted by too much thought and labour. You don't need drugs. You have been running about the country, holding forth on all sorts of subjects, to the injury of your system; and you must give it up, at least for a time. Eat and drink more ; think and speak less ; and, for a month at least, walk about the fields, or sit upon a gate and whistle; that is, if you *can* whistle."

" Thank you, Doctor," I said, laughing; " this is, doubtless, an excellent prescription, but how to take it is the difficulty."

" How to take it? Oh ! *thus :* a mutton chop every day, washed down with a glass of home-brewed ale ; lock the study-door for a month ; say ' No' to all applications, and get your brethren to preach for you."

So saying, the Doctor rang the bell, and when the footman entered he ordered him to bring some wine. He filled a glass, and asked me to drink it.

" Thank you, Sir, excuse me," I said ; " I am an abstainer."

" I know you are, but you have come to me for advice, and I take the liberty of prescribing for my patients. I give you this *medicinally*, you know," said the Doctor, with a quiet smile.

I offered him the guinea, which he promptly refused, saying,

" No, no ; put it in the mutton chops and the home-brewed. Good morning, Sir."

A few days after this, I received a letter from a gentle-man in this very town, requesting me to move a reso-lution at a public meeting. Cordially approving the object of the meeting, namely, the promotion of inter-national peace, I felt disposed to comply with the request ; but this would be an act of rebellion against Dr. Scott's law, and not only so, but he was very likely to hear of it, as the names of the speakers would, in all probability, meet his eye. He had commanded me to say " No," a short word, which I have ever found it difficult to use when a favour was asked. I therefore resolved to go.

The meeting was well attended. Several influential members of the Society of Friends were present, as they always are at the call of benevolence. They are well named. They have nobly earned their distinctive appellation. They are a society of " Friends ;" friends of peace, truth, freedom, justice, and man, all the world over. Had they confined their friendship to themselves, they would have been the most exclusive sect in the world; but, happily for man, notwithstanding that queer humility which proclaims denomination by singularity in dress, they have " not so learned Christ." Fools laugh at them. Wise men respect them. Good men love them. Patriotism may count upon their services. Philanthropy, should the world grow so bad as to chase her from every other door, may confidently cross the threshold of the Quaker. If you wish to break the arm of the tyrant, or to check the career of Mars, or to impoverish the temple of Bacchus, send for a Friend. The chair was occupied on this occasion by a well-known Friend, whose face seems to have been moulded by the right hand of benevolence; whose name is a household word in our West Indian colonies; whose patriotism ought to have sent him to the House of Commons long ago; and whose dwelling is often visited by the welcome fugitive from the doomed yoke of that slayer of souls, South American slavery. At the close of the meeting, the chairman and speakers were invited to take supper at the house of Mr. Daniel Coresound, a Friend, respected by all who knew his worth. I was Mr. Coresound's guest for the night, and on the following morning, whilst bidding me " Farewell," he put a letter in my hand, saying, " Thee can read that at thy leisure." I was about to open it at once, when he said, " No, no, friend; it doesn't require any answer. Farewell."

On leaving the town I opened the envelope, and found a ten-pound note, and a short letter, of which the following is a copy:—

" 5 *Mo.* 10*th.*

" ESTEEMED FRIEND,

" We are all much obliged for thy help at the peace meeting. My friend, James Scott, tells me thou hast been consulting him, and that he has advised rest. I would recommend thee to go to Hastings for a short time, and as I wish to bear part of the expense, I enclose ten pounds. Take care of thy health.

"Very sincerely and respectfully,

"D. CORESOUND."

Next in value to an act of brotherly kindness, is the manner in which it is performed. The ostentation of the praise-hunter was here carefully avoided. The kindness and delicacy of the Christian gentleman were finely blended. Mr. Coresound had certainly read the command of the Divine Teacher—"Take heed that ye do not your alms before men, to be seen of them; otherwise ye have no reward of your Father who is in heaven. Therefore, when thou doest alms, do not sound a trumpet before thee, as the hypocrites do in the synagogues and in the streets, that they may have glory of men. Verily, I say unto you, they have their reward. But when thou doest alms, let not thy left hand know what thy right hand doeth, that thine alms may be in secret: and thy Father who seeth in secret himself shall reward thee openly."

This most unexpected donation enabled me to enjoy that rest which Dr. Scott had recommended as essential to health. It is surprising how a little money raises one's courage! My nervous system was wonderfully braced by the estimable Mr. Coresound's gift. Arranging some matters at home, I set out for a fortnight's tour, travelling by short stages until I reached Hastings, whose sea-view, bracing atmosphere, and fine neighbourhood, were instrumental in restoring me to health. Sitting on the beach, and looking-out on the never-sleeping ocean, I began to think over the motives that prompt human action.   I thought of the Conqueror, as one naturally would in the neighbourhood of Hastings—of the statesman, the philosopher, the poet, and the Christian minister, and endeavoured to infer, from their respective pursuits, the essential nature of the motives by which they are respectively influenced; but as I could not conclude that I was *certainly* right in either case, it struck me that it would be more profitable to examine my own motives.

I reviewed my experience in life, and had no difficulty in reaching the conclusion that I was under unspeakable obligation to Him in whom I live, and move, and have my being; but what share had my own motives in shaping the course of my history?   This seemingly simple question I found exceeding difficulty in answering.   I could trace the superior motive in most cases with considerable distinctness, but was humbled to find it associated with so many of an inferior character.   I had fondly thought, sometimes, of a simple motive, a distinct, separate, all-impelling desire, acting alone in its unearthly purity, and unstained by any relation to time or self.   I had, at least, wished to be actuated by this, in reference especially to the work of the ministry.   I had desired to serve the great Master, out of pure gratitude for the unspeakable service He had rendered to me and to the human family, and to leave the success of my feeble services entirely to His own grace; but, alas! I found too many witnesses in the court of conscience to depose that I had fallen grievously short of this sublime standard. Had the fear of man never brought a snare? never modified a sermon, or shaped a sentence? never weakened resolution, or changed purpose?   Had the praise of my fellow-creatures never excited an ambition too selfish to be holy, and too earthly to be laid upon the altar of the Lord? too proud to be consistent with heart-discipline, and too worldly for one who had vowed not to be conformed to the world? Had the desire to excel in those qualities which critics praise, never tried to run abreast of the desire to win souls to Christ? Had the wish to be some one, never risen above the wish to do something for the real interests of my fellow-men? Had the cares of the world never absorbed thoughts which were avowedly consecrated to the study of revelation? And had the growth of personal piety been steadily watched, both on its own account, and as an illustration of the power of Christianity?

Ah! how are poor men compelled to cling to their strong Saviour! Even those motives which are of heavenly origin lose their lustre, and have their power weakened, by contact with that mystery of contradictions, the human heart. Yet it is a blessed compulsion which sends a man to Christ, asking pardon for what others call his virtues, and forgiveness for what others call his piety. The correct conception of Christianity is that of a power which contemplates ultimate moral perfection in all its subjects. He who fixes his gaze upon this grand purpose, cannot but feel that he is far from the goal, and this feeling will urge him to the Master, humbled, grieved, ashamed.

It may seem strange to those who have not studied the subtleties of the human heart, but it is, nevertheless, true, that Christian ministers are more exposed than other Christians to the neglect of the inner life. That, as a general thing, they *do* neglect it more than their non-official brethren is not my statement; an allegation of this sort would be inconsistent both with truth and charity; but they are *exposed* to this danger in consequence of their *official* labours. Office is proverbially dangerous. The private Christian appropriates truth; his look is introspective; and his object is personal improvement. The preacher is a benefactor; his eye rests on truth which he communicates to others; and his aim is the spiritual good of others. He may preach a true, able, and even earnest sermon, without feeling its power as much as do many of his hearers. This statement does not imply a doubt of his deep conscientiousness and decided piety—far less, of course, of his correct deportment and irreproachable life—but it illustrates the peculiar danger to which he is exposed, from office and its incessant demands, to relax that vigilance over the *inner* life which is so necessary to its healthy action. Official piety is, of all things, to be avoided as a delusion and a snare. The mechanical performance of stated duties in connexion with the Church of Christ, as if the ministers of living truth were an acting priesthood, whose office gave validity to their actions, notwithstanding the corpse-like coldness of their hearts, is as offensive to clear reason as it is opposed to the loving genius of the Gospel; and yet, the doctrine of Rome and Oxford on this matter is but the huge outgrowth of that peculiar danger to which the minister of Christianity is exposed. Terrible is that idea—" Lest, when I have preached to others, I myself should be a castaway!"

On this subject I had most distressing thoughts, tumultuous agitations of the soul, like those of the ocean before me when a hurricane leaps on its breast. I imagined myself a shivering, starving wretch, gazing from the dark street through the window of a princely mansion, where the assembled guests were luxuriating in abundance and joy; and that I had invited those guests. I foresaw the grand consummation, the splendours of a completed Church, to some few of whose members I had been the bearer of glad tidings, but I stood afar off in the outer darkness! The agitation of my soul increased. The temples throbbed, the heart sank as if a weight of lead had fallen upon it, and the whole frame was painfully affected. I fancied the sea troubled as if a storm had swept suddenly over its surface. I exclaimed, "God be merciful to me, a sinner!" and, shortly after, I thought I heard a voice crossing the sea, which whispered, "It is I; be not afraid!"

I was more than ever convinced, as the result of this short but severe visitation, that to live under the constant power of Christianity is the only way to enjoy its hallowed peace. To talk about the powers of the world to come is one thing; to feel them is quite another. Occasionally to feel the influence of the Unseen is one thing; habitually to realise that influence is another. To guide men into the way of peace, while a storm rolls over the heart of the guide, is just possible; but to be able honestly to cry, "Come!" is a higher exercise of sanctified eloquence than to say, "Go! *that* is the way." Yet the doctrine of Solomon is full of encouragement to the honest expositor of truth: "The liberal soul shall be made fat; and he that watereth shall be watered himself." The discipline of the spirit, however, cannot be made an occasional thing with safety; it must be habitual and regular. Evil creeps in at some of the heart-crevices caused by the fall, if the watchman relax his vigilance but for a moment; and pastoral fidelity can never be the substitute of personal godliness. An apparently trifling offence, in word or action, is enough to make a conscientious person thoroughly wretched; and, of all agonies, those produced by a stormy conscience are the most intolerable. It is easy to do wrong, or to omit right, but it is *not* pleasant to feel the rebound with which the spring of conscience sends back the error or omission upon the very vitals of the soul! That the severity of the training operation differs in different minds is a trite observation; yet the process which prepares a human spirit for "glory, honour, and immortality," must always be characterised by the severity of Love, which is sufficient to make the least sensitive feel the ordeal. The man who has not gone through fire and water is not prepared to appreciate the wealthy place; and he who has not known the terrors of the Lord will speak but feebly in his attempts to persuade men.

How I longed for perfection; how I hated and loathed myself; how I wondered at the Divine patience; how I envied the disembodied; how I wanted the veil that conceals the upper world to rend, that I might see beyond it; and how I felt the mysteries of being thronging around as if insulting my poor feeble soul; it were long to tell, even if it were lawful to commit such things to paper. Yet, over all this, there occasionally glanced beams of beautiful light, which seemed to resolve themselves into the words, "We walk by *faith*, not by sight."

So it is. Confidence in the word of the Unseen Lord is the condition of Christian life. To "endure, *as seeing*" the Invisible, is the authorised definition of faith. And this is power, this is consolation, this is victory. Trust, hope, wait. Time will unroll all God's parchments; or, which is the same thing, eternity will; for eternity, to a creature, is just time prolonged,—only it is time without probation, time developing the issues of that probation under which the creature was placed in the early morning of his being. We shall have disclosures, by-and-by, grand, wonderful, sublime, and, without doubt, perfectly satisfactory, "justifying the ways of God to men," and exhibiting the exact reason why heart-agonies, groans, fears, and fightings were preliminaries of happiness, health, and peace. This, certainly, is not our rest. Then,

> " Hail! the heavenly scenes of peace,
> Where the storms of passion cease!
> Life's dismaying struggle o'er,
> Wearied nature weeps no more!
>
> " Welcome, welcome, happy bowers,
> Where no passing tempest lowers;
> But the azure heavens display
> Smiles of everlasting day!
>
> " Where the choral seraph choir
> Strike to praise the harmonious lyre;
> And the spirit sinks to ease,
> Lulled by distant symphonies!
>
> " O, to think of meeting there
> Friends whose graves received our tear;
> Child beloved, and wife adored,
> To our widowed arms restored!
>
> " All the joys which death did sever,
> Given to us again for ever!
> Hail! the calm reality,—
> Glorious immortality!"

The primary object of my brief absence so far providentially gained, in increased physical vigour, I returned to my dear family and flock. I was somewhat annoyed, however, by hearing murmurs of dissatisfaction regarding the quality of the pulpit supply during the time of my absence. These rumours, I reflected, are either well-founded or not. If the former, it is hardly kind towards me to make them; for my people, knowing the state of my health, should avoid anything likely to cause excitement; but if the latter, justice to the esteemed brethren who gratuitously supplied for me, requires that I know the ground of complaint, that I may set them right with the people. An opportunity soon occurred for the investigation of this weighty matter. Some eight or ten of the friends were invited to tea, and, among the rest, Mr. Deacon Small, and a remarkably fluent little sister of his, Mrs. Hoble. The gentleman who had supplied for me on the first Sabbath was a Mr. Wilson, an acceptable "lay" preacher, residing some five miles distant from Willow-field; and on the second Lord's day, Mr. Ashley, the pastor of a Church in the neighbourhood, and an able and loving-spirited man, had kindly taken my place.

"Well, dear friends," I said, "I am happy to see you once—"

"And we you, Sir," interrupted Mrs. Hoble, "aye, that we are!"

"I was about to say," I continued, "that I am happy to see you once more, and—"

"So are we, Sir, and we hope you won't go away again."

"Why not, Mrs. Hoble?"

"O! because you have spoiled us. We can't hear any one else; now, there!"

"We want sound doctrine, Sir," said Mr. Small. "Arminianism won't do for us."

"It won't; no, indeed," affirmed the little sister.

"No," said Mr. Hedger, with a solemn shake of his head.

"Arminianism?" I asked, smiling, "what's that, Mrs. Hoble?"

"Ha! ha! tell you, Sir? you don't know what Arminianism is, I suppose?"

"Well, but what is it? You will surely give me your idea of it?"

"O yes, Sir, certainly. Why it is—Arminianism, you know; and it is not—Calvinism. Is it?"

"Very correct, Mrs. Hoble. Now, who has been teaching this?"

"Who?" said Small and his sister, speaking together, "why, that Mr. Wilson."

"Indeed! Do you remember anything he said?"

"Yes, Sir," replied both, simultaneously; "he said á great deal which shouldn't have been said."

"You are severe upon our kind brother, who, I am sure, wished to do you good, and came some way to serve you, in the absence of your sick pastor; but give me, if you can, one sentence correctly, that I may judge."

"Why, Sir, he said that Christ died for all men," replied Mr. Small, with great earnestness.

"Well, but, Mr. Small, you have heard me say that, many times, have you not?"

"No, Sir, not as I remember."

"*You* say that, Sir!" exclaimed the little sister, "no, I should think not."

"I am sorry your memory is so weak respecting my teaching; but of course you do not forget what Paul and John say on this very important subject?"

"No, I should hope not," said Mrs. Hoble, smartly.

"Certainly not," said Mr. Small, firmly.

"I trust we never shall," said Mr. Hedger, gravely.

"Then," said I, "it is somewhat strange you should find fault with Mr. Wilson for holding apostolic doctrine. The apostle Paul uses these expressions:—'He died for all;'—'Who gave himself a ransom for all;'—and, 'That He, by the grace of God, should taste death for every man.' And the apostle John says, 'And he is the propitiation for our sins, and not for ours only, but also for the sins of the whole world.' Now, I think there must be something wrong with those hearers who take offence with one who uses only scriptural language. Besides, I have so often brought this subject before you, and pointed out the relation which the doctrines of Scripture bear to each other in the economy of truth, that you cannot express dislike of Mr. Wilson's statement without also quarrelling with my views; and, what is a far more serious matter, with the language of the apostles themselves."

My worthy friends, who had evidently expected that I would condemn the preacher's doctrine, just because they wished it, and without a particle of evidence, became rather uneasy when the matter took this serious turn.

"But, surely, Sir," asked Mr. Small, after a brief silence, "you do not believe in universal redemption?"

"Friend Small," I answered, "your memory is quick enough on some matters; have you quite forgotten a sermon I preached about three months ago, in which I taught you and others that sacrifice, atonement, and redemption, are three distinct things, and ought never to be spoken of as if they were one."

"No, Sir, I have not. We all liked it very much."

"Then why do you put such a question?"

"Ah! I had forgotten at the moment."

"Well," said I, "how did you all enjoy the services last Sunday? Mr. Ashley is a favourite, and I doubt not he was—"

"I hope, Sir," said Small, hastily, "you'll never have Mr. Ashley in your pulpit again!"

This really took me by surprise. Mr. Ashley was one of the most popular men in the neighbourhood, and Small himself liked him a little.

"What!" I said, "has Mr. Ashley, too, had the misfortune to run across your views?"

"He said things that were not true."

"Not true, Mr. Small? Surely you are bearing false witness against your neighbour."

"I am not. He preached about the stars, and pretended to tell us their size and weight, and how far they are from the earth."

"Oh, he gave you some insight into the splendours of astronomy, did he?"

"You may call it what you like, Sir, but it was all wrong, or, I should rather say, it was all lies! The size of the stars, indeed! Has anybody ever been up to take their measure?"

Here there was a hearty laugh at this settler. Mrs. Priestly, who was present, joined in the laughter, and as Small had great respect for her wisdom, he drew his hand complacently over his face, evidently enjoying the imaginary compliment; for, poor fellow, he was happily ignorant that the secret of her amusement was the idea of the little tailor about "taking the measure" of the stars.

"Now, Mrs. Priestly," I said, "you have read a good deal—have you ever met with an authentic account of a person paying a visit to the stars? or anything in the shape of a narrative by an astral tourist?"

"I certainly have not," she replied, smiling.

"I thought so," said Mr. Small, elevating his head, and feeling his chin.

"Of course not," said the gratified sister.

"It's very wonderful what men do know, though," said Mr. Hedger, thoughtfully.

"It is, my friend," I remarked, turning to him, "and I wish you had had the benefit of education in your youth, for, without attempting to pay a compliment, I am sure it would not have been thrown away."

Mr. Small seemed uncomfortable, and looked at his sister, who, understanding the telegraph, pressed her lips together sympathetically.

"Thank you, Sir," replied the good-man to whom I

had spoken, "it was not the will of Providence; but, through grace, I hope I know a little about that which will last when the stars shall fall from heaven."

This fine remark, breathing as it did the language of a grateful heart, had a happy effect upon our little circle.

"You remind me, my friend, of one of the thousand suggestive passages in Milton. In 'Paradise Regained,' he describes the wild beasts of the wilderness as becoming mild and harmless in our Saviour's presence : —

> 'They at His sight grew mild,
> Nor sleeping Him nor waking harmed; His walk
> The fiery serpent fled, and noxious worm,
> The lion and fierce tiger glared aloof.'

So complete a change passed over your moral nature when the Saviour met you in your wild career."

"Blessed be His name! It is true."

"But now about my brother Ashley. I wish to restore him to your good graces, friend Small. It is by the science of astronomy that we know something of the magnitudes, distances, and revolutions of the stars. This science depends upon observations, made chiefly by the aid of instruments, and upon mathematical calculations. For instance, you know Rockhill, which is about three miles off. If you will furnish a few instruments, I will tell you its height, standing at my own door while I measure it."

"Is it possible?" asked Mr. Small.

"Quite, and very easy, too. Now I hope you will withdraw your remarks concerning good Mr. Ashley's discourse."

"Well, I suppose"—eyeing his sister, and speaking deliberately—"I suppose I must."

"Justice should be done without compulsion."

"Well, then, I *will*; but I don't think he should have spoken about such things to us in a sermon."

" That's a matter of opinion; and you have a perfect right to enjoy yours, he his, and I mine; but, on matters of opinion, we are not to condemn each other, or even entertain feelings of coldness. Liberty to differ in opinion gives one occasion for the exercise of mutual love, which would not otherwise exist. If we love men merely because they think with us on every subject, this is only a modification of self-love, or paying a compliment to our own sentiments. Let us all try, henceforth, to pay greater attention to the state of our own hearts. The growth of Christian love, forbearance, gentleness, and humility, is required by our profession, is necessary to our peace, and will greatly increase our usefulness. If we knew ourselves better, we should be more reluctant to sit in judgment on our neighbour—"

" I think, Sir, that's—that's somewhat personal," said Mr. Small, in a low voice.

" My dear friend," I replied, " I am glad you think so. I intend my remarks to be personal, and to include all present, myself among the rest. Our need of frequent heart-searchings is but too certain. If we would try and judge ourselves faithfully and repeatedly, the sentence would gradually become less severe; for the habit of self-judgment would check those weeds that grow in the heart, and leave us little time to search for the faults and failings of others."

" True, Sir, and thank you," said all present.

It had struck me during the evening, once and again, that the criticisms of my humble friends on the discourses of Messrs. Wilson and Ashley were really occasioned by something else. I fancied some cause of disquiet, yet unrevealed; but I judged it best not to search for it. If it existed at all, it was not likely to remain long in the dark, especially if my busy, bustling, and warm-hearted friend, Mrs. Hoble, knew of it; and as it was almost impossible for a stray rumour to pass through the village without paying her a visit, I felt pretty certain of a revelation soon.   I had recourse, therefore, to the philosophy of waiting.   Whilst we were talking on several subjects, Mrs. Priestly asked if I had heard of the death of Mrs. Smill, of Rowly.   She referred to the wife of a house carpenter in that parish, who had been out of health for several months.   I replied that I had not.

" She is dead, Sir; and her husband insisted on putting a copy of the prayer-book in her coffin."

" Is that *true*, Mrs. Priestly?"

" I had it from the nurse who attended during her last illness."

" But was it done?"

" The prayer-book lies on the breast of the corpse in Rowly churchyard."

" Was this by her own request?"

" No; she would not allow any one to speak to her on religious subjects."

" What was Smill's object in burying the prayer-book?"

" He said, he hoped it might be of use to her soul."

" This is sad.   Did the clergyman know of it?"

" I cannot say, Sir, but I earnestly hope not."

" Is Smill an intelligent man?"

" Quite so, in business; but his reading is confined to Moore's Almanac."

" Does he attend Church?"

" About five or six times in the course of a year."

We all remained silent for a few minutes; for who could avoid reflection on this affecting case?   Our silence was broken by the voice of Mrs. Hoble:—

" Is it true, Sir?   I hope you will tell us—"

" What, Mrs. Hoble ?"

" Oh! I hope it is not true," and tears filled her eyes.

" What *is* it?" I again asked.

" That—that—you are going—to leave us?"

My suspicion was confirmed. The cause of disquietude was revealed. But I had not thought of this, or, indeed, of anything else.

" Not, so far as I know, Mrs. Hoble; but what makes you ask that question?"

" O, Sir, people say that you want to leave us, and Mr. Walters says you have had an invitation from some place, and you have preached and made speeches at so many places, and John says he is sure you're going; and Mr. Ardphist told Mr. Hollot that you wanted more salary, and Mr. Hollot said, no minister should have more than fifty, or, at least, sixty pounds a year, because—"

" At most," I suggested.

" Yes," continued my kind little friend, " at most, sixty; because, if they have more, they won't preach experience, and—O, I hope you won't go!"

" Preach experience," I remarked, "that's a suggestive thought; but does Mr. Hollot mean his own experience, the preacher's, or Mr. Ardphist's?"

This question presented a difficulty. The thought of preaching Ardphist's experience was too droll to escape notice, hence a laugh interfered with Mrs. Hoble's tears.

" I really cannot say, my friends," I added, " whether I shall leave you or not. I think I shall remain, but how long I cannot say: for whilst, on the one hand, we should not be precipitate; on the other, when Providence seems to call, it becomes us to obey, whether it be a call to enjoyment or suffering, to increased labour or passive endurance. I confess that I have no special wish in the matter. You know well that I do not believe in what is called accident. I am convinced that all things are ordered by Infinite Wisdom, and that our duty is just to obey what we believe to be the voice of the Lord. We may err, even with this belief prompting our movements; but sins of ignorance were distinguished from sins of presumption under the Jewish dispensation, and, I need not say, that they are likewise distinguished under the Christian economy. As to my income, you know the amount; and respecting my expenditure your own common sense can judge; yet I have never asked an increase of salary, and never will. If you esteem me, as I believe you do, the very reason that leads you to desire a continuance of my services, should also reconcile you to my departure to a larger field of labour, with a corresponding increase of salary, for the benefit of my family. In the meantime, leave the whole matter to the wise Ruler, as I intend to do."

We sang a hymn of praise; I gave a short address on the religion of the heart, and the way to promote the health of the inner life; and, after uniting in prayer, we separated in peace and love, and with earnest wishes for each other's prosperity.

CHAPTER IX.

LITERATURE AND THEOLOGY.

"Twins formed by Nature; if they part they die."—*Young.*

HOW SHALL I PROVIDE FOR MY FAMILY?—PURCHASING WISDOM BY EXPERIENCE—I BECOME A SCHOOLMASTER—CASTLES IN THE AIR—TRUE LABOUR NEVER LOST — THE BOOK—ALARMING PRINTER'S BILL—THE HEART OF THE FOREST—MY RESOLUTION—FIVE HUNDRED PAGES OF MANUSCRIPT—HOW TO GET TO LONDON—UNEXPECTED LETTER AND ITS CONSEQUENCES—THE FUGITIVE SLAVE'S EXCLAMATION—LITERATURE AND CHRISTIANITY—THE PALE YOUNG MAN—CONVERSATION WITH MR. TISSUE—ST. MARTIN'S-LE-GRAND—THOUGHTS IN A COFFEE-HOUSE — LARGE CITIES AND PERSONAL PRINCIPLE — THE YOUNG MAN AGAIN — PATERNOSTER ROW—MR. ATFORD'S STORY—THE WIDOW AND ORPHANS—SALE OF MY MANUSCRIPT — PUBLISHERS — THE POET — PROOF SHEETS — THE POSTMISTRESS OUT OF HEALTH.

" IF any provide not for his own, and specially for those of his own house, he hath denied the faith, and is worse than an infidel." An indolent Christian is a solecism. The husband and father who bears the Christian name, and yet loves not his wife and children, is a hypocrite. Christianity purifies and strengthens love, and love promotes activity. But when a man's family increases without a corresponding increase in his ability to provide for them, what shall he do? A tradesman could do several things under such circumstances. But suppose the man to be a village pastor, whose congregation is as large as can be expected from the population, and as liberal as their means will afford. Shall he ask them to increase his salary? The thing would be at once useless, absurd, and impolitic. Shall he intimate his intention to leave? By all means, if he wishes to create a disturbance, and split his congregation into parties; and especially if he has no invitation elsewhere. Shall he engage in some secular business? Yes, if he desires to lose caste, and has nerve enough to brave the contempt of worldly witlings, the cold looks of his well-to-do brethren, the sneer of the squire, the withering smile of the clergyman, and the jealousy of those who are engaged in the business he has adopted. Shall he economise by wearing a smock frock, coloured necker-chief, and corduroy? Impossible! Society has con-demned the man to be a gentleman, and a gentleman he must be—aye, and a benevolent one, too. He must relieve every case of necessity, and subscribe to every charity. He must dress in a suit of black, though it be threadbare; and adorn himself with a white neckcloth, though it require ingenuity to hide its rents. His wife and children must be respectably dressed, or *his* influence will decline, and *her* reputation as a housewife and economist perish. Possibly there may be an opening for a schoolmaster in the village. Shall he appropriate the only spare room in his cottage to this purpose? He may do so—gather a few juvenile Hodges, Hodgkins, and Hodgkinsons, and find the result intolerable bondage, unfitting him for study, gnawing his temper, and inter-fering with his power in the pulpit. Shall he, under cover of pastoral visitation, eat his dinners and suppers in the houses of his people, and leave his beloved wife and children to a crust and cheese at home? Not if he has a soul, and intends to avoid becoming the medium of idle village gossip. There is one alternative left. Shall he try literature? There are many preachers, well qualified for the discharge of official duties, who could not step on the literary arena without certain failure. There are secrets in the publishing trade, of which the country pastor knows not. He may produce a good book, and, in the simplicity of his heart, believe that he has complied with all the conditions of literary success; but the printer's bill—for, of course, an unknown man must publish at his own risk, if he will publish—and the account of sales, amounting to perhaps half-a-dozen copies in as many months, effectually undeceive him. The book has passed honourably through the ordeal of criticism, and the public have good-naturedly believed the critics without the trouble of buying, reading, and judging for themselves. Besides, the said public are not in the least interested in the matter. What *does* it signify whether a little book, written by one Davis, or Jones, or Smith, living in some out-of-the-way village, be good or bad, profound or superficial, original or stale? It is a matter in which no one is interested except the author, who reads the reviewer's estimate of his labours with gratitude and hope, in happy ignorance of the fact that his " clever little work, containing passages of real eloquence," would never have been noticed in any way by the learned editor—but for the name of the *publisher.*

Self-acquired knowledge is of the highest value. Perhaps, wisdom purchased by experience is costly, but that is an argument in its favour, and an evidence of its worth. Of the possible modes of existence, or plans by which a man in my circumstances might manage to live, there were only two that I either could or would adopt, and I adopted them both in turn. With the exception of a dame's school, where little children were sent to keep them out of the way of their toiling mothers for a few hours daily, there was no " fountain of knowledge " in the village.   It occurred to me, therefore, that I should at once do good to the youth of the place, and increase the comforts of my family, by assuming the office of schoolmaster.   The table and chairs were removed from the largest room in the cottage, and a long desk and forms were substituted; the latter involving expense which I hoped to cover by the receipts of the first quarter.   There is no difficulty in advertising the move- ments of a village pastor.   He has but to mention his purpose to one of his people, and it becomes known speedily; and if he wish it extensively known, his best plan is to name it in strict confidence, as in this case everybody knows it before the sun goes down.   On the day of opening, seven boys presented themselves; a number afterwards increased by an additional three.   I felt most anxious not only to educate those lads, but to train them. I considered their moral nature as having higher claims than their intellectual; and knowing, from experience, that the sure way to enlighten the understanding is to engage the heart, I acted as any teacher under the influence of this conviction would act.   The result was as satisfactory as the class of minds with which I had to deal, and the short time during which I kept school, would permit.   Always fond of solitude and study, the noise and excitement of the school compelled me, at the end of six months, to relinquish the ill-appreciated and onerous duties of a schoolmaster.   The boys would not be silent.   They knew nothing of restraint.   Accus- tomed from infancy to roll about the fields, leap hedges, swing on gates, and live in the open air, three hours' stillness and application to books and figures were posi- tively out of the question.   Never did sturdy Protestant rebel against the Pope with more perseverance than did my rosy-faced boys against the law of "Silence!" Finding, however, that a positive want in the village had been supplied, and that the parents had begun to appreciate the advantage of a school, I did not give it up until I secured the services of a young man as schoolmaster. A room was hired in the village, my pupils were transferred to the new master, and I was left at liberty to resume my place in the study, hoping that the potatoes, cheese, and bacon, which the pedagogue had received for his six months' labour, would last the pastor until he became a—successful author!

You smile; but why? There is something really animating about these tricks of the fancy. Castles in the air keep one busy. The process of building requires activity. Energy brings its own reward. A man pursues an imaginary good; he will never overtake *it;* but the pursuit has braced his energies, and if his motive be honourable, and his object in harmony with the eternal law of morals, he will find something else as he runs, equal to, if not decidedly better, than the thing of which he is in pursuit. Saul went in search of his father's asses and found a kingdom. This curious fact has shaped itself into a proverb, and it is a proverb of much significance. It is a text for strong-eyed philosophy. The incidents of history are frequently more instructive than its chief lessons. True labour is never lost. Suppose a man should study a given subject thoroughly, and write two hundred and fifty pages upon it, and then throw his manuscript in the fire. Is his labour lost? Certainly not. He is master of one of the ten thousand streams of knowledge that flow through the universe of God. The result of his investigation and labour is treasured in his mind; and though, if he be a poor man, that gross power, money—had his thoughts been exchanged for it—would have helped him in the market-place, yet he has a mental power, as the reward of his toil, which elevates him to a position which gold cannot buy, and which the smiles of royalty cannot confer.

Suppose, again, that, deceived by hope, he arrange with printer and publisher—give his thoughts to the world— receive high praise from the critics—and at the end of three months a printer's bill demanding £37 10s. at once, and a publisher's statement exhibiting the sale of twenty copies only; whilst at that moment he is unable to pay his quarter's house-rent, or purchase decent raiment for his family,—what then? You condemn him? Well, *I* submit! You have condemned me; for this last supposition is a fact in my life and struggles. Just restrain your anger, and look in for a few minutes. You see that neat-looking little cottage on the brow of the hill. There is a lawn in front. There is a monthly rose in full bloom beneath each of the windows, and the lady of the house shows her taste by exhibiting several pots of splendid geraniums. It is the month of May, in the fifth year of my ministry. Step in: we have just finished a plain breakfast. I have an open letter in my hand; but, fearing lest its contents should agitate my wife, I have gone to my study. My head rests on my hands, and the printer's letter and account lie open before me. "Thirty-seven pounds, ten shillings! What is to be done? Is *this* the result of my anxious toil, and sleepless nights, and aching head? Is this the way by which I am to support my dear ones, and maintain my character, and escape from galling misery? Thirty-seven pounds, ten shillings! Lord, help me!" You see this sight and hear this soliloquy. Are you angry still? More than ever, perhaps. Yet if that book had sold rapidly—that identical book, observe—and not another, either better or worse—and the publisher had remitted fifty pounds to the author, you would have praised me. *Then*, it would have been the reward of merit, the result of perseverance, the rising of mind to the surface, or some other neat little compliment—would it not? Ah! then, how fragrant the monthly rose, and how fine the geraniums! how beautiful the situation, and how happy the life of the student, with the body of heaven in its clearness over his head, the flower-spangled carpet beneath his feet, and the music of the forest swelling on his ear! How you would congratulate—how you would almost envy him then! But why? Is he not the same man? Has he not the same head and heart, the same energy of character, decision of purpose, and love to humanity? Are non-success and non-merit the same thing? Does failure in a good purpose change the character of that purpose? "No; but no man should undertake liabilities which he cannot reasonably expect to be able to meet." True, that is as clear as an icicle, and equally cold to the man who is struggling to scale a lofty mountain with stones falling on his head, and the spray of the cataract piercing to his skin. But never mind, good censor, this money *shall* be paid, and that, too, without lightening *your* purse one shilling. All I want is life, health, and time. God will give me the first and second, and I shall ask the printer for the third.

I locked the letter in my desk, put on my hat, crossed two fields leading to a dense forest through which the villagers had trodden a narrow footpath. Entering this, I wandered without motive or object until I came to a little bubbling spring, almost concealed from the light by the thick foliage overhead. By the side of this miniature fountain I sat down upon a stone. The rooks were chattering above; the magpie flitted past; the squirrel sprang from branch to branch, with the agility of thought; the grasshoppers chirped in the long grass around me; and the frog leaped at its own will. These were all *free*, but I was in bondage. These were without care, but I was the victim of corroding anxiety. I, a man, an immortal—and, through grace, a Christian—I knew not what to do. The contrast was too painful to be pursued long; but the thought that I was under training for a higher state of being, while they had reached the highest degree of existence of which their nature was capable, reconciled me to the seeming anomaly. I looked forward to heaven; they were enjoying theirs. " Fowl, beast, insect and reptile," I exclaimed, " enjoy yourselves during your short hour! I shall not disturb your elysium any longer." My purpose, however, was taken. As the boy of Bethlehem beheaded the champion of the Philistines with his own sword, so I determined to wrest from the hands of literature a weapon which should make it serve my purpose, instead of plunging me in deeper difficulties. Without a figure, I resolved that my pen should pay the printer's alarming bill. That evening I projected a work of greater pretensions than its predecessor, on an historico-theologic subject which I had never seen satisfactorily treated. I wrote to the printer, asking if he would allow the account to stand over for six months, promising to pay him with interest then. I also wrote to a London publisher, offering him the sheets of my former book at the price of waste paper, and inclosing a syllabus of the intended publication, which, I said, would be ready in four months, and of which he should have the first offer. The printer hesitatingly agreed to my request; the publisher, in the course of a week, sent me £12 10s. for the sheets, and wished to see the manuscript of the new work when ready. I immediately sent the £12 10s. to the printer, thus reducing his account to £25, and greatly strengthening his faith in the probability of an ultimate settlement. By unceasing labour, and without giving up one public duty during the time, at the end of two months and a half, I had 500 pages of manuscript ready for the press. To attempt a description of my feelings when the last word was penned, is out of the question. But, even then, the battle had not been fought. I had furbished the weapons, but the enemy was yet before me. Would Mr. Tissue purchase the manuscript? Everything depended upon that. If he refuse, I had laboured in vain, so far at least as the pecuniary object of the toil was concerned.

But there was still another difficulty,—namely, how to get to London. To forward the precious manuscript was dangerous. It might never reach its destiny. It might be lost. Or the publisher might neglect it. What then? Send it by a friend? No; that would not do. A man always conducts his own business best. But the expense of going and returning was utterly beyond my power. Besides, I should in all probability have to remain some time in town; for Tissue might refuse to buy, and the copyright *must* be sold. On that I was firmly resolved, unless Providence should make it an impossibility. I pondered this matter for eight days; but, of course, could make nothing of it. I thought of asking my treasurer for an advance on next quarter's salary of £3; but dismissed the idea, partly because I should sorely miss that small sum when it came to be deducted, and partly because he would be curious to know what I intended to do with the money. About my literary labours, my flock knew nothing as yet; and to circulate the intelligence that I was going to London, would have been to the villagers as difficult a riddle as that which Samson proposed to his wife's kindred. Jealous already of my frequent occasional services elsewhere, this mysterious journey would have added fuel to the smouldering fire.

The newspapers had for some time advertised a forthcoming Conference in London on an important subject. The wish to attend had crossed my mind; but, of course, it was merely a wish. The Conference was to consist of delegates representing districts or congregations agreeing in the object contemplated. On the morning of the ninth day, a letter arrived from a gentleman residing many miles distant, suggesting that I should get my people to appoint me as their representative, and pressing me to attend the proposed meeting. I replied at once that my people sympathised with the object, but both pastor and flock were unable to give any substantial proof of it. Two mornings afterwards, another letter came, enclosing a post-office order for £3, which the writer said he had much pleasure in placing at my service, and which, he supposed, would cover all my travelling expenses. I shall not make any commentary on this remarkable incident, but simply ask, how an atheist or a believer in chance would account for it?

Our weekly lecture took place on the evening of that day. At its close, I brought the claims of the Conference before the people, told them I wished to see them represented there, and asked whether they would delegate me? They consented; and it was formally proposed, seconded, put to the meeting, and carried, that I represent the congregation. At five o'clock on the evening of the next day, had you been in Paternoster Row, you might have seen a man, with a brown-paper parcel under his arm, looking at the numbers on the publishers' doors, and, in all probability, you would have said, with a smile, and a feeling of inward satisfaction, because of your own superiority, " That's a country parson, who fancies himself an author. How tightly he holds his manuscript! Precious, no doubt!"

A fugitive slave from South America, a fine, tall, intelligent-looking young man, entered a bookseller's shop in Paternoster Row a few years since. He glanced rapidly around on the bending shelves, enriched by the contributions of intellect, the mental wealth of the poets, philosophers, moralists, and divines, of a country where slave and tyrant are alike unknown. The young man's eyes sparkled. Smiting his hands together, and looking up to heaven, he exclaimed, in a voice of startling gratitude, " THANK GOD! I HAVE SEEN PATERNOSTER ROW!"

Thus felt and spoke a self-taught man, under the glorious excitement which a love of literature creates, when the eye wanders over the thousand proofs of what a free press, conducted by a free people, can accomplish, as those proofs are exhibited in the crowded warehouses of this famous little street. I could enter but partially into my coloured brother's feelings on this occasion, for I had seen " the Row" before; and I could not enter into his feelings at all, as a man who was able to contrast slavery with liberty in his own person; for, blessed be God, I could say with Paul to the tribune, " I was free born." Yet my imagination—as I waited until the publisher, on whose " Yea" or " Nay" so much depended, should have time to speak to me—busied itself with those mysterious parcels and packages, crowded shelves, and huge piles of books, bound and unbound, of all sorts and sizes, that everywhere met the eye. Here was one of the great temples of literature, and I, having already entered as a noviciate, stood, with trembling heart, wondering whether I should be admitted now as a humble priest, or rejected as unworthy of the distinguished honour. I thought of Literature and Science as twin sisters, nourished, cherished, and adorned by Religion. Where were the mighty achievements of mind, but for the awakening impulse given to it by the celestial fire of Christianity? Where were the fame of Paternoster Row, but for that herald of intellectual emancipation—Protestantism? And where the millions of printed books that issue from these warehouses annually, and find their way to every nation and kingdom on the face of the earth, but for that great illuminator of humanity—the Bible? Strike the superhuman book out of the list of publications, and you aim a fatal blow at all healthy intellect, curb the spirit of man, and hand human souls over to a dark and cruel despotism. It is a miserable misbelief that the progress of literature can in any way weaken the authority, or nullify the purposes of religion. The Christian Scriptures will ever be far a-head of the age. The light that shines from heaven will always precede the investigations of philosophy, like the star that led the Persian magi to the feet of the Child born for universal empire. The attempt to separate literature and religion, is a more atrocious crime than the effort to dismember a prosperous and united empire. The intellectual man who spends his days in the condemnation of Christianity, alleging that it is the enemy of free inquiry and human progress, is guilty of treason against both literature and humanity. England is pre-eminently the land of Bibles, and for that very reason it is the land of a literature unequalled in the history of mind. The language of prophets and apostles is familiar in the lips of her sons, from the palace of royalty down to the fisherman's hut; and the greatest poets, philosophers, orators, mathematicians, astronomers, patriots, statesmen, moralists, and divines have, as a matter of course, been produced by the country of which this grand fact can be predicated. The intellectual opponent of the doctrines of Jesus, therefore, who anticipates the millenium of literature as a consequence of their destruction, is like a man administering a deadly poison with the assurance that it is the elixir of life. Had I no higher reason for wishing the universal dissemination of the Book upon whose pages the Sun of Righteousness pours His immortal beams, I would say—that we may have a world of *free men*, ennobled by the influence, and adorned with the graces of a healthy *literature*, cast the Bible on every shore, and place it in every human hand, without note or comment, to tell its own tale, and to accomplish its own work! But to stop the fountain is not the way to purify and perpetuate the streams. If you wish to cherish a vivid fancy, a fertile imagination, and a profound intellect, lay open the pages of that wonderful volume, which brings the spirit-world within the province of human investigation, draws man into sympathy with the elder sons of God, and shows the same Almighty hand which created the worlds of a universe, and placed them in their orbits, ever open with blessings to the sorrow-smitten children of men. If you wish to wreathe the brow of Literature with a halo of imperishable glory, lead her to Him, the God-Man, in whom heaven and earth meet; and she, too, shall receive a " well done!" from the great Prize Distributor, at the end of the race. But let her not set up as a rival sovereign over human hearts, or attempt to usurp the throne of Christianity; for in this case, if she do not speedily die of inanition, she will be speedily covered with infamy and disgrace, and she and her rebel abettors will be hurried to destruction together. This is the unalterable law of the case; and the wise in all worlds say, " It is holy, just, and good !"

At this moment, a man, apparently about five-and-twenty years of age, came from the inner office, and the clerk informed me that Mr. Tissue was at liberty. I was attracted for a moment by the appearance of the departing stranger. His eye met mine, and a slight blush passed rapidly over his pale, thin face. In his hand he held a small roll of paper; his clothes had evidently been long worn, and frequently brushed; and altogether I felt certain that I was looking on one whose heart knew care, and who had often, and at that moment too, met with severe disappointment. He glanced at me again, just as he disappeared at the door, as if his soul longed for a word of sympathy.

I entered the inner sanctum, where sat one of the judges of literature—a member of that irresponsible tribunal, whose lightest word or look may crush hopes which have borne up the soul of the patient student during months and years of continuous toil. He looked at me with a pair of keen grey eyes, evidently accustomed to study the countenance as the index of the soul. He was sitting at a low desk, on and around which were letters, accounts, and one or two proof sheets; while a pile of manuscript lay within reach on another table. I gave him my name, and told him my business.

" I have no recollection of the matter," he said. I then handed him his own letter, requesting to see the work when it should be finished.

" O, yes, now I remember, Sir. Is it done ?"

" Here it is, Sir, ready for the press."

" Ah, our hands are quite full at present—things are very dull—never knew business so slack—have just refused an offer of what seems a telling subject; but I am much obliged for your offer. I shall have great pleasure in publishing for you." He was turning over the pages of my manuscript all this time, with a rapidity which rendered it impossible for him to read the shortest sentence. "Yes, Sir," he continued, "I shall be happy to publish for you—it seems a very good subject—only there is so much of this kind of thing in the market— on the usual terms, and I shall do my best for you."

Was it pride, or what was it, that made me feel at that moment as if I had been placed opposite a burning furnace, or caught in some criminal act? My face became intolerably hot, and I wiped the perspiration from my brow. "Thank you, Mr. Tissue," I replied; "but I have no intention to publish in that way."

"Oh! well; why not publish by subscription? Many do that. Some of our greatest men have published by subscription. Indeed, it is getting quite common now. It seems to answer the purposes of all better than running the risks of trade, or casual sale."

This long speech gave me time to collect energy, and I said, with an abortive effort at a smile—

"Your *great men* may do as they please, Sir; but I will not publish by subscription, nor publish at all on my own account. I have come to town expressly to sell the copyright; and you, according to engagement, have the first offer. If it does not suit you to buy, I go elsewhere." So saying, I put out my hand to pull the manuscript towards me.

"How much do you expect for it?" he asked, detaining the parcel.

"What size of a book will it make?" I inquired.

He looked at the quantity of copy, and said, "About four hundred pages, small octavo."

"What price should be put upon such a volume?"

" Can't say exactly; perhaps six shillings, or six-and-sixpence."

" In that case," I replied, " I should ask fifty pounds for the copyright, transferring all right in it to you."

" Fifty pounds!" exclaimed the publisher, with a loud laugh; " why, Sir, you can't be serious! It is clear you know nothing about the risks, and troubles, and losses of trade. Why, I had the offer of a little thing just now—and little books pay better than large ones, sometimes—for five pounds."

" I wish you had taken it, Sir," I said.

" You do? Why, how, what do you know about it?"

" Nothing, Sir; but that the man who left this room just now is nearly broken-hearted; and, possibly, five pounds would save him from madness or suicide."

" You know him, then, and his circumstances?"

" Neither. Never saw the man before."

Mr. Tissue was moved. He had a heart; of that I was certain. Men with grey eyes are generally keen, energetic, and at first cold; but you may depend upon their sympathy with real sorrow. Search the ranks of our benevolent men, and you will agree with me. The publisher snatched up a bit of paper from the desk, on which two or three words were written, and left me for a minute or two. What this meant, of course I knew not; but a pleasing thought struck me.

On the publisher's return he said, " Sir, I have no intention at present of buying your manuscript—the risk is too great, even at a reasonable price; but you will, perhaps, leave it for a day or two, that I may glance over it."

" Certainly, Sir, with great pleasure. When shall I return?"

" The day after to-morrow, about this hour?"

I now *felt* that it was time to look after refreshment, as it was six o'clock in the evening, and I had tasted nothing, except a biscuit, since seven in the morning. I went to St. Martin's-le-Grand, and enjoyed the refreshment of that best of beverages, tea, in one of the numerous coffee-houses that gladden that busy region of Old London. There were, perhaps, twenty persons in the coffee-house, who were apparently as much strangers to one another as they all were to me; for each was attending to himself, without reference to his neighbour. And the mind was being fed as well as the body. One read the *Times;* another, the *Sun;* a third, *Frazer;* a fourth, *Blackwood;* a fifth, the *Record;* a sixth, the *Nonconformist,* and so forth; according as the literary, ecclesiastical, or political taste dictated. Conversation there was none for a considerable time, nor was there anything to distract the attention of the reader, except the rustling of the papers, the pleasant rattling of coffee-cups, and the quick, short, professional remarks made by the waiter to something like a dark cupboard, which appeared to have the faculty of leaping up and down at his word. I glanced rapidly at the profiles of my companions, but they were all strange to me; a circumstance which, whilst it induced a momentary feeling of loneliness in the midst of company—if the *paradox* be admitted —suggested a thought in relation to London, which had not before occurred to me; namely, the need of strong *principle* in the case of individual men. Here, I reflected, if anywhere, a man is left so much to himself, as a consequence of the myriads that surround him, that if his mind be not moulded and fortified by correct moral *principle,* he may be carried away by any temptation, under the idea that he may sin with impunity, so far as his fellow-men are concerned. In a small population, where every one is known, the fear of losing character acts beneficially on many persons, who, though they may have no higher motive for correct deportment, know that success in life depends greatly on a fair reputation. If the eye of God be disregarded, the eyes of men suggest the need of caution. But in the centre of London, if the fear of the Great Witness rule not the heart of a man, he may feel, generally speaking, as if he dwelt in the centre of an American forest, so far as detection in folly is concerned. The effect of a great multitude is, in this sense, similar to that of absolute isolation. Whilst, however, on the one hand, great cities furnish facilities for sin, which cannot be found in sparse populations, on the other hand they have the advantage of throwing a man of real principle more emphatically upon himself. I should, therefore, conclude, that strong personal principle finds in large cities, and especially in the metropolis, just the sphere where its value may be most surely tested, and its growth most powerfully developed. God is everywhere; in the wild wilderness, the hamlet, the village, the town, and the city alike; but as the storm strengthens the roots of the oak, so the consciousness of facilities to sin, without much hazard of exposure by one's fellow-men, leads the man of high Christian morality to take firmer hold of those eternal principles, from which his spiritual nature derives its nourishment and strength.

Whilst these thoughts were occupying my mind, several of the coffee-house customers had departed, and others had come in. Among the new comers was a young man, who took his seat opposite to me. He paid no attention to what was going on around, but, after ordering something from the waiter, pulled out of his pocket a little note-book, and entered some memoranda in pencil. I heard a sigh escaping once or twice, and yet it was not altogether of a mournful sound, like that which bursts from a heart ready to break, but indicated rather that sigh of relief which the burden-bearer heaves when his load is removed from his back. Sighs, like tears, are sometimes the children of grief, and sometimes the offspring of joy; and though sighs are sighs, and tears tears, all the world over, yet there is not much difficulty in detecting the difference to which I allude. I looked at the sigher for a moment. Our eyes met. He coloured slightly. Could I be mistaken? No. But where is the small roll of paper? It was the author of the rejected manuscript. For a reason which the reader understands, I felt disposed to speak, and, of course, began in the orthodox fashion, by some truism about the weather.

"We have met before, I think, Sir," I said, after we had exchanged opinions concerning the state of the atmosphere.

"Yes, Sir," he replied, "I believe I had the pleasure of seeing you in Paternoster Row."

He paused, but evidently wished to say more. That some general remark might give him time, I said,

"How one's expectations are disappointed by this famous Row!"

"Yes," he replied, "frequently, no doubt; but publishers are not likely to understand the feelings and circum—"

"I mean," said I, hastily interrupting him, "one's expectations of the *street*. A person living in the country, and who has never seen London, concludes—at least, I did—from the immense number of publications issued thence, that it must be a fine, broad, clean street, with magnificent shops, whose windows are clear as crystal, and as attractive as books in all languages can make them; but, instead of that, it is a narrow, dirty, inconvenient place, with pavements scarcely a foot wide, rendered slippery and dangerous by the incessant traffic of butchers, and offensive by disgusting smells from the tallow works; whilst the street is so narrow that carts cannot pass each other without great difficulty."

"Yes," he said, smiling, "but the Row is the manufactory, and printers do not require the finest locality for their trade."

"Exactly so," I replied. "Such is life. We form conclusions on insufficient data, and find ourselves mistaken. We are captivated by the splendour of the mansion, forgetting that there may be frightful misery within; and we pass by the mud cottage, ignorant that angels visit there. We pass on the streets persons whose history and experience would shame romance. We meet, shake hands with, and bid good-bye to, acquaintances of whom we know but little, but whose memory is the depository of facts and feelings, the faithful record of which would utterly astonish us. We come in contact with greatness in unpretending forms, and disgusting meanness in costly attire. Unable to see beneath the external coating, we fancy gold and diamonds from the glitter of the casket, and imagine only dross from the paltry case. Seeming cheats us out of reality, and the appearance of the covering deceives us regarding that which is covered. But I suppose we must be content with this partial knowledge at present, and submit with the best grace we can to the tricks thus daily played upon us, in the hope of clearer light some day soon."

"And yet, Sir," said my new acquaintance, "it would be as dangerous to reverse the rule of judgment; for appearance is sometimes a correct guide to reality."

" I quite agree with you, Mr.—"

" Atford."

" Thank you, Sir. I quite agree with you, Mr. Atford; and therefore I have only two rules of judgment in the case of strangers,—the face, and the tones of the voice. The latter sometimes deceive me, the former seldom does. There is, for example, the extensive publisher, in whose warehouse we met this evening. His voice is by no means such as to inspire hope in a young author—and I presume I speak to one—but there is something in his countenance which a physiognomist would cling to with pleasure."

Mr. Atford smiled, and said,

" Well, Sir, I know very little of that science, if it be one; but Mr. Tissue is a riddle to me. I need not affect concealment of the fact that I offered him to-day the copyright of a small book, for you must have inferred as much. He viewed the thing only, of course, through the medium of trade, and with that it would be unreasonable to find fault; but, from all that I had heard, I expected a little more of the gentle in tone. Yet, strange to say, after refusing to buy, he sent for me, about twenty minutes after I had left his office. I had given him my address—I should rather say, I left it on the desk without his consent—and, being tired, I returned here, for I lodge in this house for a night or two. I have just come from the Row, and, I am happy to say, he has taken my manuscript."

" Indeed! I am glad to hear that. Did he assign any reason for changing his mind?"

" Yes, Sir; he said that, out of respect to the name I bear, he would risk the publishing, and that he hoped I would do my best to promote the sale among schools known to me."

" Your manuscript is on education, then ? "

" Yes."

" May I ask what he meant by 'the name you bear ?' "

" Are you not a Nonconformist minister, Sir ? " asked Atford, after a minute's silence.

" I am."

" So was my dear father. Mr. Tissue knew him, and out of respect to his memory he has bought my manuscript. Sir, the memory of my father is unspeakably dear to me. It was the legacy he left me—the legacy of a consistent and holy life, and many have regarded me for his sake. How I wish that wisdom and piety were hereditary ! But it is perhaps well that it is not. I love Mr. Tissue for speaking well of my sainted father. Sir, you sympathised with me, if I mistake not, when I left the publisher's warehouse ; and, if you will kindly listen for a few minutes, I will tell you my story as briefly as I can, and that not to pain you, but as one of the many sad tales which, I have heard my father say, are suggestive and useful to preachers of the Gospel."

" You favour me," I said, " by the confidence, and you already have my sympathy."

" I was born, Sir, in a village in Gloucestershire," said Mr. Atford, " my father being at that time pastor of the only Dissenting Church in the parish. His income was, of course, very small ; yet, by the exercise of that economy which righteous principles teach, and the help of my excellent mother,"—here a deep sigh escaped from the speaker,—" who ever cheered her husband in his trials, he managed to keep out of debt, and to retain his character and influence. I was the eldest of five children, two boys and three girls ; and when I was sixteen years of age—that is, six years ago—"

"What," I asked, interrupting him, "are you only twenty-two?"

"Not more, Sir, although circumstances make me look older."

"I beg your pardon; proceed."

"When I was just sixteen my father died. Grief and care evidently shortened his days. Unable to make any provision for his widow and children by insurance, the funeral expenses paid, we were left at his death without a shilling in the world. The house in which we lived belonging to the Chapel, we, of course, had to leave it, to make room for my father's successor. The people showed us all the kindness that lay in their power, but that was not much, from their circumstances in life. I had received a plain education, and the clergyman of the parish, a kind, Christian man, of the school called 'low,' or 'evangelical,' sent for me, and suggested that, if I chose to open a school for young children, he would patronise me as far as he could, out of respect to the memory of my late father, and out of pity to my mother and her children. He said, 'William, I deeply sympathise with your mother, left a widow with five children. May the Lord graciously look upon her, and support her! You, my dear boy, are the eldest, and it becomes you, in humble dependence upon Providence, at least to try if you can support, though it be but partially, your mother and the younger children. Will you?' I replied, thanking him, that I would do anything he might think best. Arrangements were made, under his judicious management, for the opening of a little school. The effort was so far successful, that for three years my dear mother, sisters, and brother, were almost entirely supported by my exertions. Poor and mean, indeed, was the support, but my mother never complained, although

I sometimes found her in tears when she wished to conceal them. At last, her health gave way, and she lived, I know not how, but I may say, on nothing. She taught my eldest sister the use of the needle, and dear, gentle Emma went about the village asking, almost begging, plain sewing. About four years ago, Emma, the sweetest and most lovely sister that ever brother had, was seized with consumption, and shortly afterwards died—went to sleep, rather, in the hands of the Redeemer. This was a sad blow to me, for I loved her with the purest love; but why do I mention self? The blow fell on our rapidly sinking mother with terrible force. For six months she could not leave her room, and her nurse was little Jane, a delicate thing, not more than nine years of age. Twelve months afterwards, Jane followed Emma to the land of holy peace. My mother, strange to say, seemed to grow better after this additional bereavement; but it was a false recovery. She was not really better in health; but a strange and mysterious working of the brain made her think so, and I sometimes had terrible suspicions that her mind was affected. Whenever this fearful thought occurred, I trembled, and not unfrequently ran into the fields to seek relief in tears. I continued my school for five years, with as much success as such a poor place could afford. Twelve months ago, however, the clergyman, my kind patron, received church preferment, which he well deserved, and a man of very different stamp was sent in his place. At the same time a division, which ultimately came to blows, occurred in the Dissenting Church; and what with the bigotry of the new clergyman, and the uproar and scandal occasioned by the Dissenters, my scholars were withdrawn, one by one, until I had only two or three left. We were reduced to the verge of starvation! A few kind neighbours sent us little presents occasionally, but whilst we felt grateful, we were, at the same time, pained to receive them. I committed to paper my thoughts about education in general, and the management of schools for the children of the poor in particular; and, after many months' severe struggles, I found my way to London in the hope of getting five pounds to—to—b—"

Here the young man burst into a flood of tears, accompanied by sobs, which attracted the attention of several persons in the coffee-room. Some of them rose from their seats, and gathered around us, which greatly embarrassed me, and greatly distressed poor Atford. I begged the gentlemen to resume their seats, as the young man was affected by some painful circumstance of a personal nature, at the same time thanking them for their sympathy with one evidently suffering. In a short time he recovered, and said,

"Forgive me, Sir; I wished to say that I came to London yesterday, in a farmer's waggon partly, and partly on foot, in the hope of getting five pounds to bury the body of my beloved mother."

"Your mother, my tried young friend?"

"She died, three days ago, Sir; and if God had not made my journey successful, she must have been buried as a pauper."

"May an Almighty hand help you!" I exclaimed, very earnestly.

"Thank you, Sir; may it be so!"

"But what about your brother and sister?"

"A distant relative of my father in Birmingham has kindly given them shelter in the meantime," said he; "but about the future I know nothing. All is dark. And I must leave, too; but where to go, I know not. We have hardly anything left in the house, except the few books which once formed my dear father's library. My mother would rather have died than allow one of them to be touched. She used to go daily to the little room where they stood, and press them to her breast, saying, 'These darling books! They were *his* treasures; *his* hand touched them; *his* eyes fell on them;' and then she would kiss them, and weep and smile by turns! Poor, affectionate mother, God has taken thy soul, and I can lay thy body honourably in the grave, and then—"

"You have taught me a lesson, Mr. Atford," I said; "and at the same time created gloomy forebodings."

"Indeed, Sir," he inquired; "how is that?"

"You have taught me to be contented with, and thankful for my lot in life; but you have compelled me to throw my thoughts forward to the possible experience of my widow and children, should it please God to take me away."

"Fear not, Sir; I trust you have many years of honourable usefulness and happiness before you."

"I do not really *fear*," I said, "but I *feel*."

"True, Sir, and every one in your position—I mean, every husband and father—I suppose, must feel, when the uncertainties of life and the future are thought of."

* * * * * *

And yet,—I reflected, on leaving Mr. Atford,—is not feeling respecting the future a modification of fear? My remark indicated a distinction without a difference; and I have not honoured Him to whom the future and the present are one and the same thing, by stating that I feel while I do not really fear. There is truth in the statement, but it is a truth calculated to make a false impression, as it suggests more than it means. What is feeling—of course, the word is metaphorical thus applied — but anxiety? and what is anxiety but a kind of fear? And what, after all, have I, or any other man, to do with the future, as far as it relates to this present world—to bread, water, and raiment? "Give us *this day* our daily bread," is an authorised petition. "Take no thought for to-morrow," is a binding law. Is it not wrong, therefore, to read the petition as if it meant to-morrow, and to overlook the law as if it were without significance? Still, forethought is one thing, and fearful apprehension is another. The former tends to action; the latter unnerves energy. A healthy appreciation of what is due to one's dependents must be salutary in its effects; but the cry of the spirit which, translated, reads, "There is a lion in the way," can neither do good to the creature, nor be in harmony with the purposes of the Creator. To work is scriptural; to be careful and anxious about the issues of work is not. "In the morning sow thy seed, and in the evening withhold not thine hand; for thou knowest not whether shall prosper, either this or that, or whether they both shall be alike good." Labour, patience, faith, seem then to be the general conclusions. Results belong to the Great Disposer of all events.

At the appointed hour I stood at the publisher's door.

"Walk in, Sir," said a shopman. Mr. Tissue was at his desk. My manuscript lay before him. His face indicated conflicting thoughts. I was not kept long in suspense; Mr. Tissue was a man of business, and "time is money."

A conversation, with which the reader would neither be edified nor amused, having taken place, the worthy bibliopole offered £25 for the sole right to print and publish my book. Beyond that figure he had determined not to go. A single sovereign more would have gladdened my heart; but the countenance of the tradesman indicated the very limit of liberality; and the ghost of the printer, with his twenty-five pound bill in his fingers, glared down upon me from the ceiling. I hesitated, struggled, reasoned, and accepted. That evening the printer's account was discharged, interest being generously foregone in consequence of the payment being made before the stipulated time

And now I was as poor as ever. No, not so. I had not laboured in vain. I had discharged a just debt. I was no longer under obligation. I had preserved my character—my only capital. I was free, and the reflection that my own labour, though it was severe and trying, had, under the blessing of Heaven, accomplished the result, was a source of serene satisfaction. I went to my lodgings and bed that night a happy man! What of to-morrow? Let it take care for the things of itself. I did not sleep much, but fell into a half-dozing, half-waking reverie on the value of character, the proverbial hard-heartedness of publishers, and the sorrows and joys of literature.

That publishers are frequently misunderstood, and consequently misrepresented, might have been expected from the peculiarity of their business. It is not to the intrinsic merit of a book that they look exclusively for its success. Works of very little importance sometimes " hit the market," whilst valuable treatises are often commercial failures. Things that are intellectually contemptible and morally pernicious too often find crowds of readers, whilst productions at once profound, elegant, and pure, find their way only in narrow and select circles. The inane tale has a run; the thoughtful essay is admired by the few thoughtful men, and lies in sheets in the publisher's warehouse. The petty newspaper that retails blasphemy, advocates Sabbath desecration, and exhibits the atrocities of the cruel man and the murderer, counts its subscribers by tens of thousands, whilst the journal that keeps itself pure, and advocates the interests of humanity on the basis of revelation, struggles hard for existence. A book that makes men laugh, pays both author and publisher; but a volume that asks the rational immortal to think, seldom remunerates either. I am not under obligation to the publishers, nor are they likely to offer a consideration to an anonymous advocate; but simple truth suggests the conclusion that in "Memoirs" and "Lives" they have sometimes been harshly treated. They must view all transactions in the light of mere trade. As a general rule they can do no other. It would be a fine sight to look upon a publisher who should become the pioneer of every struggling genius, and the champion of every poor author, regardless of pecuniary consequences; but this magnanimity would necessarily be of short duration. It would soon reduce itself to the condition of the poorest poet that it had tried to elevate to opulence and fame.

Undoubtedly, publishers have repeatedly made mistakes, which to posterity seem unaccountable. They have rejected, or given a nameless trifle for the copyright of works which will endure as long as the world has a literature; but to condemn them for errors in judgment, so long as they do not pretend to infallibility, is scarcely equitable. Depend upon it, no publisher will reject a manuscript whose success he foresees. But, as publishers are fallible as other men, common sense requires caution in the investment of their capital. There is one thing exceedingly desirable, which I would, however, earnestly recommend to them all, or at least to those of them whom it concerns, and 'that is—the cheap virtue of politeness. They have to do with the most sensitive minds of the community—the literary, the cultivated, the refined; and minds, too, which are sometimes rendered doubly sensitive

by the action of poverty and trouble.   Let them, therefore, speak courteously to the stranger, even when they
judge it proper to reject the offered manuscript.   It is
surely enough for the man who has spent months or years
in the preparation of a work, on which he has expended
thought, and which he has adorned and beautified from
the resources of a refined imagination, or a poetic fancy,
to have his hopes blasted by the fact of rejection, without
the additional woe of gratuitous insult from a purse-
proud tradesman.   That I am not prescribing for an
imaginary ill, several authors can testify, and the following
fact, selected from others that have come to my knowledge,
will prove.   An author, whom I know well, gave me the
following anecdote:—He wrote, some years ago, an historical and descriptive poem, to the merits of which critics
in England and America have since borne honourable
testimony.   He offered the manuscript to two or three
publishers, who declined, each in his own way, to risk the
work.   He then went to a house well known in the trade,
and asked for the head of the firm.   That personage
happened to be the individual to whom he spoke, and who
was at that moment doing business with a gentleman
over the counter.   " Well, Sir, your business?" inquired
the head, in a hasty tone.

" I wish to show you a manuscript, Sir, when you
have leisure," replied the author.

" A manuscript! Oh! what is it?"

The author uncovered it, and laid it before him.

" Pooh, pooh, pish! *Poetry!*"—exclaimed the worthy,
in a harsh guttural, pushing the MS. from him, as if it
had been infected with the plague.   " No! *no poetry—*
take it away!"

Of course, the stranger, and all the shopmen and
clerks, instantly fixed their eyes on the poor author, who

snatched his parcel, as a father would snatch his child from the hands of a ruffian. He felt, he said, that the eyes of a nest of snakes would not have been so intolerable to him at that moment. Having covered his derided property, he looked at the person, and remarked—

" I merely wished to show you the manuscript, Sir, in the way of business."

" Precisely; yes, poetry—*stuff!* Will have nothing to do with it."

" Which a *gentleman* would have said in different terms," remarked the author, as he indignantly left the place.

Now it is worthy of notice, that this house was not one of those that serve a sect, or deal in a class of publications bearing on the same particular topic; but one from which poetry, travels, and general literature regularly issued. The insulted poet, therefore, could say with Antony :—

" Sometimes we see a cloud that's dragonish
A vapour sometime, like a bear or lion,
A towered citadel, a pendant rock,
A forked mountain, or blue promontory
With trees upon't, that nod unto the world,
And mock our eyes with air."

He had expected, at least, courtesy; but he found— barbarism; and this, to a member of the singing brotherhood, is not particularly gratifying.

I had the pleasure of being introduced, during my week in town, to several authors, and literary men, some of whom were then eminent in their profession, and one or two have since received fresh laurels from the public. Friendships then formed have been cemented by subsequent occasional interviews; and though no other result had sprung from my labour, so far from con-

sidering it lost, I should have judged it highly rewarded.
Three or four authors and ministers, of noble intellect
and high position, became my friends, have continued so
ever since; and two of them, especially, have so often
given evidence of the genuine character of their friendship, that, but for reasons already stated, it would
gratify me to mention their names.

Good Mr. Tissue put my work to press without
delay, and, of course, posted the proof-sheets for revision to my quiet country retreat. This event occasioned
a kind of trouble, of which I had not thought. The
repeated arrival of large letters at the village post-office,
addressed to me, was a circumstance not likely to pass
unnoticed by the inquisitive grocer who superintended
that establishment, and his friends and customers.
What could all these double letters be about?

Mr. Watkins, the grocer and post-master, " did not
know;" but he " thought it likely they were from some
missionary office, asking subscriptions."

Peter Pimple, the letter-carrier, " never zeed nothing
so odd; and he hoped the parson would not forget to
give him a 'ansom box at Christmas."

Jem Black, the sweep, " had heerd as parson wor an
hather; though wot it meant he didn't pertend for to
know."

Mr. Small was of opinion, that " a church meeting
should be called, to investigate the mystery."

John Pry " thought Mr. Watkins should open one of
the letters, as he had heerd as how Sir James Greem
had a-done it."

Mrs. Watkins " would hear of no such thing;" but
at the same time she inquired whether the letters were
sealed with wax or wafers. Her worthy husband having
informed her that the latter substance was employed, she

told her customers not to meddle with other people's business, and retired with a meaning look.

Joe Doubtful was afraid "they might be summonses from the Government, as the minister had not said what he was doing in London so often."

Mary Stall exclaimed, " Dear-a-me ! "

Mrs. Hoble "would ask the minister himself; that she would."

Mr. Hedger " thought she had better not. They had known their minister for a long time, and he was sure it could be nothing bad."

Adam Kib " was not sure about that. He had heard of ministers dealing in railway shares. He thought this was the meaning of it; and, if so, they would all be ruined soon."

William Quick " thought neighbour Kib had better attend to his own affairs, and to those of Mr. Height's Chapel, to which he belonged."

Salfy Pulp " had heard from Peter Pimple that the letters were printed, and therefore she felt quite uneasy about them."

Mary Grey " thought Mr. Small had better write first to the minister, and ask an explanation; and if he did not give it, then have a church meeting."

Mr. Small felt his chin, and agreed with the sensible suggestion; but Grocer Watkins was afraid that the minister would hear of their conversation, and perhaps write to the General Post-Office, finding fault. The thing was sorely perplexing ! And when Mrs. Priestly prophesied that their silly gossip *would* drive any gentleman from the village, they knew not what to do. One morning Pimple brought me a proof, the envelope of which had evidently been tampered with. It was partially torn, and a bit of filthy wax, with the impression of a thimble, lay where the wafer should have been.

"What does this mean, Peter?" I asked.

"What, Sir?"

"This. Look." So saying, I pointed to the torn envelope.

"I'm sure I don't know, Sir. Just as I got it from the office."

"Who gave it to you?"

"Who gave it to me?"

"A direct answer, if you please."

"Yes, Sir, yes—why, who should give it to me?"

"I will have no trifling, Pimple."

"O, beg your pardon, Sir; why, why, it was Mrs. Watkins."

"That will do. You will be at the post-office at five o'clock this evening?"

"Yes, Sir."

"So shall I; as I wish to see Mrs. Watkins in your presence."

"Sir? I—what, Sir?"

"You heard me distinctly, I think?"

"Yes, Sir; certainly."

"Very well. Good morning."

At five o'clock I stood in the grocer's shop. Watkins himself was behind the counter, and bowed very politely. I asked for Mrs. Watkins. She was very unwell, and in bed.

"I am sorry to hear it," I said; "this is surely a sudden attack."

"She was taken very suddenly, Sir," said Watkins.

"When?"

"About an hour ago."

"Has Pimple been here?" I inquired.

"No, Sir, not—yet," answered Watkins, uneasily.

"What! not since the morning?"

"N— oh, yes; he was in, buying a piece of cheese, not long since."

"That was," said I, carelessly, "before the illness of Mrs. Watkins?"

"Yes," said Watkins; but a thought striking him, he coloured to the forehead.

"Well, now, Mr. Watkins," I said, "I am sorry that a pretended illness should add to the crime of trifling with the letters of the public. I shall not expose you for this offence; but repeat it, and take the consequences."

"I am very sorry, Sir; but it was an accident."

I looked in his face; he turned away, and I left.

CHAPTER X.

A NEW FIELD OF LABOUR.

" Our voluntary service He requires,
Not our necessitated; such with Him
Finds no acceptance, nor can find; for how
Can hearts, not free, be tried whether they serve
Willing or no, who will but what they must
By destiny, and can no other choose? "—*Milton.*

MAN'S HIGHEST HONOUR—WILLING SERVICE—POWER OF LIFE—FACTS IN CHRISTIAN EXPERIENCE—IMMORTALITY—PLACES OF SERVICE—AN AUTUMNAL EVENING—CREATION GROANING—AN ANGRY FEMALE—A HAZARDOUS PROMISE—APOSTROPHE—PASTORAL VISITS—JACOB MOORE—THE BOOK AND THE LETTER—ALL BURDENS NOT HEAVY—REQUEST FROM PRELATESTON—MINISTERIAL REMOVALS—SETTLEMENT IN PRELATESTON—ONE THING WANTED—WILL THE READER HELP?—GRIEF OF MY LATE FLOCK—MR. SELF—MR. MITHALL—CHURCH AND SUNDAY SCHOOL—BIBLE CLASSES—PREACHING—RATIONALISM AND RITUALISM—FIDELITY IN VIEW OF THE TIMES—AVOIDING POLITICS—MR. POTTER AND THE REV. MR. SPALKS—A " PALTRY SCHISM SHOP "—EXCELLENT CLERGYMEN—MUTUAL DESIRE FOR UNION—THE REV. CHARLES ARBOUR—CHRISTIAN LOVE AND CHRISTIAN " EVIDENCES "—ALL TO BLAME—VOICES OF THE SECTS—FEROCIOUS LANGUAGE—BETTER DAYS—BEAUTY OF UNION—UNITY WITHOUT UNIFORMITY—PEACE AND WORK.

THE honour put upon the intelligent creature, when he is called to the service of his All-wise Creator, is the highest which it is possible for him to receive. Elevation in the scale of being is measured by the earnestness and devotion which characterise the services rendered, and not by the position in which the servant stands in relation to his fellow-servants. Place is of little importance, compared with filial and faithful obedience. The utterance, " I am Gabriel, that stand in the presence of God," suggests a glory and honour that strike the imagination with wonder and awe. The effort to realise the dignity and majesty of such a being is necessarily a failure. We think of the most powerful potentate with which the history of nations has made us acquainted, and instantly reject the similitude, as feebleness itself; for, keeping out of view the moral contrast between a polluted mortal and a holy immortal, the greatest monarch that ever swayed a sceptre over his fellow-men cannot be brought into comparison, for a moment, with the radiant intelligence that *stands* in the presence of God—no more than the mole, that casts up a hill an inch or two higher than surrounding mole-hills, can be compared with the eagle that passes beyond human vision, with its eye fixed on the sun. Yet the readiness for service, indicated by this remarkable utterance, is equalled, and, if all the circumstances be taken into account, surpassed by the declaration once made by a poor man :—" What mean ye to weep and to break mine heart?" asked the persecuted " teacher of the Gentiles," when his friends endeavoured to dissuade him from prosecuting a perilous journey, " for I am ready not to be bound only, but also to die at Jerusalem for the name of the Lord Jesus."

In the first case, we see one of the immortal princes of heaven, invested with the highest honour within the reach of creaturehood, standing in the presence of the Great King, and watching the slightest intimation of his Sovereign's will to pass, with the velocity of thought, to any world, on any mission with which he may be honoured. Service is his happiness, obedience his glory, the approval of God

his reward. But we cannot forget that, go where he
may, he is safe. Neither stripes nor imprisonment,
neither bondage nor death, neither insult nor weariness,
are possible. In the second case, however, we see a *man*
—a man, feeble as others, encompassed with infirmity,
hated, hunted, persecuted, ever in peril, bearing the
marks of the persecutor's scourge in his body, with
nothing before him but a life of tempest, and a death of
violence; yet this man, rising above the weakness of
humanity, so far as he was personally concerned—while
sorrow, on account of the grief of others, almost broke his
heart—was so completely absorbed by the one great
thought of serving his Master, that neither bonds, nor
torture, nor death, could change his purpose, nor cool his
holy ardour. Heaven's angels are seen, in the apocalyptic
vision, surrounding the throne, and they are heard saying,
with a loud voice, " Worthy is the Lamb that was slain
to receive power, and riches, and wisdom, and strength,
and honour, and glory, and blessing." Sublimity and
grandeur characterise the scene; earnestness and devotion belong to the service. The position of the worshippers is on the heights of glory; the worshippers
themselves bloom with the beauty of undecaying life and
moral perfection; and the sincerity of their adoration is
evinced by the unanimous shout with which their
doxology rolls over heaven. But there are other servants elsewhere. There are two men, feeble from loss
of blood, covered with the marks of the lash, hurried to
a prison, forced into an inner cell, where their feet are
bound to a beam of wood: " And at midnight Paul and
Silas prayed, and sang praises to God." Here, the position of the worshippers is a loathsome pit, in an oriental
prison; the worshippers themselves are covered with
gore, and smarting with fresh wounds; but they, too,

worship—notwithstanding the pain, the gloom, the bondage, and the disgrace; and the sincerity of their adoration needs no plea in its favour. In the cells of the prison at Philippi, the strange melody of Christian song falls upon the ears of the prisoners, winds its way through the labyrinths of the dungeon, ascends to heaven, and is answered by an earthquake which shatters the building to its foundations, opens all its massive doors, and unfetters all its inhabitants! This scene, though as different, in one sense, from that seen in the Apocalypse as it is possible to conceive, is, in another sense, almost equal in sublimity. The living soul of both scenes is voluntary, intelligent, and intense adoration of the exalted Redeemer of men. In both cases, the idea of service without compulsion is prominent. We see mind adoring Him who is all mind—intelligence, whether on earth or in heaven, converging upon its source—gratitude recognising the spring of all happiness—the love of purity instinctively attaching itself to the Holy One—and life owning its glorious Giver in the language of living song.

A wonderful thing is life; and its astonishing capabilities teach at once that there is a living God, and that to serve Him is the highest honour and the chief felicity of existence. Illustrations of the surprising power of that mysterious thing which we call *life*, would require volumes instead of a paragraph. The record of what man has purposed, done, and suffered—the acts of statesmen, heroes, and chiefs—the immortal monuments of genius, learning, and piety—the testimony of witnesses, and the patient endurance of martyrs—the annals of nations, and the history of all time—are proofs and exemplifications of this marvellous power. These things compel every rational being to conclude that man is more than he seems, that the service of God is the liberty of intellect, that threescore years and ten cannot be the limit of existence, and that the doctrine of immortality is no poetic fable. In support of this conclusion, there are facts which every *Christian*, whatever his sect, admits, and which no unbeliever will have the boldness to dispute, simply because of his utter inability to give a verdict on a matter which lies so far above the region of his cold speculations.

It is a fact, then, that every "Christian"—I use the term in its legitimate, not in its conventional sense—has seasons of conscious communion with spiritual realities, and with his invisible Lord and Saviour—seasons of hallowed joy, when the world and all its cares are left behind, as troublers whose unhallowed feet cannot ascend the mount of vision, or defile the holy scene—seasons when anxiety is rebuked, fear is scattered, sorrow is lightened, darkness is banished, and faith, hope, and love are invigorated with celestial energy—and seasons when the truth, value, and divinity of Christianity are *felt* to be absolutely impregnable, notwithstanding the acknowledged weakness of the individual Christian, and the admitted strength of malicious foes. It is a fact, that though the individual Christian may be poor in pocket and obscure in place, destitute at once of the world's gold and the world's greatness, he feels himself a child of God, a disciple of Christ, and an heir of a blessed immortality. With him, it is not the vocal repetition of part of a creed, far less is it a cant phrase—yet he says, amidst his seriously-felt infirmities, with all the self-possession of a man who can give a reason of the hope that is in him, "I know in whom I have believed, and am persuaded that He is able to keep that which I have committed unto Him against that day." There is no fanaticism about the man—he is too humble for that; no self-confidence—he knows the conditions of salvation, as well as his own weakness and folly, too well for that; and no affected superiority over others—he knows how much he is indebted to grace for that. In this case, the capabilities of that Life which is connected with, but both intellectually and morally distinct from, the body, are remarkably manifested. It is surely note-worthy, and, as I think, a conclusive proof of immortality, that this spiritual intelligence in man can be raised so far above surrounding influences and external circumstances, as to realise the unseen and eternal, and to feel that they exclusively form the realities of the universe, and the only objects worthy of rational desire. It contemplates that which the bodily eye hath not seen, and that which the bodily ear hath not heard—feels earnest and ever-growing sympathy with the pure and lofty instructions of revelation—and gathers around itself a spiritual atmosphere, in which it lives, moves, and has its being. It loves and serves a Master on whom the eye of sense hath not looked for many a century of time, and breathes holy aspirations for that promised moral perfection which will qualify it to adore Him without interruption and without hindrance; and it knows, as a matter of settled conviction—rendering all questions both superfluous and profane—and anticipates as the perfection of joy and the glory of existence, that to be with and see that Illustrious Master is the contemplated end of redemption, and the purposed crown of immortality.

All this is simple matter of *fact*, as myriads of persons, separated from each other by language, climate, and government, can at any moment testify. Two other facts, equally indisputable, will make this point complete. It may be objected,—" All this may be; such feelings and convictions are just possible in the case of certain persons; but they are only the results of religious preaching, and of associating themselves with certain parties whose creed, written or understood, embraces these notions." I have a short and sufficient answer to this objection. It is a plain matter of fact that, whilst the men under notice love their Bibles, their brotherhood, and their pastors, they view them all only in the light of mere instrumentality, whose efficiency depends entirely on a superior power, and affirm, to a man, that the awakening of their once-dormant inner life was the result of supernatural influence—the Spirit of the living God communicating to their spirits the purifying and exalting truths of Christianity. Now, surely, testimony borne with such unanimity, under such a variety of external circumstances, ought for ever to silence every speculative objection brought against the matter. The adherents of a sect may be mistaken, the members of a given Church may assume an untenable position; but the concurrent voice of all Christians, everywhere, and in all ages, may not be set aside, to clear the way for any adversary of the Gospel doctrine of a future life.

The other fact to which I alluded is, that so far from materialism, or mere organisation, accounting for all this, the Christian men referred to maintain a constant struggle against the degrading propensities and appetites of their own bodies. One of them, in a letter to certain parties, writes thus :—"I keep under my body, and bring it into subjection." And the same man, in another letter, says to the persons addressed, "If ye live after the flesh, ye shall die; but if ye through the Spirit do mortify the deeds of the body, ye shall live." Is it not, therefore, clear as facts, reasoning, and the obvious import of language can make it, that there is a spirit in man—a wondrous tenant in these temporary tabernacles—a life of amazing capability in these frail houses of clay, which are daily crumbling to the dust of the earth ; and that to teach that the sexton and the grave close the career of man, is to degrade and deceive humanity, and to rob it of its glorious crown ?

Instead of teaching this cold and withering dogma, which is alike improbable and absurd, is it not more rational, more ennobling to humanity, and more consistent with revelation, to build upon the powers of life and its grand destiny an argument for the hearty, voluntary service of God, by every intelligent man? Respecting the destiny of intelligent life, I may ask the opponent of immortality—Are all these intuitions, aspirations, and hopes, in vain? Are they given only to excite desires which cannot be satisfied, and to arouse expectations which cannot be realised? Is human consciousness only a tantalising delusion? And are these admitted capabilities so much waste power, which cannot find sufficient field for exercise here, and yet have no hereafter in which to serve? I may inquire further—If it be consistent with the ordinary procedure of God, to call forth such powers only to cast them aside, before the period of maturity, and to leave undeveloped fruit whose seed He has himself sown and watered? Decay and re-production is the law everywhere around us, in the material universe. There is nothing lost, far less annihilated. Shall the greatest thing in the world—the only thing capable of moral action, of noble deeds, and deathless anticipations— cease and determine, and be dissolved into air, or reduced to nonentity, when the feeble body, in which it has lodged for a time, shall be gathered to its original dust? Is it necessary that the tenant die when the house falls? Why should it, especially as it is demonstrable that he has inhabited several already, without loss of personal identity? If the Creator has *said* that the intelligent existence ceases for ever on the dissolution of the body—if He has anywhere said this in so many words—then, perplexing and strange as the oracle would be, I will immediately believe it; but in that case I must also believe that the body, with all its frailty, changes, and mortality, is a greater thing than the living spirit, and that the latter is entirely dependent upon, and subservient to, the former. I must further believe that the purpose of humanity is served, when the grave receives its loathsome portion—that God's ultimate design concerning his noblest earthly creature was to cast his carcase among the worms of the earth—that all the hopes held out by the Book which millions have gladly received as a Divine revelation, are only so many exciting promises never intended to be performed—and that, as a logical consequence, the best thing—if there be a best and a worst in this starless chaos—we can do, under these gloomy circumstances, is to eat, drink, and die! But I do not choose to believe all this, or any part of it. It is too negative for my creed—too cold for my heart—too absurd for my understanding—and too dishonouring to my God. I need a positive creed and a loving religion, and in Christianity I find them both; and in the destiny of the Christian soul I find the sublime development of both.

Here, then, I take my stand, and find a cluster of arguments for consecration to the service of God. Let mind, life, and love, serve Him who is all three!

> " All within
> Awake to glorify the ' Wonderful ! '
> And from the throbbing heart, with heavenly fire
> Burning to utter his unmeasured praise,
> Pour out an anthem to the glorious One !

Thought, feeling, memory, hope, and faith, and love,
The mind, the soul, the spirit, all would praise.
My very sins shall praise Him ! Worthy He,
For what He is, has done, and yet will do,
Of loudest celebration ! "

The position may not be such as one would choose, if the power of election were granted; but locality is nothing; the motive that prompts and the principles which regulate service, are everything. Whether the hamlet or the town, the centre of Africa or the shores of England, the sunny fields of the East or the eternal snows of Greenland, the dungeon of Philippi or around the throne of Heaven, it matters little. If the work be of God, and the heart be in the work, all will end well, and the difficulties of a position are generally intended to be tests of faith and obedience. When these are sufficiently tested, either the difficulties vanish, or the Master calls his servant to another sphere. Let him not, however, deceive himself with the hope that the new sphere will be all sunshine and flowers, all odours and song. Such scenes of labour are not appointed for servants, who, whilst *in* the service, are being personally trained *by it*. The instrument must be polished and brightened by action, and then, at " *that* day," to which time and eternity both steadily point, " They that be wise shall shine as the brightness of the firmament, and they that turn many to righteousness as the stars for ever and ever."

I trust these remarks will neither be considered out of place, nor as standing in need of apology. They are intimately connected with the substance of this narrative, and, indeed, in some measure necessary to its coherence. Besides, in such musings I have often found solace to the spirit chafed with cares, and calm consolation when

O

dark clouds were overhead, and thick walls of perplexity in my path. To trace everything to its original source, or to detect *every* link in the chain of events, is more than man can do; but to try to reconcile seeming contradictions between the facts of experience and the promises of revelation is a profitable task, and a study which cannot be honestly undertaken without profit to the student.

Much perplexed from a cause which a very small portion of the gold that perisheth would have removed, I had reasoned as above; and, humbly resolving that, though the suggestion that the market-place offered a better field for success than the church, had pressed itself on my thoughts, I would not yield to it, but wait patiently and consecrate myself afresh to the service of my Redeemer, happen what might, I went out to enjoy the refreshing breeze of a fine autumnal afternoon. My book had been published, and had passed safely and honourably through the ordeal of criticism. So far well, and for the publisher's sake I hoped it would obtain a remunerative sale, although, personally, I had no interest in it, and expected nothing from it. I also hoped that the doctrines it taught, and the arguments it exhibited in favour of those doctrines, might be of service to some of its readers. Beyond this I thought little concerning it. It was now drawing towards the end of October. The crops were nearly all secured. The sheaves, which had stood on the fields, like saints on the morning of the resurrection, ripe for glory, had been gathered in, as the immortal bodies of the redeemed will be gathered on that day, to enter the kingdom prepared for them from the foundation of the world. I walked about two miles, until I reached an eminence from which an extensive view of the country could be obtained. The air was cold, clear, and bracing, and from the top of this little hill I looked around on field and woodland, admiring the soft and solemn beauties of that peculiarly suggestive season of the year.

> " Nature seemed
> In silent contemplation to adore
> Its Maker. Now and then, the aged leaf
> Fell from its fellows, rustling to the ground ;
> And, as it fell, bade man think on his end.
> On vale and lake, on wood and mountain high,
> With pensive wing outspread, sat heavenly Thought,
> Conversing with itself."

Reciting these lines, which I had committed to memory many years before, and which were vividly recalled by the time and circumstances, I continued in thought until a rough voice and a torrent of curses arrested my attention. I looked and saw a man lashing and kicking a poor horse, that had fallen with its heavy load at the foot of the hill. The blood was oozing from the animal, which had evidently put forth all its strength, and was now suffering the ill-treatment of its savage master. I ran to the man and rebuked him for his cruelty. This sudden and unexpected remonstrance had the desired effect; but I received the compliment of a muttered oath for meddling with things that did not belong to me. The remarkable statement of Paul in his letter to the Romans came forcibly before me :—" We know that the whole creation—every creature—groaneth and travaileth in pain together until now. And not only they, but ourselves also, who have the first-fruits of the Spirit, even we ourselves groan within ourselves, waiting for the adoption, to wit, the redemption, of our bodies." And when will that time come? I mentally asked—when will the jubilee of creation come? And when will the second Adam restore Paradise to our miserable world, in which man and beast have groaned, suffered, and died, for so many doleful centuries? I was returning to my

house, pursuing the course of thought which these questions suggested ; but, instead of fixing upon the attractions
of that day of emancipation, I thought of the dark and
dismal present, of the sins, woes, and miseries of man—of
the labours, endurance, and sufferings of the brute creation
—of death, corruption, and the pit of wrath, until my mind
became terribly agitated, and I fancied something hissed
into my ear—"The Bible is not true !"* I gazed around,
and seeing no one, I left the road, and fell on my knees
by the side of an old tree, and with clasped hands looked
up to that Being in whose ear a stream of wailing rushes
without interruption, from the beginning to the end of the
year, from the dwellers on this earth. I thought of
Nathaniel, the fig-tree, and Jesus, rose up and went to
my house. One of my children had been ailing for some
days, and my dear wife was sad at heart.

I was in the act of lifting a cup of tea to my lips, when
the door opened suddenly, and a tall, masculine woman

---

* I may here remark, in a note, for the benefit of young readers, to
whom the thought may not occur, that the suggestion, " The Bible is not
true," was, under the circumstances, not only false, but stupid. The
question as to the truth of the Bible had *nothing to do with* the subject
of my gloomy musings. The Bible is not accountable for the sins and
woes of man, and the sufferings and groanings of creation. These exist,
as matters of fact, independently of any question of this sort; but if the
Bible be not accountable for them, it accounts for them, and tells us how
they are to be removed. Hence its value, and glory. They are *in* the
world, were there no Bible. It is in the world, and tells us that *they
must leave it some day.* This is a part, but only a part, of its inestimable
value. A redeemed soul, a redeemed body, a redeemed creation—these
are its wonderful announcements ! " If these Scriptures," says Coleridge,
" impregnable in their strength, sustained in their pretensions by innumerable prophecies and miracles, and by the experience of the inner man, in
all ages, as well as by a concatenation of arguments all bearing upon the
point, and extending with miraculous consistency through a series of fifteen hundred years ; if all this combined proof does not establish their
validity, nothing can be proved under the sun, but the world and man
must be abandoned, with all its consequences, to one universal scepticism."

rushed in, and without either sitting down, or beginning her speech with the usual " good evening," she threw her arms about her violently, and poured out the following tirade :—

"I want my money—you, Sir! I want my money!* I wish we had never seen your face! *You* a gentleman! The money—the money—the money! You can find it for others! The account—the account, immediately! No excuses! I must have it, have it—now—now—*this moment!* A minister indeed! A—"

" Hold!" I exclaimed, rising and pointing to the door. " There's the door, madam; you will oblige me by departing, and your small account shall be settled *to-morrow.* You never had occasion to ask me for money before—you never shall again!"

She hesitated, and continued talking with wild rapidity, as if she had been excited by more than mere passion. The children, trembling and pale, clung to their mother, who sat in the centre of the terrified group, with the tears streaming from her eyes.

" Do you hesitate?" I asked. " Cross that threshold *instantly!*"

She flung herself out, almost bursting the door from its hinges by the violence with which she pulled it after her. I locked it, and embracing and kissing my loved ones, said, " Weeping may endure for a night, but joy cometh in the morning!"

" But, my dear," said my trembling wife, " why did

---

* This woman kept a small grocery in the village. Though her goods were inferior in quality and higher in price than those which I could procure in a town five miles distant, I had always dealt with her, paying her regularly every quarter. It was now nearly two months past quarter-day, and I was fifty shillings in arrear, which I could not pay at that time; we had been living very narrowly for some weeks, and it seems she thought I was paying ready money elsewhere, which was not the case.

you say to-morrow? You know there is not a shilling in the house."

"I said to-morrow, love, because I mean it; and as to there not being a shilling in the house, why *that* is nothing new;" and I tried to smile.

That was a sleepless night, a night of tossing and trouble, and I arose with the dawn, and went out to seek in the frosty air the repose which my bed denied. Everything around was dream-like. Nature seemed to be slowly opening its lids, after a refreshing sleep. The sun had sent his herald light to the atmosphere, as if instructing it to say to man and beast, that he himself would look down upon them soon, and call them forth to new life and labour. And, punctual as a faithful lover, he came. Kind sun! he shineth on the evil and the good, and exhibits the grandeurs of creation to the eye of the poor as well as to that of the rich. But what should I do? My promised "to-morrow" had come. Reluctantly—but there was nothing else that could be done—I had resolved to ask an advance of fifty shillings on the next quarter, to enable me to pay my gentle visitor of the previous evening; but what was to be done *then?* Fifty shillings would discharge the grocer's account, but I was literally without money, and how were household wants to be supplied in the meantime? "Well, the silver and the gold belong to the Lord. He knows my wants, He knows my heart, He knows that I wish to serve Him, and to owe no man anything but love. He may try me—but I *will* trust in Him! Although the fig-tree shall not blossom, neither shall fruit be in the vines; the labour of the olive shall fail, and the fields shall yield no meat; the flock shall be cut off from the fold, and there shall be no herd in the stalls: yet I will rejoice in the Lord, I will joy in the God of my salvation. The Lord

God is my strength, and He will make my feet like hind's feet, and He will make me to walk upon mine high places. Light is sown for the righteous, and gladness for the upright in heart. Why art thou cast down, O my soul? and why art thou disquieted within me? Hope thou in God: for I shall yet praise Him who is the health of my countenance, and my God." Thus recalling Scripture, I returned to my lowly lodge in the wilderness, intending, after breakfast, to call upon Mr. Small for the purpose of asking the amount of money necessary for that day.

Ye rich men, ye children of "fortune," ye who spend in feasting, pleasure, jewels, dress, and theatres, more, far more, in a single day or night, than would provide for the wants of a poor man's family for a year, think, O think, if the Great Master can pass you by without demanding an account of your stewardship? I would not have you want for anything. Far from it. But would it not sweeten your cup of pleasure to know, that the sons of struggle are, in some few instances, made thankful to the "Lord of all" because of your liberality? Your servants, your horses, and dogs—let none of them want, because they minister to your pleasure, and are dependent upon your care; but the poor Dissenting preacher, and the frequently still poorer curate of the rich Establishment—men whose labours, if they do nothing else, help to secure your parks, mansions, property, and persons, from the hand of violence, by teaching the people honesty and the fear of God—think if ye might not so arrange as to add a fresh zest to your providential enjoyments, by adding an unmissed trifle to theirs. Believe me, they deserve it. The country is the better for their services; and though I cannot see my way with respect to the propriety of a compulsory Establishment, yet I do see how the voluntary gifts of your abundance would cause thanksgiving to God, and greatly increase your enjoyment of lawful pleasures—*provided always the motive from which you act be in harmony with the mind of the universal Lord !*

In pursuance of my resolution I called on my worthy friend Small, about ten o'clock. He had gone out, and would not be back until twelve. I occupied the time, therefore, in paying some pastoral visits, when I tried to soothe the sad and to cheer the disconsolate, although my own heart was not remarkably buoyant. I entered one house, where an old man, who had seen seventy-eight winters, was sitting cowering over as much fire as would have filled a table-spoon. His back was bent with hard labour and age, and around his bony and withered body there was a pile of old rags, obviously fit only for the dunghill. There was nothing between his bloodless feet and the cold brick floor, but some wretched bits of leather, which had once borne the shape of shoes or slippers. The furniture of his hut was like the human inhabitant,—old, broken, and, to all appearance, useless. An earthen cruse, containing about half-a-pint of cold gruel, stood by the mock fire, waiting in vain for a little heat. A tear stood on the old man's cheek when he heard my voice. The few straggling grey hairs which clung to it, like ivy tendrils to a decayed oak, intercepted the descent of the solitary tear, and there it sparkled, between me and the rag-stuffed window, like a diamond lying on a moss-covered rock in the desert. An old copy of Henry's Bible lay open on a deal table within Jacob's reach, and on the Bible lay the tortoise-shell spectacles which had been Jacob's companions during many years of his pilgrimage. " What a miserable place ! " you exclaim, young man, with health dancing in your veins, and hope in your heart, and Delusion, in gay attire, beckoning you on to—what? But wait a minute or two, until you hear Jacob Moore's own account of matters. He should know best, whether the place be miserable or not, for he was born in this very cottage, has lived in it nearly fourscore years, and has never been twenty miles from it in his life. Now, listen. Just take your place behind the old chair there. Jacob will not look around, so you may hear all that passes without being discovered.

"Well, Mr. Moore, how do you feel this morning?" I asked, drawing the wreck of a chair close to the bundle of rags, and laying my hand on the old man's knee.

"O Sir," said he, "don't call me Mister, if you please, for I am a poor guilty creature.

> ' A guilty, weak, and helpless worm,
>   On thy kind arms I fall:
> Be thou my strength and righteousness,
>   My Jesus, and my all.'

But I am glad you have come. This is one of the thousand answers I have had to prayer. I asked the Lord to put it into your mind to visit me this morning, if you were not better engaged, and whilst I was speaking—though I fear it is sinful in me to think of the greatly beloved Daniel and my poor self at the same time—but, whilst I was speaking in prayer, the door opened, and you are here! God bless you, dear Sir!"

"Why did you wish to see me this morning, my aged friend?"

"Why? 'Come and hear, all ye that fear God, and I will declare what He hath done for my soul.'

> ' Buried in sorrow and in sin,
>   At hell's dark door I lay;
> But I arise, by grace divine,
>   To see an heavenly day.'

That's why I wanted to see you, Sir."

" Good tidings, indeed, Jacob; but," said I, smiling, "I have heard all this before. Have you nothing different to tell me? Are you not tired of religion yet?"

A heavenly smile lit up the old saint's countenance, as if his guardian angel had just passed before it—a smile which made the solitary tear reflect new beams between me and the light, as he caught my meaning, and replied,

" Tired of religion?

> ' Her ways are ways of pleasantness,
>   And all her paths are peace.'

But I wonder that Jesus is not tired of me. O, what grace *He* has!

> ' Grace, 'tis a sweet, a charming theme;
> My thoughts rejoice at Jesus' name;
> Ye angels, dwell upon the sound;
> Ye heavens, reflect it to the ground!'

No, Sir, I have nothing new to tell you. Yes, I have, though—

> ' Thus far the Lord has led me on,
> Thus far His power prolongs my days;
> And every evening shall make known,
> Some *fresh memorial* of His grace.'

He makes the outgoings of the morning and evening to rejoice. Great is His faithfulness. Bless the Lord, O my soul!"

" But tell me, now, my friend, have you *no* fear?"

" Fear! ah! Sir, the enemy was busy with me last night. I really thought it was my last. You know, I have nobody in the house with me during the night. My poor daughter-in-law looks in every day about twelve, but, poor dear, she has her children to look after, and can't come oftener. I tried to sleep, but was obliged to sit up for the cough. I thought, once or twice, I was going. The enemy told me there was no mercy for me, and I looked to myself and saw nothing but sin and corruption, and I was all fear."

"But how do you know it was an enemy that said that? Might it not be a friend?" The venerable man moved his head a little to one side, so as to catch a glimpse of my countenance.

"If my poor memory serves me," he said, "you have often told us that every voice that contradicts the voice of Jesus, is false; and I know it was the enemy that said that to me last night, for my Lord says quite the contrary. He says, 'Him that cometh to me, I will in no wise cast out;' and again, He says, 'Come unto me, all ye that labour and are heavy laden, and I will give you rest.' Now, that's me. I'm one of them.

> 'Come hither, all ye weary souls,
> Ye heavy-laden sinners, come ;
> I'll give you rest from all your toils,
> And raise you to my heavenly throne.'

What can a poor sinner want more?"

"Then you have no fear, when you look to Jesus?"

"No, blessed be God!" exclaimed the humble believer, lifting his thin hands, "no fear then.

> 'But if Immanuel's face appear,
> My hope, my joy begins;
> His name forbids my slavish fear,
> His grace removes my sins.'"

And then, in a lower voice, he added, "'All have sinned and come short of the glory of God.' 'Where is boasting, then? It is excluded. Therefore we conclude that a man is justified by faith without the deeds of the law.' Precious doctrine! glorious Saviour!

'When I see thee as thou art,
I'll praise thee as I ought!'"

My heart was full. This was a scene of real sublimity.
Here was a chapter on the "Evidences of Christianity."
I asked Jacob if he wished me to read with him.

"O yes, Sir, if you please—read, read the sure word,
and pray."

On taking my leave Jacob thanked me. "No," said I,
"no thanks; I am the obliged party. Selfishness brought
me here. I came to be refreshed, and I have not come
in vain. Peace, peace be with you!"

As I departed, I heard my hoary friend saying,

" Peace shall attend the path they go,
And light their steps surround."

From this " vestibule of heaven," I went to the cottage
of a poor labourer, whose wife I found holding a little
child, which was at that moment struggling for breath
in a severe fit of hooping cough—that sharp scythe of
death, which cuts down so many little flowers, and wrings
the hearts of so many bereaved parents. Poor little
sufferer! The man of seventy-eight still waits for the
Master's wished-for call; and thou, who hast just entered
on the race, art already fighting with the last enemy!
Poor child, if thou knewest all, thou wouldst, perhaps,
choose to fall now—for fall thou must, some day! How
dismal were this world but for the Gospel, which points
to the " restitution," the " kingdom," and the " glory!"

Twelve o'clock having come, I went to friend Small's,
and obtained the sum wanted very readily. I then
walked to my fair friend, the grocer, and paid the
account. She held down her head, received the money,
and handed me a receipt, but spoke not. She had lost a
customer, and I had gained a little more experience.

Reflecting on the scenes of the day—a penniless purse,

an empty cupboard, a full Bible, and a complete Saviour—we retired to rest, and I fell asleep with the words on my tongue, " Take, therefore, no thought for the morrow ; for the morrow shall take thought for the things of itself. Sufficient unto the day is the evil thereof." The morning came, beautiful, clear, exhilarating, and I thought I should go to a neighbouring town; but if asked why, or what to do, I could not have answered. We had just enough in the house for breakfast, but nothing for dinner except a few potatoes. After breakfast, my old friend Pimple, the letter-carrier, whom the reader has met before, gave his legal double rap at the door, and handed me a letter, bearing the London post-mark, but the superscription was in a hand new to me. A cheque for £10 lay in the letter, the contents of which follow :—

" *London, 29th October, 18*—

" MY DEAR SIR,

" I have read your work, recently published, with great pleasure and satisfaction. It is highly suggestive, which is, I think, about the best compliment that can be paid to a modern work. Accept my best thanks for the contribution you have thus made, in your village retirement, to a subject of great importance at the present day.

" I have received a letter from the deacons of the Church in Prelateston,* inquiring whether I can direct them to a suitable minister, as their pastor has lately resigned office. The statements I have heard respecting you, together with the impression made by your book, lead me to think you might supply the pulpit for a Sabbath

---

* Of course, the reader will not find this name in the " Gazetteer," nor was it in my correspondent's letter; but though I have changed the name, the designation I have substituted is very appropriate.

or two, as I understand you are moveable. I have named you to the deacons, and probably you will hear from them. The Chapel is not large, and the congregation are not numerous at present, but the population of the town is large, and the *right* minister would, doubtless, be of service to the cause of truth there.

" I beg your acceptance of £10, being an exhibition from a fund with which I am connected.

" Wishing you every blessing, I am,

" My dear Sir, yours faithfully,

"———— "

I have not forgotten the emotions produced by this letter; but all I shall say respecting them is, I called my wife into the study, and, after reading it to her, we knelt together, and thanked our Father in heaven. I did go to the town that day, and returned with a large parcel of provisions on my shoulder, and gold in my pocket. My step was much lighter with my burden than it had been, several days before, without it; thus proving that all burdens are not heavy. In addition to the well-timed relief, and the hope excited by the letter of my excellent correspondent, there were two sources of pleasure which I cannot omit to mention. The first was, the high position of the writer, both as a minister and an author; and the second, the fact that my literary labours had not been altogether fruitless. I had written under the pressure of difficulty, to pay a printer's account. The amount realised had just done that, and no more; but here was, at least, a prospective advantage, of which the book was clearly the occasion. My doctrine, that true labour is never lost, was once more verified; for, even supposing that I should hear no more of Prelateston, the voluntary testimony of such a man as ———— to the work I had published, and the substantial proof he had given of the sincerity of his testimony, were exceedingly gratifying. Two days afterwards I received a letter, of which the following is a copy :—

> "*Prelateston, 31st October,* 18—
>
> "REV. AND DEAR SIR,
>
> "As one of the deacons of the Church in this place, I have been instructed by my colleagues to write to you, and to inquire if you will kindly preach to us, the pulpit being vacant by the resignation of our late esteemed pastor, on the second and third Lord's days in November. I need not say that your compliance, if possible, will greatly oblige us all. Hoping to hear from you by return of post,
>
> "I am, yours very faithfully,
>
> "J. C. ELLIOTT, Sen."

The striking language of Job—"Thou hast granted me life and favour, and thy visitation hath preserved my spirit"—expresses my feelings on the receipt of Mr. Deacon Elliott's letter. To what this might lead, or whereunto this might grow, I could not foresee; but under all the circumstances of this case,—the unsought and unlooked-for interest taken in me by my metropolitan friend—the official letter I have transcribed above—the pressure of care which had long borne me down, and which, but for the sustaining influence of Divine promises and providences, would have crushed me—and the certainty that the village afforded no rational prospect of amelioration,—I judged it my duty to reply that day, expressing my willingness to visit the Church at Prelateston. It is simply a matter of fact to state, that strong mutual attachment existed between my flock and myself; and I foresaw that uneasiness and anxiety would be created by the announcement of my intended absence for a fortnight. Yet that announcement had to be made, in some form. To break loose from a people to whom one is strongly attached—to sever ties formed under the most sacred circumstances—and to leave a people whose minds and habits have been to a great extent moulded by the constant labours of several years in the Christian ministry, is very painful; and though the intended visit might not lead to such a severance, yet my good flock were sure to anticipate this result, should they hear that I was about to supply a vacant pulpit. Those who love a minister most, are just those who imagine that others will feel towards him as they do; and they are, at the same time, the very persons whom he is most anxious not to depress by the forebodings of separation. The congregation, too, had continued as large as ever, and the state of the Church—to which additions were being made from time to time—was such as to call forth unfeigned gratitude. Happily, I have had no experience of this kind, but I should think it very painful to leave a divided, distracted, and decaying Church; but perhaps it is more painful still, to resign the pastoral connexion with one that is united, peaceful, and prosperous. Yet, when one is called to do so, with the prospect of increased usefulness elsewhere, if he be a man who habitually recognises the movements of that Hand which the world sees not, both wisdom and piety indicate the course he ought to pursue. Truth is one; the normal state of the human mind is everywhere the same; the influences of the Gospel produce similar results, without respect to locality; and, therefore, the enlargement of the scene of labour is an argument for increased zeal in precisely the same work which had been carried on elsewhere. If the motive of service in the village be such as has been traced in a previous chapter, it must not be changed on entering the populous town. The doctrine proclaimed cannot, must not, be changed, if it be that commanded by the Master, proclaimed by His apostles, and demonstrated by the experience of eighteen centuries to be the power of God unto salvation. All these considerations led me to leave the matter without personal preference either way, confident that I had " one thing" to do, wherever the *place* might be, and that He in whose service I was engaged would not and could not forsake me.

" Thou wilt keep him in perfect peace whose mind is stayed on thee, because he trusteth in thee," is one of those inexpressibly valuable assurances of the Divine book, which have the advantage of being put to the test of actual experience. Multitudes have tested this assurance thus, and have found its literal truth. But how strong is the evidence of human depravity in the reluctance which men feel to trust implicitly in God! That the *creature* should hesitate to rely upon the CREATOR is utterly unaccountable on any hypothesis but this old, true, and sad one. Yet, when through gracious influence this reliance becomes a fact, the perfect peace of the mind becomes a fact too. Thus, amidst change, difficulty, trial, sorrow, and uncertainty, it is the happy privilege of the man who has committed *all* to the disposal and government of his Lord, to enjoy hallowed serenity of soul. Sometimes this peace is violently invaded; but it is the work of an enemy, and a sure proof to the disturbed mind that it hath not yet attained, neither is already perfect.

With much agitation at first, and deep consciousness of unworthiness, I went to accomplish the service to which I was committed; but after a while I felt the perfect peace spoken of by the prophet; and as this book is avowedly an illustration of Providence in the life of an individual,

I feel under voluntary obligation to record the fact here. How unspeakably happy a man becomes, when he entirely excludes the idea of self-dependence, and self-wisdom, and with holy confidence casts himself and all his interests, for time and eternity, at the feet of his great Saviour! It is surely a foretaste of heaven. Entire passiveness, with the heart clinging to the Master's feet, and the ear open to catch His slightest word, to act, to rest, or to suffer, seems the very ideal of a happy faith, under the present economy. Who would not covet that state of mind which enables a man to say, I am ready to labour, to be bound, or to die, for the name of the Lord Jesus? Yet why is it not possessed by all who bear that "worthy name?" It was a fully recognised Christianity, as the embodiment of Divine love and truth, that enabled Paul to speak thus. Christianity has lost none of its original splendour, none of its original power, and none of its original attractions by the lapse of ages. Why, therefore, do not all who trust Paul's Saviour, and serve Paul's Lord, say so at this hour? "Because of temptations?" Had Paul none? What are the trials of modern Christians compared with his? What, especially, are they in this highly honoured and happy land, where liberty, peace, and light shed their united influence on palace and cottage, city and hamlet alike?

* * * * *

Three months after the correspondence named above, I preached my first sermons in Prelateston, as the unanimously elected and recognised pastor of the Church. I found the congregation, during my temporary visit, few in number compared with the great population of the town, and even with the capacity of the Chapel, though it was, and still is too small, and suffering all the inconveniences of a small Chapel in a populous neighbourhood.

Influences of an injurious character had also been at work for some time—influences having no relation to any question of morals, but still they were sufficiently powerful to call for great courage in the new pastor, and for united action on the part of the diminished Church, if lost ground was to be regained, and new ground acquired. The locality of the Chapel, the building itself, the unsatisfactory state of the congregation, and the influences to which I have alluded, were all seemingly against me. I hesitated for a considerable time before I determined to accept the invitation ; but the size of the town, the devotional spirit of the Church generally, and the conviction that it was *duty*, induced me to comply with the request. And though, so far as income is concerned, twice the amount received in the village, with a family, through the favour of God, doubled in number, in a wealthy and consequently expensive town, the change does not appear a remarkable improvement, yet as I care not for luxuries, and never coveted wealth, the change is in most respects beneficial ; and, above all, I have been permitted to see so many proofs of successful labour, that I have never for a moment doubted the propriety of the removal.

Before I refer to the feelings of my village flock on the occasion of my departure, and enter on a brief history of persons and events in connexion with my present charge, I would take this opportunity of saying that there is one thing very much needed, and the possession of which would, *I am certain*, greatly increase my usefulness—one thing for which I have hoped and longed for several years, but which, in consequence of the great expenses of property, cannot be realised, except by some manifestation of Providence, of which I know nothing as yet—that one thing is a *large, commodious, well-situated, and plain* CHAPEL, *with one-third* of its sittings entirely free for the use of the poor; and with *school rooms* attached, for the unsectarian, scriptural education of the children of the humbler classes. Could I see this, my heart would rejoice; I should feel that I have not lived altogether in vain; I should look upon all the past as blessed training for much future service; and as my health is good, habits simple, energies unimpaired, standing in the town all that a Christian minister need desire, and hope unabated, I should hail the event as a voice from Heaven, to proclaim with increasing fervour that grand old Gospel which is the eternal antagonist of Popery and Puseyism on the one hand, and of Infidelity and Rationalism on the other—fatal foes of man, which daily surround me, with their blighting and destructive agencies! The thought has occurred to me more than once, that perhaps *this hope*, too, shall be realised. How? I cannot answer. If it be for the honour of the Great Friend of man, and the good of my neighbours and their children—not to speak of following generations, when the hand that holds this pen shall have ceased to move— I hope, I think—nay, I go so far as to believe—that it will. Was it a mere play of the fancy, or a pleasant dream? the whisper of an angel passing by, or a faint foreshadowing of a coming reality? I know not; but the thought suddenly struck me, a few days since, that He in whose hand are all hearts, and to whom the silver and the gold belong, *may* put it into the heart of some steward of His, who shall read this volume, to consecrate as much of his gain to the Lord as shall enable me to realise this fondly cherished desire. Time will tell whether this thought was a prophetic intimation, or a mere wish, born of hope and fancy. I think it right, however, thus to relate the impression, assuring every reader who may be so far interested in the well-being of his fellow-men, and the diffusion of that Divine light which has already made Great Britain the most remarkable nation on the face of the earth, that it will afford me sincere pleasure to impart to him or her, confidentially, all the information and particulars which may be required.

When I determined to remove, I handed in a written resignation to my village flock. It did not take them altogether by surprise; but it tested the sincerity of their feelings, and gave me evidence, at once painful and agreeable, of their deep attachment to my person and ministry—painful because I felt it an act of violence to leave a simple-minded people who loved so tenderly—and agreeable, because the evidence of esteem, under such circumstances, is one of the gratifying rewards of faithful labour. There were tears shed and lamentations uttered, on that occasion; and when I bade them farewell, the Chapel was crowded to the doors and the ceiling with deeply affected hearers. The evening previous to our departure, my house was filled to a late hour with old and young, among whom were literally the lame and the blind, all testifying, some by tears, some by prayers and blessings, and some by little trinkets to my children, the interest they felt, and the regret they experienced in our departure. This parting scene would have looked simply ridiculous to the cold-hearted worldling; but I both felt and understood it. It was the result of cherished ties of the purest nature, of religious associations, hallowed scenes, and good communicated and received; it was a time of remembrance, on the part of some, of happy hours of benefit—and, of others, of calls and warnings neglected or slighted; and it was another illustration of the uncertainty of every thing in this ever-changing world. On the following morning early we undertook our journey, but the doors of the cottages were open, and many a final blessing, waving of hands and wiping of eyes, surrounded our path through the village. I could almost have returned, at that moment, to the house I had just left for ever, that I might live and die among my affectionate *first* flock; but, as that could not be, I was glad when I found myself seated in the train, which bore us rapidly away from the neighbourhood of poor, beautiful, romantic, and still-loved Willowfield.

It is vain to speculate upon non-existing circumstances, or to say what I might have been or done, had my lot in life been different. Had I possessed what is conventionally termed wealth, perhaps I should have remained in my rural home, enjoying the beauties of much-loved natural scenery, and ministering to the bodily and spiritual wants of my congregation; but perhaps, upon the other hand, those sympathies which personal experience evoke, would not have been so keen and sensitive as they are. Doubtless, it is well to struggle; and, bating imperfections, follies, and sins, I should submit to a similar course again, on condition of similar experience of an ever-working and most gracious Providence, who leads the blind by a way they know not, and establishes men in the truth by the sweeping hurricane, as well as by the milder action of the sunlight and the showers of the Christian dispensation.

My first care, in my new field of labour, was to examine narrowly the state of the Church, the peculiarities of its members, the tone of religious feeling, and the dispositions entertained by one member towards another. Upon the whole, the result of the examination was satisfactory; but there were two or three symptoms of personal coldness, and something like official jealousy, which required at once to be traced to their sources and rectified. When a Church is long without a pastor, it requires much wisdom and much mutual forbearance to keep the wheels moving smoothly; in this case, the pastorate had not been long vacant—indeed, I was the first and only minister whom the people had heard with a view to settlement; but the influences to which I have slightly referred already, had been in operation sometime before my predecessor's departure. It seems that one of the members had departed from the faith on an essential doctrine of the Christian revelation, and that excision was deemed a duty by the pastor and the majority of the Church; but, strange to say, a minority opposed this decision, on the ground that the errorist was an amiable and benevolent man, and that his error was merely one of judgment, not of heart. Two parties were consequently formed; and, as in all such cases, the original cause of division soon gathers to itself tributary streams, until a turbulent river is formed—so it was in this. No sooner had the pastor resigned, than the disaffected minority sought to re-open the question, and to recall to church privileges the member who had been cut off. In this, being a minority, they were of course unsuccessful; but as the affair was a thing with which I had nothing to do, I would not permit it to be re-examined under my presidency, having first ascertained from the man himself, that he put a negative upon one of the most positive doctrines of the Gospel. The result, however, was some slight division among the people, and a strong feeling of jealousy respecting one of the deacons on the part of the other three. Time, however, together with the action of the holy and humbling doctrines of the Cross, cured this; and I have long had as loving and harmonious deacons as ever helped the hands of a pastor, or aided a Church by their deliberations.

My next care was to look at the working of the Sunday school. The attendance of children was very good, but I found that the superintendent and teachers did not work with the greatest harmony. Mr. Self was a naturally strong-minded, but rather pompous and dictatorial personage. I was surprised to find that he never even consulted the teachers, but introduced his plans, changes, and alterations, without intimating his intention, and with a preposterous frequency which rendered successful labour in the school out of the question. Overweening convictions of his own importance was poor Self's rock-a-head. He was fond of office, and so ridiculously vain, that if his slightest dictum did not meet with instant obedience, he went off like a rocket. He once dictated to me an alteration in the mode of conducting the public service; and when I intimated that "every star shines best in its own orbit, and that if he would do his best for the school, I should do my best for the congregation," his egotism was terribly wounded—he threatened to throw up his office of superintendent, leave the Chapel, and go elsewhere. It was a pleasant riddance. One of the deacons suggested to me that I should express regret at his decision, and ask him to remain, as we should be sadly at a loss for a successor.

"What?" I said, "Mr. Mithall, would you have me do violence to truth? I do *not* regret Self's decision; and, so far from wishing him to remain, I hope he will go at once. The prosperity of the Sunday school is a greater thing to me than the foolish huffs of all the Selfs in the kingdom. And as regards the Sunday school, it will get on when he leaves, and no sooner. I have already determined on a suitable superintendent."

"Indeed, Sir? Who is that?" asked Mr. Mithall.

"It is a man who loves children, and Sunday schools,

is esteemed by all the teachers, and is not too proud to ask their advice in the conduct of the school."

"I am glad to hear it, Sir, but pray who—"

"A man that has my fullest confidence, and who, if I mistake not, will deserve it long."

"But, perhaps, the teachers—"

"Will be very glad to see him at their head. I have no fear of any objection to his appointment except it come from yourself; but I hope, to please me, you will forego any such feeling."

"Me, Sir? What objection can I have, if the gentleman be as well qualified as you say? Of course, I shall be glad of his appointment."

"You will start no objection?"

"Certainly not, Sir."

"Then it is *yourself*, my friend."

The worthy deacon coloured, then smiled, and at last said that he was "committed, fairly or unfairly he would not say."

The teachers unanimously solicited him to take the office of superintendent. He did so. His diligence, punctuality, and zeal are proverbial, and the school has prospered ever since. It is wise to have as close a connexion between the Sunday school and the Church as possible; and to secure that, were there no higher reason for it, try to have all your teachers members of the Church, and your superintendent, if possible, a deacon. This is a point I have kept in view for years, and I am more than ever convinced of its propriety. Let the dear little children feel that they are the adopted of the Church, and that Christian men, as such, care for them, and good must be done. I visit the school at least once a month, and deliver a plain address to the little ones, generally winding up with a few words to the teachers;

P

and, at the close of the address, we spend about three-quarters of an hour in prayer and praise.

My next object of solicitude was, the senior children of the school, and the young people of the congregation—those who think themselves too old or too wise to remain scholars any longer, and too young to be considered a regular part of the stated congregation. These young persons are at a very critical period of life; and, for that reason, should come peculiarly under the watchful care of the Church. Pondering what could be best done for them, I introduced two Bible classes—one for males, and one for females; taking them on alternate weeks, and conducting them entirely myself. Several of both sexes came, and pleasing instances of profitable instruction occurred. I did not see quite so many of the class of youths for whose benefit this labour was especially intended; but an advantage sprang from it which I had not anticipated. The Sabbath-school teachers came with gratifying regularity, and made the substance of the information they received material for instructing their Sunday scholars. Often have they thanked me for this aid, and as often have I felt gratified that a new and deeply interesting link was thus formed between the pastor and the dear little ones—the children, generally, of mechanics and the labouring poor.

I have also frequently delivered gratuitous lectures on profitable subjects in literature, evidences of Christianity, or history, during the winter months, to the young men and others of the town who chose to attend.

But, of course, the great scene of labour has been, and I hope ever shall be, the pulpit; and the great agent of successful labour, under the influence of the Spirit—the preaching of the everlasting Gospel. This is the theme, the power, the energy, by which the nations have seen astonishing moral and intellectual changes effected. It is "the power of God unto salvation to every one that believeth." It has demonstrated its divinity by its deeds, and raised up for itself millions of witnesses who unanimously declare that it came from and leads to God. But instead of these general declarations, which might be multiplied to any extent without the fear of contradiction, even from the most unscrupulous foe of Christianity who has any regard to his own reputation as a man somewhat acquainted with the history of nations, it will be better to produce one or two cases which have come under my own observation. It is true that the life of one man, at the longest, is but short, and that that portion of a man's life which is spent in public service is still shorter; but even the ministerial life of one who has been in any degree honoured of God, as a blessing to his fellow-men, will furnish instances sufficient to prove the position that the Gospel, in its fulness and integrity, is the sole and exclusive agency that successfully meets man at the point of his greatest wants and deepest woes. It is not ecclesiastical systems, not church ceremonies, not philosophical essays, not rationalism, not moral homilies, but the truth as it is in Jesus that softens and purifies the heart, wins the affections back to God, enlightens the understanding, and draws the man into that path which leads to "honour, immortality, and eternal life." I have *reasoned* with the ungodly and the sceptical, met their objections—intellectual, theoretical, and historical—and always silenced, but never, so far as I have ascertained, *thus* convinced any of them of the infinite value of the Gospel, except in one instance—and, even in this solitary case, the reasoning did not of itself accomplish the desired result; but it led the man, out of curiosity, to hear me, and whilst listening to those truths which stand out on the pages of the New Testament radiant with Divine lustre, he heard words whereby he was saved. His home, formerly the scene of filth, misery, and cruelty, became the home of peace, happiness, and love. Humility took the place of his Christ-opposing pride, and he proved the depth of his sincerity by urging his former infidel companions to attend the house of God.

Another case was that of a man of fifty years of age, who had heard the Gospel frequently, in different places and at different times; but his object in visiting Church or Chapel was to spend part of the day in comparative quiet, his own house offering no attractions of this kind. I had frequently noticed this man; but one Lord's-day evening, my subject being the love of Christ, his manner peculiarly attracted my attention. At the close of the service, he came into the vestry, desiring to speak with me. He sat down, and instead of speaking, burst into tears—tears which flowed freely and long. What followed, need not be repeated; but that man is now a member of the Church—earnest, devout, humble, and zealous. His very appearance is remarkably improved; and his once turbulent family sit with him in earnest attention every first day of the week, and his home, though humble, is orderly and peaceful. The infidel Sunday newspaper and noxious serial have been removed to make way for the Bible and the Christian magazine, and the man's temporal circumstances are greatly improved by his religious life.

I could select at least fifty cases, extending over the last fifteen years, which have come under my own eyes, in which old and young, rich and poor, grossly profane and boldly infidel, have become regenerated followers of Jesus Christ; and, in *every* instance, the acknowledgment was, that His Gospel was the power by which the heart was influenced and the conduct changed. Doubtless, many of my fellow-labourers in " this ministry " can furnish a still greater list ; but the point to be established is, " After that in the wisdom of God the world by wisdom knew not God, it pleased God by the foolishness of preaching to save them that believe. For the Jews require a sign, and the Greeks seek after wisdom: but we preach Christ crucified, unto the Jews a stumbling-block, and unto the Greeks foolishness; but unto them who are called, both Jews and Greeks, Christ the power of God, and the wisdom of God. Because the foolishness of God is wiser than men : and the weakness of God is stronger than men." "But," it is said, " Paul reasoned— shall we not reason with men?" "Yes," I reply, " reason with all the eloquence of Demosthenes, and all the demonstrative skill of Socrates; but if Paul be cited as a precedent, let Paul be honestly followed, for he " reasoned *out of the Scriptures,* opening and alleging that Christ must needs have suffered, and risen again from the dead."

The times that are passing over Europe and the world—the critical position of all religious systems and institutions—the unusual energy with which hostility to Revelation is inspired—the yearning anxiety of real Christians to draw nearer to one another, as if they had instinctive apprehension of a fearful storm—the rapidly multiplying omens that a crisis is imminent— the anxiety of governments, and the restlessness of nations everywhere—the doleful cries of war, famine, and pestilence—and the rapidly spreading belief among students of prophecy, that a new era hastens to accomplish the most wonderful changes over the face of the whole earth—*demand* fidelity, unwavering and earnest, in all the ministers and servants of the Lord Christ.   We have nothing but the Gospel of His grace and kingdom that can be of the slightest avail in " turning men from darkness to light, and from the power of Satan unto God, that they may receive forgiveness of sins, and inheritance among them who are sanctified by faith." Exclude this, and we have *nothing* left; no weapon, no armour, no argument, no hope! This is not the time either to engage the attention of men rushing on to judgment, with the childish ceremonies of an effete superstition, or to please their intellect by logical disquisitions on a Christless philosophy. The doctrine that began at Jerusalem, and not that borrowed from either Rome or Germany, will receive the effectual blessing. Woe be unto us if we preach not the Gospel! Our hearers will rise up against us in the day of Christ, and cover us with speechless confusion if we do not.

I have before stated my convictions on the subject of national ecclesiastical establishments with sufficient clearness; and the facility with which some of the worst errors of the Papacy have of late years clung to the English branch of this old tree, is one among many historical and contemporaneous proofs that they are unwise, unjust, unscriptural. But a man may denounce apostate nominal Protestantism, and laugh at the absurdity of a merely mechanical religion, whilst his own instructions are nothing better than the old error, which attempted to reconcile Christianity with a pagan philosophy. It is obvious that the ministry, if it would realise instrumentally the end for which it has been instituted, must be faithful to its high commission ; it must be " the ministry of reconciliation;" for otherwise it not only ceases to be what its distinguishing name imports, but it becomes a hindrance and an injury, a blight and not a blessing, to men. It is worse than nothing. A religious blank, if such a thing can be, is better than the systematic inculcation of false doctrine; for this latter, whilst claiming recognition as a message from the Lord, is an underground attack upon the Divine system, through which alone man can be reconciled to his God. This is the spirit of Antichrist—teaching in the name of the Redeemer doctrines upon which he Has set the mark of His displeasure. If this definition be correct, it will include in its sentence of condemnation many who have no written platform, and no practical sympathy with the grossest form of nominal Christianity now existing in the world. Whatever may be the name of his religious community, he opposes who does not co-operate with Christ. He who is not with Him is against Him; and he that gathereth not, scattereth abroad. There is no denominational safety, and no denominational guarantee of scriptural orthodoxy. A church is but the shadow of a sanctuary, not the thing itself. Hence, within the enclosure of the orthodox fold, errors as deleterious to the soul as arsenic to the body, may be administered by the professed servant of Him who "came to *save* men's lives." The folly of Ritualism must not blind our eyes to the danger of Rationalism. It is small consolation to the sufferer that he imbibed the poison in the company of a brotherhood removed to the greatest distance from Rome, rather than in that of Rome's nearest kindred. The Geneva gown may enrobe a blind guide as well as the Italian surplice. And, to pass to the other extreme, the man who denounces white, black, and grey, and pities the formalist for his gross conceptions of the spiritual and the invisible, may become so bewitched with his own ideal of intellectual ability, as to set up the goddess Reason in the place which belongs exclusively to Him who is the Wisdom of God. In a word, fact and history, together with the nature of the case, concur in proving, that there is no guarantee for the fidelity of the religious teacher, but in his *strict* adherence to the law and the testimony ; his rigid purpose to know nothing among men, as a religious teacher, but Christ, and Him crucified, and his settled determination to search the Scriptures daily, so that he may be able intelligently to proclaim *just what they contain.* " When nations," wrote a devout and true man,—

> " When nations are to perish in their sins,
> 'Tis in the Church the leprosy begins ;
> The priest, whose office is with zeal sincere
> To watch the fountain, and preserve it clear,
> Carelessly nods and sleeps upon the brink,
> While others poison what the flock must drink ;
> Or, waking at the call of lust alone,
> Infuses lies and errors of his own.
> His unsuspecting sheep believe it pure ;
> And, tainted by the very means of cure,
> Catch from each other a contagious spot,
> The foul forerunner of a general rot.
> Then Truth is hushed, that Heresy may preach ;
> And all is trash that Reason cannot reach ;
> Then God's own image on the soul impress'd,
> Becomes a mockery and a standing jest ;
> And faith, the root whence only can arise
> The graces of a life that wins the skies,
> Loses at once all value and esteem,
> Pronounced by greybeards a pernicious dream :
> Then Ceremony leads her bigots forth,
> Prepared to fight for shadows of no worth ;
> While truths, on which eternal things depend,
> Find not, or hardly find, a single friend :
> As soldiers watch the signal of command,
> They learn to bow, to kneel, to sit, to stand ;
> Happy to fill Religion's vacant place
> With hollow form, and gesture and grimace."

I foresee distinctly the reception which will be given to these remarks by different classes. Some will trace

them to " fanaticism;" others will denominate them
" cant;" and a third party will conclude that the writer
is "no philosopher." But these verdicts will neither
alter the facts of the case, nor break the force of an appeal
which conviction, founded on an acquaintance with painful reality, renders necessary. I think as I have written,
and under such impressions I began, and have continued
to this day, my humble ministry in this place. Again
and again I have been solicited to take part in political
movements, and to identify myself with projects involving
ecclesiastical controversy; but ever since my settlement in
Prelateston, I have uniformly refused. I think it is
superfluous to tell the reader that, in all religious and
educational matters, I am strictly and entirely a voluntary. The doctrines of Christ in the pulpit, and the law
of Christ as the motive-power of every effort to educate
the young and to save the adult, express my settled convictions on the questions to which they respectively refer.
And, on general politics, I go as far as any lover of
justice and humanity on the one hand, and law and
order on the other, can go. But it does not follow that
I should therefore stand on the polemical platform, or
shout from the hustings to an excited crowd. Hail to
the right and the true! And all honour to the men who,
believing these things to be their duty, nobly come forward to discharge it; but it is hardly fair to attribute
unworthy motives to the man who, whilst agreeing in
the desirableness of the end sought, feels that he is committed to another work, whose success he would not
willingly check by a voluntary act, which men not so
committed can do better than himself. Concentration of
effort, and division of labour, are two excellent maxims.
I have endeavoured to give my chief attention to the
pulpit; and slowly, but surely, the Chapel, which was

almost deserted when I came, was filled; and an amount of good has been accomplished which, under all the disadvantages already referred to, and others of a more private and personal nature, that need not be named, calls for fervent thanksgiving to the Father of lights, from whom every good and perfect gift cometh down. And it is a somewhat suggestive fact, that, in the Church and congregation, I can point to more than a dozen persons who have left the Establishment, and who are now not only professed voluntaries, but really anxious that everywhere the Church of Christ should be free from secular control. I do not know, certainly, that these persons would have remained in the Establishment, had I followed the course which I have avoided; but I do not believe one of them would have become a Dissenter had I done so. Nor do I mention this fact at all as a triumph; but still, possibly, there may be something like cause and effect in it; and, to my mind, it is one among many reasons which satisfy me that the rule, "This one thing I do," is both good and wise. Two of the gentlemen to whom I refer are the most liberal in the Church; they are ready to every good work, according to their ability; and the faith that is in them manifests itself by a life of consistent devotedness to that truth which is higher than systems, and to that Lord who is Head over all things to the Church, which is His body.

The circumstances which led to the secession of one of them, Mr. Potter, are worth relating; and, should any clergyman ever see the paragraph, it may suggest to him the propriety of prudence in speaking of neighbours, who, for aught he knows to the contrary, may be as anxious for the prosperity of truth as himself. Mr. and Mrs. Potter and their family had always attended the Established Church until about four years since, when Mrs.

Potter was afflicted with an illness, which caused her to keep her room for several months. When convalescence ensued, she wished to go to her usual place on the Sunday, but she was advised that the distance was too great for her strength. My Chapel being quite near their residence, it occurred to them both that, as a mere matter of convenience, there could not be much harm in going there for once. Accordingly, they did so; and finding that the short walk had not been injurious to his wife, Mr. Potter thought they might go again, until she should be restored sufficiently to attend their own Church. Perhaps they had been at Chapel ten or twelve times, when one day the teacher of the National School attached to their Church called on Mr. Potter for his annual subscription. The guinea was given as usual, " But," said Mr. Potter, as he handed it to the teacher, " I think I shall discontinue giving it. You need not call again."

" Indeed, Sir! Why?" asked the teacher.

" Because I am not satisfied with certain things which are taught in the school. I do not think they are quite scriptural."

" I, Sir! why, I wish to—"

" No, I don't blame you, but other parties; and it is from no desire to save the trifling subscription. I don't mean to save it, but to give it elsewhere."

The teacher reported the matter to the clergyman, and, the following evening, the Rev. Mr. Spalks visited the Potters. Kindly inquiring after their health, he said,

" I have missed you from Church for some time."

" I have been unwell for several months," said Mrs. Potter, " and since I got a little better, we have attended a place near our house."

" Your own Church is the nearest to your house, I
think," intimated Mr. Spalks.

" There is a Chapel quite near us," said Mr. Potter,
" and we have found it quite a privilege, in my dear
wife's weak state, to go there."

" A Chapel?" asked the clergyman, in a musing tone,
as if studying the geography of the town, " a Chapel!
I don't know any—Oh! you cannot mean that—no, of
course, you can't—that paltry schism shop;" and Mr.
Spalks laughed at his own cleverness.

" That *what*, Sir?" inquired the lady.

" O! I mean those heretic Dissenters, you know; it is
impossible, of course, for true Church-people to go among
them."

Now, Mr. Potter is a thorough man of business, and a
Christian, ready to do good to all men as he has opportunity, but he is not much read in theological controversy and theological terms, and at the time of this visit
he knew but little even of the first principles of Christianity; but it struck him that the terms " schism" and
" heretic" sounded harshly; and that, moreover, they
conveyed something very like a personal reflection on his
judgment; so with all modesty he said,

" I beg your pardon, Sir, I hope I have not done
wrong—"

" Yes, you have, Mr. Potter, wrong, very wrong, in
encouraging those people; they are the enemies of the
Church, and—"

" Sir, I am sorry to interrupt you in turn—I was
going to say, that I hope I have not done wrong in worshipping God among a people who are not heretics, if I
know what that means; and in hearing a minister whom
I like increasingly, and whose preaching has done us
both much good."

" It has, indeed," said Mrs. Potter.

" Well," said Mr. Spalks, rising with dignity to " the height of this great argument," and evincing his earnestness by his manner, " well, my friends, this is a severe trial to me, to see you both, with your interesting family, joining with persons who, but for the weakness of our laws, should not be tolerated; but as you, Mrs. Potter, were out of health, I shall say no more, only exact a promise that you will not, *on any account*, go there again. I shall expect to see you at Church next Sunday."

Neither of them replied, for as they both informed me afterwards, they were " so much surprised at being thus dealt with as children, and at being forbidden to enjoy religious liberty, that they could not speak."

The result is, that Mr. Spalks has not seen them since. Mr. and Mrs. Potter are both members of the Church under my pastoral care; and the illness, which was the occasion of suggesting a visit to the Chapel, is now looked back upon as one of those many providential blessings which come to men in unwelcome forms.

Let it not be supposed, however, that Mr. Spalks is the representative of all the clergy in the town and neighbourhood. Happily, he is not. There are two or three " district churches," the worshippers in which are blessed with the services of good and true men—men of understanding and heart, who, whilst they conscientiously think an Establishment a boon to the country, rejoice in the success of all evangelical denominations, and heartily give " the right hand" to all who love our great Lord and Saviour. With these clergymen I have the pleasure of being on terms of intimacy and friendship. In every good work, in which the absurd restrictions of the Establishment will allow co-operation, we cordially labour together, forgetting denomination in the feeling of a sacred brotherhood, and partizanship in the effort to promote the knowledge of salvation. The following conversation will illustrate the sentiments of these devoted men, and show—if it be necessary to bring an additional proof of a thing so obvious to every enlightened Christian—that there is real unity in the midst of visible diversity among all the disciples of the " One Lord."

The occasion was the anniversary of the local auxiliary to that eminently honoured institution, the British and Foreign Bible Society. The committee and speakers had been invited to dinner by the Chairman—a wealthy and benevolent gentleman, who was and is anxious to promote the best interests of men by placing in their hands the Revelation of God. There were present three clergymen of the Establishment, and two Dissenting ministers, of whom I was one. The conversation at table related, in the first instance, to missionary operations in foreign lands, and the harmonious action of the Society, on whose behalf we had assembled, with the Missionary Societies of various religious denominations. Several points, growing out of this well-known fact, were examined and freely discussed; and had an entire stranger been present, the idea that three different denominations were represented by the little company would not have occurred to him. Whilst walking about the elegantly furnished drawing-room after dinner, and conversing in little groups, waiting the hour at which the public meeting was to be held, one of the clergymen, the Rev. Charles Arbour, said to me, with a smile of genuine brotherly kindness, " I wish, my dear Sir, we were more closely united. I am sure we are one in heart, and one in all the great principles of our holy faith."

" And one, you might have added," said I, " in the desire to bring the whole of our fallen race to Christ, the only Saviour, and the only Head of the Church. The desire for union, which you express, has been long felt by me; but how to make it visible, otherwise than by co-operation where we can, and kind feelings and generous words always, I know not. Those who think as I do, cannot conform; and you, dear Sir, and many like you, who feel the fetters of your system holding you back when you would embrace brethren not within your denominational fold, will not secede."

"Say, rather, that we cannot secede," said Mr. Arbour. "Not because 'once a priest always a priest,' but because we as firmly believe in the propriety of an Establishment, as you do in the duty of Nonconformity. What I wish to see is a reform of the liturgy, the removal of those errors which time has introduced, and such alterations in the general machinery of our Church as would obviate the objections of evangelical Dissenters and bring them into union with us."

"Well," I said, "I cannot but admire the feeling which dictates your wish, but I fear I must utter a very sectarian-looking opinion—"

"Which is?"

"That your wish cannot be realised without such an alteration in the Establishment that you would not know it as the Church of your fathers; and that, though the reforms you desire—and which I, for the sake of conscientious clergymen, desire too—were all conceded by the secular authority, still Dissenters, as a body, would refuse to conform."

"But is not that bigotry?"

"No; not in the case of those to whom I refer. That there are multitudes who are Dissenters just because their fathers were, and that there are also very many who object to the State Church—"

" Say, ' National Church,' " said Mr. Arbour, smiling.

" To please you, I shall; but if it were, we should not be talking about Dissenters. That there are many who object to the National Church, not as an institution, but simply as a corrupt one, I know; and perhaps, by the introduction of an extensive reformation, you might secure them; but there remain all those who, like myself, think the principle unsound, and who would not join a State Church, though its machinery and working were both as perfect as the united wisdom of Queen, lords, and commons could make them."

" Are there really any considerable number of Dissenters who think thus? "

" Indeed there are, Sir."

" But is not this a modern doctrine? "

" I admit it, generally speaking; but would you condemn it on that account? "

" No, not exclusively," he replied; " but if the evils, which gave rise to the conviction in the minds of good men long ago that it was their duty to dissent, were all removed, I see not why a real union might not be effected between all who hold the Head."

" That is to say, we should remain Nonconformists only so long as certain grave errors attach to the National Establishment; or, in other words, make the opinions of our religious ancestors ours, and be guided solely by them. My dear Sir, where would this principle conduct us? "

" Ah! hold, brother," said my friend, " I see you have the best of it. But you will be too merciful to push me in a corner. But what are we to do? Union is so desirable in these days of conflict and reproach, and, more than that, it is such an obvious Christian duty, that we should be ready to make any sacrifice for it."

" Most true, Mr. Arbour.   As to what we are to do, 'Let us love one another: for love is of God; and every one that loveth is born of God, and knoweth God:'—We can do that.   Let all bitterness, and wrath, and anger, and clamour, and evil-speaking, be put away from us, with all malice; and let us be kind one to another, tender-hearted, forgiving one another, even as God for Christ's sake hath forgiven us:—We can do that.   Let us seek every opportunity of cultivating friendship:—We can do that.   Let us prove to the Argus-eyed world that the things which divide us belong to *it*, and that the things which unite us belong to our *common faith*:—We can do that.   Let us distinguish, in our sermons, speeches, and conversation, between men and systems, and especially between conscientious men and popular systems:—We can do that.   And let us meet on the recently-erected platform of the Evangelical Alliance, and there, in the presence of the public, speak of and to, and pray for, one another, until hearts shall be melted by the fire of Divine love, and the partitions of sect shall be rent by the hand of spiritual brotherhood, like the vail of the temple when our Divine Lord was crucified:—We can do that."

Mr. Arbour's eyes were full, and his hand was held out to grasp mine, as I ceased speaking.   The other two clergymen were standing by, arm in arm, listening. They, too, were deeply moved.

" What a glorious thing is Christianity!" exclaimed one of them.

" Talk of its evidences here!" remarked the other.

" As to the evidences of Christianity," said Mr. Arbour, " I am afraid Christians themselves have caused the need of works on that subject.   Had they followed the direction of the Master, and cultivated the spirit of the

system, the world would not have cried, 'Give us proof!'
Had they continued the practice which led to the remark,
'See how these Christians love one another!' volumes
on evidences could scarcely have been required."

"We are all to blame," said the gentleman whose
reference to the "evidences" had called forth these
remarks.

"And I shall not be behind you in confession," I
said. "We *are all to blame*.   And I hope the time is near
when we shall honour ourselves by mutual confession,
according to the direction of James—'Confess your faults
one to another;' and honour our Lord by mutual affection, according to his test of brotherhood—'By this shall
all men know that ye are my disciples, if ye have love
one to another.' I hope *that* time is near; and I, for one,
shall not willingly retard its advent."

"Nor shall we," said Mr. Arbour, speaking for himself and his brethren; a promise to which they willingly
committed themselves.

It is almost needless to say that our public meeting
was one of harmony, love, and hope. The spirit that
animated the speakers inspired the audience, and all felt
that, in the presence of the Bible, we were lifted above
meeting-house and cathedral, sect and party, and stood on
the sublime heights of that mount of vision which Divine
faith climbs when she anticipates the glorious future.

"To blame." Yes.   And where is the sect, or party,
or denomination, that is not blameworthy? All are verily
guilty before God.   And there is no excuse.   Churchman and Dissenter, Episcopalian, Presbyterian, Congre-
gationalist, Wesleyan Methodist, Moravian, Quaker, all
have sinned.   All have imbibed the spirit of a cold sectarianism, to a degree at once inconsistent with Christian
charity and Christian power in diffusing saving truth

among the nations of the world. Each sect, whilst commendably jealous of the truth, has gratuitously assumed that *it* is the depository of the whole truth, and that all others are right so far only as they hold truths in common with it. The point of divergence is the symbol of error. Truths in common are generally admitted; but then, in every *other* sect, they are so encumbered with fallacies that their power is neutralised. The difference is magnified and exaggerated, but the telescope is reversed when the point of harmony is inspected. And the spirit of the body is ingenious in the invention of motives—family considerations, or self-interest, or the fear of singularity, or wilful rejection of the truth, keeps the man in connexion with *that* system. It must be so. How otherwise can you account for the fact, that a person of such intelligence, and even seeming sincerity, remains where he is?

"I am a Churchman; and, of course, every loyal subject should be. Dissent is founded on ignorance, error, and disloyalty. Every one knows that the primitive Churches were episcopally ruled and governed. The Church of Rome, with all its mistakes, is right in this respect. Our own Church is the purest and most scriptural on the face of the earth. I pity those who have left her bosom. She is the bulwark of Protestantism, and the glory of the land. Without her, the nation would sink in infidelity, or go back to barbarism. I dislike persecution—but, for the sake of the souls of those perishing wanderers, I think they should be compelled to come in."

"Every man of education knows that Presbyterianism is the divinely appointed mode of church government. All the first ministers of the Gospel were presbyters, and every Church had its ruling elders.

Post-apostolic history proves this, even to demonstration. It has never been disputed, except by those who had a cause to serve. Diocesan episcopacy is an invention of Antichrist, and England's black prelacy is the eldest daughter of the mother of harlots. This is well known; but the prelates and the clergy of that rich hierarchy wilfully shut their eyes to the glaring proof, because they are so much in love with the pomp and pageantry of this vain world And as to Congregationalism, it is no system at all; a mere rope of sand—an aggregate of particles without cohesion—a brotherhood without a creed, without symbol, and without government; for, where all are rulers, there is nobody to be ruled except the poor parson, who crowns the farce by dubbing himself 'Independent!'"

"It is certainly extraordinary that Christian men, who have the New Testament in their hands, and especially those among them who make the early history of the Christian Church their study, should fail to see that in its best and purest days every Church was self-governing, strictly Congregational, and of course entirely independent of those that were without. For no other system is there the shadow of proof; indeed, all the evidence goes the other way. So irresistible is this fact, that candid Episcopalians and Presbyterians have been compelled to acknowledge that Churches did not interfere with each other's internal management; that the New Testament bishop was strictly the pastor of the Church; that all pastors were equals; that pastor, bishop, and elder are in fact synonymous terms, designating the same office; and that bishops and deacons are the only orders of officers known to the Apostles of our Lord."

"What a fearful state the Church of England and the various Dissenting sects were in, when the blessed Wesley arose! The rapidity with which Wesleyanism has covered the land, can be accounted for only by the fact, that it is in exact conformity with the apostolic plan. The Apostles were circuit preachers, and called out the pious and gifted men of the society as local preachers. The Wesleyan system is the apostolic restored, and this is quite enough, together with its purely apostolic doctrine and discipline, to account for its extraordinary success, at which the ignorant and the indolent have wondered so much. Indeed, it is clear, that the system thus restored to Christendom by the immortal and blessed founder of our society, is destined to become universal."

" Fearfully have all other bodies departed from the faith once delivered to the saints; but the Church of the United Brethren traces its descent from the holy Apostles to this hour, in an unbroken line of succession. Combining, as it does, the episcopal, the fraternal, and the missionary elements, it stands forth before the world an unostentatious but a living and truthful representative of the primitive Church."

" Absurd! to sprinkle a few drops of water on an unconscious babe, and then to call the poor little crying thing baptised! It is a solemn, or rather an impious, mockery of the Divine ordinance. No wonder we have infidels! It has been satisfactorily shown that this rampant heresy lies at the root of all the errors of Christendom. Simple-minded believers, who cannot open their Testaments without seeing that Christ was baptised by immersion, and that all the primitive believers were thus baptised on a profession of their faith, have often expressed surprise that intelligent Pædobaptists do not see the same thing. They *do* see it! They cannot help seeing it; but they stifle their consciences rather than give up the popular delusion!"

" The Steeple-house people and the Dissenters have not very much to choose between them. They are mostly—it is to be lamented—in darkness, not having the inward light. But while they carnally read our Saviour's words, we, as Friends, must remain faithful to our testimony."

Such is a fair report of the Voices of the Sects, only it is mildness itself, compared with the asperity in which the controversialists of the last age delighted; and if they were wild on ecclesiastical government, they became perfectly furious when Christian doctrine was the subject. It is difficult to realise, in these days of civilised literature and growing charity, the tempests of passionate invective in which they disported. I intended to have given a specimen or two, from the controversial works of last century, exhibiting the choice strains in which Calvinists and Arminians sang each other's praises; but I find it impossible to cite even a short passage without polluting these pages, and as I am anxious that they shall, at least, have the merit of purity, I have altered my purpose. Let the abomination sleep, and may the branches of the Christian Church never again be hurled into such wrathful collision.

A nobler spirit has visited the Churches generally. Better days have dawned. There are still to be found men of the old stamp—fire-and-faggot men—representatives and descendants of the thumb-screw and rack school, who would argue for their gospel in the logic of the two alternatives—submission or death. But their number is limited, and their power is utterly gone. Of the facts of the great world they know little; of the lessons of Christianity, nothing; yet they linger among us as shadows of the huge incarnations of fanaticism that once trampled on the liberties, and traded in the lives, of saints, under the miserable delusion that they were doing God service; or as the fossils of ecclesiastical geology, which remind us that if there were " giants," there were also monsters in those days.

Whatever be the cause, it is certain that such dictatorial infallibles have few apologists now. The majority of Christians of the several denominations exhibit less of the Ishmael, year after year. Perhaps one of the causes is to be found in the grand catholic efforts of modern times to aggregate Christian strength for benevolent and missionary objects. The missionary spirit has been the greatest discoverer of the present century. It has laid open the condition of humanity over the whole earth, and so touched the springs of Christian hearts in Great Britain and America, that " the disciples, every man according to his ability, have determined to send relief to " those who are perishing in ignorance of the true God and of His Son Jesus Christ. Even denominational effort for this purpose has exerted a beneficial influence; but the great meeting, representing the several sections of Protestantism, and having for its ultimate object, not the proclamation of forms of Church government, but the universal dissemination of the doctrine of salvation through the redemption that is in Christ Jesus, has necessarily tended to suggest to the minds of Christians the immeasurable superiority of their position over that of the worshippers of idols, and the holy privileges which they enjoy in common, notwithstanding visible diversity. It is impossible for Christian men, as such, to be drawn together for any object worthy of the name they all bear, without having their mutual mistakes and their mutual jealousies, to a great degree, removed. Thrown into each other's company, they feel the sacred and uniting influence of brotherly love drawing heart to heart. This is part of the reward of their associated labours for a common end. Missionary, Bible, and Tract Society meetings are conspicuous targets for the shafts and small shot of cynics and gentlemen who live by their wits, for they can indulge in the laugh-general, without running the risk of deeply wounding any person in particular; and no friend of these Societies wishes to interfere with their very harmless sport. The man who considers Christianity much the same as geography, and with whom the Church is confined to a brotherhood of clerics, holding his own particular *ism*, may see great danger in these manifestations of catholicity. With palpitating heart, and an ominous shadow on his brow, he may exclaim, " The Church is in danger !" but he goes without sympathy, and his cry of apprehension scarcely elicits the poor condolence of a solitary echo. The rigid sectary, too, who has elevated a single doctrine of the Gospel to the loftiest niche in the Christian temple, and whose grasp of his *ism* is tenacious in the ratio of the smallness of his sect, may mourn over the " latitudinarianism" of these latter days; but the secret of his affliction is so obvious, that any one may prescribe a grain of charity without much danger of administering the wrong medicine. But those whose faith stands in the power of God, and whose hearts have been warmed in the presence of incarnate Love— whilst they know that the Church is *not* in danger, and that the worthy " Hyper" has fallen into the slight mistake of supposing a part equal to the whole—rejoice in such occasions of meeting with their brethren, that they may interchange sentiments of Christian courtesy, and intermingle feelings of gratitude around *that* Name which they wish to fall upon every human ear.

Voluntary Christian Union is the most beautiful thing in the world.

> " 'Tis pleasant as the morning dews,
>   That fall on Zion's hill;
> Where God His mildest glory shows,
>   And makes His grace distil."

It is the beauty of intelligence and affection blending together in the presence of an unseen LORD. It is a virtual declaration to every spectator that the Gospel is the Catholicon for rent and torn humanity. It is the voice of a fact powerful enough to answer all the objections of anti-scriptural theories. It is the law of attraction operating in the very highest region—the region of thought and conviction. It is a spontaneous avowal that all the disciples of the Supreme Prophet are animated by "One Spirit." It is a testimony to the world that its woes and wars come not from the mysterious decrees of the Sovereign, but from a different source. And it is an undesigned prophecy that the Babelisms of men shall shortly be healed by the consummated act, of which the miracle of Pentecost was but the beginning and the pledge.

It is melancholy to reflect how Christian men misunderstand each other, in consequence of that jealousy which keeps them apart, and of that sectarianism which assumes that Truth has taken up her dwelling with it, and that she has no palace in the world elsewhere. I shall here relate an illustrative anecdote. Some years ago, a clergyman had business in the town, in which he could not succeed without co-operation. What that business was, matters not. His object, at all events, was one in which I could not fully sympathise, nor, though I saw the bills announcing the meeting he wished to hold, did I give it a second thought, for I had no intention to attend where I did not feel decided interest in the movement. The thing was too sectarian to secure my sympathy; and although I was not so weak as to fancy that this could be a matter

Q

of any consequence, yet as the most obscure Englishman has a right to his own sentiments, the consciousness of limited influence did not amount to the same thing as seeming to approve a Society, whose constitution I disliked, by attending the proposed meeting. On the afternoon of the day, in the evening of which the meeting was to be held, a card was handed to me, and the reverend gentleman whose name it bore was invited to " walk in." I confess this visit took me by surprise. What could Mr. ——, the agent and representative of an exclusively High-church Society, want with *me*, a Dissenter, and " a poor fellow of Jesus College, in the university of Christianity?" I begged my clerical visitor to be seated, and, by way of saying something, as it was evident from his manner that stress of weather had driven him into *this* harbour, I remarked that I had seen his name on the placards announcing a meeting of the —— Society.

" Yes, Sir," said he, " and I fear the meeting will be but small. I understand there are other meetings in the town this evening."

" Has the thing been sufficiently made known, Sir?" I inquired.

Visitor—" It was put on some of the Church doors."

Myself—" Why not on the doors of Chapels as well? For if it be a thing in which Christians of one sect should engage, as Christians, of course Christians of other sects might be invited to co-operate."

Visitor—" No, Sir, it is not connected with *any sect*. The Committee belong to the National Church."

Myself—" O, indeed, Sir; I know that the Society is supported by friends belonging to the Establishment; but—pardon my seeming rudeness—I included it among the sects, though in no offensive sense, I assure you."

Visitor—" O! yes, Sir; well, I have called to ask if

you will favour me by coming on the platform this evening, and taking a resolution. We shall feel very much obliged to you, indeed."

Myself—"It is very painful to me to refuse any such request, Sir, especially from a stranger; but, with the greatest respect for you, I shall be compelled to decline attending."

Visitor—"I am sorry for that, Sir. Can I remove your objections? You are a thorough-going Protestant, I suppose."

Myself—"Undoubtedly, as much so as any gentleman belonging to your own Church; but then, you know, we differ, probably, as to the best way of treating the points of controversy between Roman Catholics and Protestants. I would remove prejudice from the minds of the former, by uniform gentleness in speaking of them; and I would attract them to us by the exhibition of that unity which ought to subsist among all Protestant Churches, without the dead uniformity which the Roman Catholic is in the habit of praising as the exclusive glory of his Church."

Visitor—"Very excellent, indeed—a suggestion of great value—but how to get the people back is the difficulty."

Myself—"Back, Sir? I fear I misunderstand you. My idea was, that we should all teach the people to forget the past, and to go forward to a more excellent thing."

Visitor—"Ah! ahem! I mean, back to the unity of the Church."

Myself—"That is to say—"

Visitor—"I meant uniformity, but perhaps you were thinking of something else."

Myself—"My hope is that Protestant Christians will prove their essential unity, while they maintain their distinctive principles; and that they will be one in heart, and one in Christ, while they obey the dictates of judgment respecting opinions which are neither essential to salvation, nor hindrances to co-operation in every good work."

Visitor—" Sir, I am glad I have called on you. I have been somewhat deceived, by those who told me you were sure to attend the meeting; but agreeably disappointed in the charity of your sentiments."

Myself—" Why, Sir, some Churchmen do not understand the principles of Dissenters. Tell me now, honestly, what you thought of us."

Visitor—" I shall offend if I speak the truth."

Myself—" You can offend only by a contrary course."

Visitor—" Well, I thought you all wished to destroy the Church."

Myself—" Then you gave us credit for being half savage, half infidel."

Visitor—(Laughing.) " Something like it."

Myself—" Then be assured, my dear Sir, that we are not infidels, and that we hardly esteem it a compliment to be suspected of barbarity."

Visitor—"I have been terribly deceived! Everybody says that you Dissenters wish to destroy the Church, if the Government does not give you a portion of her revenues, and—"

Myself—" That will do at present, before you enumerate other absurd, malicious, or ignorant charges—for, practically, it matters little which of the three is their source. Instead of wishing to destroy the Church, we wish to purify and save her. All we wish to destroy is the golden chain which binds her to the State, and makes her the slave of politicians while they promise her liberty.*

---

* As this volume may meet the eye of some who have formed no nobler idea of the work of Nonconformists than that which was entertained by my reverend visitor, I beg to say that the great end and aim of all religious Dissenters is conservative, not destructive. They wish to preserve and invigorate the religious life of the community, and to circulate over

As for coveting a share in ecclesiastical revenues, the babe weaned from the breast might see, that if that is our object, we are seeking it by the most clumsy method that even insanity could dictate. Surely, if I wished patronage, I would try to please the patron; and if I longed for a living, I would humbly seek fellowship with the system which has livings to give."

Visitor—" But it is said, by some parties, that you anticipate the time when Government will yield to the force of what is called popular opinion, and—"

Myself—" We are highly honoured, truly! That is to say, in old-fashioned Saxon, it is thought that we are playing the hypocrite, and longing for the time when a State bribe shall tickle our hands, and reduce our sweet voices to the melody—' We have no king but Cæsar.' My dear Sir, you don't know the descendants of the Puritans."

the land, and over the world, the GOSPEL, with its laws, its light, and its freedom. They wish to remove everything that prevents the Word of God having "free course." Many of them, but not all, think the union of Church and State *one* of those obstructions; and for *that* reason they would dissolve it. In loyalty to the throne they cannot be surpassed; but, in the great matter of religion, they desire that all should be subject to Christ. *Positive* truth is their object. To build up, on the true foundation, is their chief work. The State-church question is only one of many, and it does not rank in the first, nor in the second, nor even in the third rate class. The purity of the Churches, missionary work, efficient pulpits, education, social morality, truth, righteousness, salvation—*these* form the grand ends of their labour.

Dr. John Campbell is supposed by many to possess a representative character. If so, I presume it arises chiefly from the fact that he speaks the sentiments of many, whilst uttering his own well-formed judgment. He waves his BANNER; but it is for literature, liberty, humanity, and religion—not violence or destruction: and he bears WITNESS; but it is to the Gospel of love, purity, and brotherhood. Power, decision, charity, are remarkably united in the oracle of Bolt-Court.

It is really surprising, at this hour of the day, to find educated Churchmen so utterly ignorant of the character of Nonconformity!

Visitor—"I am greatly gratified that I have had the pleasure of meeting you, Sir,—although I confess I came with reluctance; and if you will only come to the meeting this evening, I promise you I shall never forget this interview."

Myself—"I have an engagement at the hour at which you begin; after that I shall look in; but I cannot ascend the platform, for the reason I have already mentioned. I wish you every blessing."

Visitor—"Good evening, dear Sir, I shall often think of you. Good evening!"

The meeting was announced for seven o'clock. I had to visit a beautiful young female on the borders of eternity, from the power of that scourge of the loveliest portions of our race,—fell consumption. My heart was chastened and afflicted by the rapid decay of the amiable sufferer, but cheered by the unquestioning faith she had in her faithful Saviour. After bidding her farewell for, as I anticipated, the last time, I went to the public room in which my clerical friend held his meeting. And I shall find it difficult to forget the ridiculous picture presented by that meeting. There were about a dozen chairs on the platform. In the centre sat the Chairman, a respectable barrister, well known to me. On his right sat the clerical visitor of the afternoon. There were about a hundred chairs and five-and-twenty forms in the body of the hall. These, together with two old ladies, a man on crutches, and a little boy, composed the entire assembly. I entered the hall, but no sooner had my eye taken in this ludicrous scene than I withdrew, and who will blame, if I confess to something very like a hearty laugh?

"What's going on here?" asked an acquaintance of mine, a worthy member of the Society of Friends, whom I met in the street.

" A Quaker's meeting," I replied.

" Ah," said he, " none of thy drolleries!"

" Well, go in," said I, " and if you hear a word spoken, I shall say it is *not* a Quaker's meeting. That's all."

My friend ran up stairs. I waited his return. He was soon by my side, when he said, " No, it is not a Quaker's meeting, according to thy idea of that, for the Chairman has announced an adjournment."

" O, then, I must beg forgiveness," said I.

The object for which I have introduced this anecdote will be realised, if it illustrate the remark, that good men fall into serious mistakes regarding the opinions of others, in consequence of ignorance and non-association. The prevalent idea is, that unity and uniformity are one and the same thing. Now, so far from this being the case, either of them may exist without the other. So far from being identical, they are not even mutually related. There may be unity without uniformity, and uniformity without unity. Unity is the result of principle and conviction. Uniformity may be the result of system, of law, or of dictation, where there is no mutual attraction, and no internal influence causing adhesion. Rome and State-churchism seek uniformity; Religion and Freedom tend to unity. Law shapes uniformity, which it may obtain instead of life. Gospel creates life, and realises unity. Real unity is a thing of living love. External conformity to a given standard, is no proof of inward vitality. There is great uniformity in the grave; but the living, if they enjoy liberty, seldom show it; and if they do not enjoy liberty, it is only the symbol of bondage. Let men think freely, without any standard but the Bible, and the more they reverence its oracles, and love Him, of whom they speak, the more will they be drawn together. But if they do not reverence the truth of God, and believe in the Saviour whom He has sent, to ask them, under the terror of penalty, to say the same thing, and to utter the same creed, is an insult to reason, a mockery of religion, and a violation of liberty. If Christians differ, let it be on their own responsibility; but let no Church, no minister, no law, compel them to differ by erecting an exclusive hierarchy, or proclaiming an infallible dogma. Let not the children of the same family be compelled to be of the same stature, and to wear exactly similar garments. Let them all love their brethren and their heavenly Father; but let it be *love*—spontaneous, free, unbought, uncompelled, earnest, sincere, and intelligent! Let no secondary motive intrude. Let no voice of man be heard in the recesses of the heart; and let no external influence check the rising incense of a grateful soul.

And what a mighty impulse this unity without uniformity would give to the action of the Christian Church! She has a great and honourable work to perform—a truth to proclaim to the ends of the earth—a noble testimony to bear for the honour of the Lord of all—a protest to issue against the errors of the nations— a cry to raise as the herald of the coming Prince—a rugged wilderness over which to shout, " Prepare ye the way of the King!"—and a Gospel of reconciliation to preach in all the languages of the world. How surprisingly would her strength be increased, her spirit cheered, and her hope animated, if she felt the joy of unity without the fetters of uniformity! All the sections of the brotherhood of faith have work—work the most blessed in which creatures can engage; let them all have peace among themselves, that they may do it without distraction. Let them not have to stop repeatedly to settle party disputes, when a world lies before them to be conquered in the name of their King. Let not the enemy have occasion to mock because of their family disputes; let not the regiments of the hosts of the Lord make themselves ridiculous in the eyes of on-lookers, who neither understand their true character, nor appreciate the sublimity of the enterprise to which the Lord of Hosts has called them. Let them be all of one mind, having compassion one of another—let them love as brethren—let them be pitiful and courteous, not rendering evil for evil, or railing for railing, but, contrariwise, blessing, knowing that they are thereunto called, that they might inherit a blessing. Let them ponder the holy oracle, which speaketh in this wise:—"For as the body is one, and hath many members, and all the members of that one body, being many, are one body, so also is Christ. For by one Spirit are we all baptised into one body, whether we be Jews or Gentiles, whether we be bond or free, and have been all made to drink into one Spirit. For the body is not one member, but many. If the foot shall say, Because I am not the hand, I am not of the body; is it therefore not of the body? And if the ear shall say, Because I am not the eye, I am not of the body; is it therefore not of the body? If the whole body were an eye, where were the hearing? If the whole were hearing, where were the smelling? But now hath God set the members every one of them in the body, as it hath pleased Him. And if they were all one member, where were the body? But now are they many members, yet one body. And the eye cannot say unto the hand, I have no need of thee: nor again the head to the feet, I have no need of you. Nay, much more those members of the body, which seem to be more feeble, are necessary. And those members of the body which we think to be less honourable, upon these we bestow more abundant honour; and our uncomely parts have more abundant comeliness. For our

comely parts have no need: but God hath tempered the
body together, having given more abundant honour to
that part which lacked: that there should be no schism
in the body; but that the members should have the same
care one for another. And whether one member suffer,
all the members suffer with it; or one member be
honoured, all the members rejoice with it. Now ye are
the body of Christ, and members in particular. And God
hath set some in the Church, first apostles, secondarily
prophets, thirdly teachers, after that miracles, then gifts
of healings, helps, governments, diversities of tongues.
Are all apostles? Are all prophets? Are all teachers?
Are all workers of miracles? Have all the gifts of healing? Do all speak with tongues? Do all interpret?
But covet earnestly the best gifts: and yet show I unto
you a more excellent way. Though I speak with the
tongues of men and of angels, and have not charity, I am
become as sounding brass or a tinkling cymbal. And
though I have the gift of prophecy, and understand all
mysteries, and all knowledge; and though I have all
faith, so that I could remove mountains, and have not
charity, I am nothing. And though I bestow all my
goods to feed the poor, and though I give my body
to be burned, and have not charity, it profiteth me
nothing. Charity suffereth long, and is kind; charity
envieth not; charity vaunteth not itself, is not puffed
up, doth not behave itself unseemly, seeketh not
her own, is not easily provoked, thinketh no evil;
rejoiceth not in iniquity, but rejoiceth in the truth;
beareth all things, believeth all things, hopeth all things,
endureth all things. Charity never faileth: but whether
there be prophecies, they shall fail; whether there be
tongues, they shall cease; whether there be knowledge,
it shall vanish away. For we know in part, and we

prophesy in part. But when that which is perfect is come, then that which is in part shall be done away. When I was a child, I spake as a child, I understood as a child, I thought as a child: but when I became a man, I put away childish things. For now we see through a glass, darkly; but then, face to face: now I know in part; but then shall I know even as also I am known. And now abideth faith, hope, charity, these three; but the greatest of these is charity." "Let love be without dissimulation. Abhor that which is evil; cleave to that which is good. Be kindly affectioned one to another with brotherly love; in honour preferring one another; not slothful in business; fervent in spirit; serving the Lord; rejoicing in hope; patient in tribulation; continuing instant in prayer; distributing to the necessity of saints; given to hospitality. Bless them who persecute you: bless, and curse not. Rejoice with them that do rejoice, and weep with them that weep. Be of the same mind one toward another. Mind not high things, but condescend to men of low estate. Be not wise in your own conceits. Recompense to no man evil for evil. Provide things honest in the sight of all men. If it be possible, as much as lieth in you, live peaceably with all men. Dearly beloved, avenge not yourselves, but rather give place unto wrath: for it is written, Vengeance is mine; I will repay, saith the Lord. Therefore, if thine enemy hunger, feed him; if he thirst, give him drink: for in so doing thou shalt heap coals of fire on his head. Be not overcome of evil, but overcome evil with good."

Thus speaketh a Book whose Author is Divine, whose genius is charity, whose doctrines are unchangeable, and whose precepts are binding on all who profess to hold the Head. "WHOSO READETH, LET HIM UNDERSTAND."

CONCLUSION.

THE PAST AND THE FUTURE.

"Where burns the loved hearth brightest,
    Cheering the social breast?
Where beats the fond heart lightest,
    Its humble hopes possest?
Where is the smile of sadness,
    Of meek-eyed patience born,
Worth more than those of gladness,
    Which mirth's bright cheek adorn?
Pleasure is marked by fleetness,
    To those who ever roam,
While grief itself has sweetness,
    At home, dear home!"—*Barton*.

INFLUENCE OF TROUBLE ON DIFFERENT MINDS — LESSONS I HAVE LEARNED DURING LIFE—NO MAN ABLE TO JUDGE BEFOREHAND WHAT IS BEST FOR HIM—HAPPINESS THE RESULT OF PRINCIPLE —CONTENTMENT—CONSTANT EMPLOYMENT—HUMAN NECESSITIES MET — CHRISTIANITY A DOMESTIC AND PHYSICAL BLESSING — INTELLECT AND THE GOSPEL—THE FUTURE—THE CHURCH A SOCIAL HOME — A HOME IN THE HEART — A HOME IN HEAVEN— FAREWELL!

OCCASIONAL troubles have great power over men accustomed to health and prosperity; they sink under them, become sickly, dispirited, and gloomy, and are ready to interpret every seemingly untoward circumstance into the most dismal reading, as if all the archers in the universe stood, with drawn bow and ready arrow pointing at them; while men who are used to the music of sighs, with the accompaniment of tears, scarcely believe in their personal identity when glimpses of prosperity and joy fall upon their path. I have known several men of both classes. I myself should belong to the last named, but for one remedial fact—the possession of an unyielding hope, which has held my head above water, even when wave followed wave with untiring rapidity. The PAST, as the reader sees by this time, although I have not told him the half, has taught me several important lessons. This is the appropriate place in which to enumerate these lessons, before I mention those hopes respecting the FUTURE, which are the balm of my spirit amidst the perplexing mysteries of humanity, and bid a courteous farewell to those who have patiently listened to my narrative.

First.—I have learned that no man is able to judge, before the event, what is best for him. To borrow, and use metaphorically, a phrase from the lapsed science of astrology, from an early age I tried to construct a " horoscope " of my destiny. I schemed, planned, proposed; adopted *this*, and rejected *that*; endeavoured to draw the veil from the face of the future; and determined that no ordinary difficulty should check the course I wished to follow. Listening to the fallacious dreams of youthful poetry, I fancied a beautiful and happy future, a garden without a concealed serpent, a crystal lake without a sweeping hurricane. I had begun to *live*, after the almost lifeless existence of one of the feeblest of infancies, and found in imagination a new world, although, as will be remembered, its morbid action sometimes plunged me in great distress. But experience has taught me that all these efforts to anticipate the purposes of Divine Providence are worse than useless—worse, because they create a false idea of real life, and make trouble, when it comes, doubly painful to endure. That which we call disappointment, is only the thwarting of our plans, and the

setting aside of our ideas, to make room for the execution
of the designs of the Lord God, whose thoughts and ways
are above our thoughts and ways.   The moral discipline
through which it is necessary for a man to go, is never
taken into account by the youth who creates his own
future.   *That,* though of all things the most important,
is not an item in the aggregate of his intended experiences.   The best thing is left out of the list.   When
planning her voyage across the ocean of life, Fancy
omits the ballast; and were it not for the care of Him
whose "way is in the sea, and whose footsteps are
not known," the ship would inevitably founder.   "All
these things are against me!" is the natural cry of the
grief-stricken; but they are only intimations that our
pre-judgment of the best for us, was erroneous.   We
change our verdict when Time collects all the evidence,
and places it before us; and then, if we be loyal men—
loyal to the laws of the great King—we exclaim, "All
is well!   What hath God wrought!"   The impatient
boy thinks the order and discipline of his father's house
needlessly strict, and very irksome; he pants for liberty,
unconscious that his idea of liberty would speedily
entangle him in fetters from which his father's rule is
intended to preserve him; he wishes to be a man, whilst
utterly ignorant of the serious responsibilities which manhood involves; and he longs for the day when he shall
be his own master, not knowing that no man is capable
of ruling either himself or others, who has not first submitted to the rule and authority of parents or guardians.
So in our non-age, our anticipations of the future
are formed in the midst of entire ignorance of what is
best for us, and, consequently, were there not a Father
and a Guardian to correct our false notions, to shape
our course, and to hold us in by strong and merciful

law, we should plunge into one of the thousand pitfalls which Fancy saw not in her aërial flight. And now, how different the retrospect of the man of forty, from the prospect of the boy of fifteen! Yet, if different, it is better *for him.* I would not have it otherwise, excepting sin, folly, and infirmity. There has been ONE to care for me, though I have not seen Him; and the great object of early desire has been realised, though the scenes through which I have reached it, and the circumstances in the midst of which I have found it, were utterly unthought of.

Secondly.—I have learned that happiness is not the result of position but of gracious principle. The colour and shape of the world depend very much upon the state of the eye that views it. The miserable at heart see nothing but dark colours and wretchedness. Everything is wrong with such persons. The earth is a land of woe. All men are bad. Sorrow is universal. Joy is insanity. Repose is impossible. The curse is omnipresent. Suicide is wisdom. The grave is the only palace in this doomed world. Or, with the lovers of pleasure, gold is God. Broad acres are Paradise. Horses and hounds are angels. Wine is nectar. Power is life. Fame is heaven. Hold, brethren! Ye are all wrong! This world is not Pandemonium, though it sometimes looks like it to him who wars against its true Sovereign; and it is not Heaven, though the man who thinks that happiness consists in external possession fancies so. The eye that is connected with a pure heart sees things differently. Happiness must dwell within, or be an entire stranger. She is particular in choosing her residence, and nothing short of the human heart will please her taste; but when she is admitted there, she pays liberally for her lodgings, for she imparts colours of beauty to everything without, and turns into blessed prophecy even the darkest scenes of being. She enrobes the globe, hurrying to eternity with its load of dead, and dying, yet immortal humanity, with a mantle of Divine love, and enables the eye of the poor man to see all the beauties of nature, and his heart to enjoy them, as truly as if he were proprietor of the whole. The chosen home of happiness is the heart; and if it be reconciled to the blessed Father, through the Son, how large it becomes, and how are its powers of enjoyment strengthened! Appropriation of all that is good, and rejection of all that is evil, become intuitive then! The man may be very poor, his name unknown on the banker's books, and his person strange to the merchant-princes of the world; but the flowers of the field bloom, and the songs of the forest are warbled, for him. Under his feet, and around his path, lie the works, and over his head dwells the bright smile of a "reconciled God." He may be swimming against the stream, but the banks thereof are adorned with trees of *his* "LORD's planting." He may tremble at the face of a fellow-creature whose claim he cannot satisfy, but his conscience approves the principles he has adopted, and the oracle he believes whispers in his ear, "Light is sown for the righteous, and gladness for the upright in heart." Human praise may seldom greet him, but the desire to have a conscience void of offence towards God and man holds him up in the warfare of life. The nobles of the nation may not hail him in the street, but the visits of ministering angels make his humble dwelling one of the portals of heaven.

> " A languid, leaden iteration reigns,
> And ever must, o'er those whose joys are joys
> Of sight, smell, taste. The cuckoo-seasons sing
> The same dull note to such as nothing prize,

But what those seasons, from the teeming earth,
To doting sense indulge.   But nobler minds,
Which relish fruits unripened by the sun,
Make their days various, various as the dyes
On the dove's neck, which wanton in his rays.
On minds of dove-like innocence possessed,
On lightened minds that bask in virtue's beams
Nothing hangs tedious, nothing old revolves
In that for which they long, for which they live.
Their glorious efforts, winged with heavenly hope,
Each rising morning sees still higher rise;
Each bounteous dawn its novelty presents
To worth maturing, new strength, lustre, fame;
While Nature's circle, like a chariot-wheel
Rolling beneath their elevated aims,
Makes their fair prospect fairer every hour;
Advancing virtue in a line to bliss;
Virtue which Christian motives best inspire!
And bliss which Christian schemes alone ensure!"

Thirdly.—" I have learned, in whatsoever state I am, therewith to be content."   Why should I not?   Will impatience or murmuring mend my lot, or better my condition?   Or have I any right to quarrel with the arrangements of the Almighty?   I have merited nothing but His anger.   I am a tenant-at-will.   The Great Proprietor has undoubted authority over me.   He may withdraw the boon of being at any moment without premonition.   All things are His, and He giveth to every man severally as He will.   Times without number have I felt the keen pang of anguish, because I could not do as I would; but He who gave me principles knew that the ability and the will did not harmonise with each other.   I would, but could not; better this than to reverse the position of the verbs!   Believing, not in Chance but in Providence, not in self but in God, contentment is at once a duty and a joy.   " Bread and water" are promised.   These are enough to him who feels that they are more than he has merited.   Besides, when the claims of necessity are satisfied, to the demands of fashion or of luxury one may boldly say—"You are not named in the covenant!" Artificial wants may be supplied by opulence, which demands payment for its wares in the shape of artificial diseases; but the requirements of nature are instinctively limited to that which is beneficial to health. And, rising above that which is merely personal, whilst I have frequently desired to strengthen the hands of benevolence and charity, and lamented the inability which prevented the gratification of that desire, yet here, too, the wonderful Book gave out this consolatory utterance, " For if there be first a willing mind, it is accepted according to that a man hath, and not according to that he hath not." But contentment with the allotments of Providence does not involve the cessation of efforts to struggle for the haven. Though it is right to bow to Him who sends the storm, it is also right to "row hard" to escape from it; and vigorous effort, when faith keeps the heart quiet, and hope nerves the arm, is seldom unsuccessful.

Fourthly.—I have learned that constant employment is a duty, obedience to which tends to cheerfulness and health. Work, considered by itself, is no curse. Heavy labour, with the drops on the forehead, and the thorn and the thistle rushing into one's hands and feet, may well remind him that his father was driven out of Paradise; but work, under the present economy of things, is a medicine and a joy. Compulsory idleness is an affliction; voluntary indolence, a vice; mischievous activity, a crime and sin; but persevering toil in good work, with a good aim, is a moral duty and a real pleasure; and, as I have before said, such labour is never lost. All successful men have been hard workers. All good men are active from a necessity of their new nature. No man is crowned, except he strive; and as a matter of course, if he wish to be crowned, he must strive lawfully. Angels are not idle; they are ministering spirits, and swift messengers. And Jesus, the greatest worker, said, " My Father worketh hitherto, and I work." With such examples and precedents, who would be idle ? " What can *I* do ? " may sound humbly, but a close inspection of motives would check the query. Men of lowly lot have done great things. " There was a little city, and few men within it; and there came a great king against it, and besieged it, and built great bulwarks against it : now there was found in it a poor wise man, and he by his wisdom delivered the city ; yet no man remembered that same poor man."

Now this was exceedingly ungrateful. Such men deserved to have been carried into captivity, all but the poor man and his kindred. Nevertheless, the saviour of the little city did not work in vain, nor has he gone without reward, for Solomon has immortalised his wisdom and courage. " Then said I, Wisdom is better than strength : nevertheless, the poor man's wisdom is despised, and his words are not heard." Such is the world; but the " poor wise man," who folds his hands because the world is slow in its appreciation of active worth in the case of those who have neither a patent of nobility, nor the wealth before which nobility itself sometimes stands uncovered, is in danger of losing his reputation for wisdom. Work and tire not, is the motto which I would recommend to all who wish to see this fine old world turned round, with its face to the sun. It has long run the career of the prodigal, and had long experience of the prodigal's woes. Let good men use the lever which Mercy hath placed within reach, and results will follow which will make the weak say, " I am strong ! "

Besides, activity in some work of usefulness aids the enjoyment of Christian truth. Those of my flock who are thus engaged are just those who most fully appreciate the Gospel and value its privileges. The tract distributors, the visitors of the poor, and the Sabbath-school teachers, grow in knowledge, " understand doctrine," and " draw water with joy out of the wells of salvation;" whilst those who are indisposed—happily, in the case of the Church under my care, *their* number is small—to any effort of this kind, and who centre all their religious ideas on personal comfort, receive least of that which they exclusively seek. The discontented, and the troublers of Churches, are generally found only among those who are not at work in the " Father's vineyard." What may be called the philosophy of this fact is easily apprehended. Men busy doing good have no time for mischief; but the idle generally wish to be thought great friends of truth, purity, and Church prosperity; hence " they wander about from house to house, tattlers and busybodies, speaking things which they ought not." There were some of them in the Apostle's days, as appears from more than one of his letters. " For we hear," he writes, " that there are some who walk among you disorderly, working not at all, but are busybodies." Indeed, this characteristic of humanity appears to have belonged to it at an early period of the world's history. The Egyptian despot prescribed more work as a remedy to the murmurs of the Hebrews; and if Milton be accepted as an historian, Adam said to his wife,

" Would thou hadst hearkened to my words, and stayed
With me, as I besought thee, when that strange
Desire of wandering, this unhappy morn,
I know not whence possessed thee; we had then
Remained still happy, not as now, despoiled
Of all our good, shamed, naked, miserable."

He had before advised her,

> " And let us *to our fresh employments rise*
> Among the groves, the fountains, and the flowers ;"

but she determined otherwise, and, alas! she has many followers.

Fifthly.—I have learned that the Gospel of Christ meets the necessities of men of every class and condition. This may seem a trite saying; but I speak of what I have personally seen, and the testimony of real experience is valuable when it supports a doctrine of so much moment, especially at a time when " false witnesses are risen up." I have seen the effect of Christianity on the day-labourer, the mechanic, the shop-keeper, the man of literature and cultivated intellect, the wealthy and the noble, the young and the aged, the strong, the infirm, and the dying; and in every case it was *the same.* When the results are similar, notwithstanding much variety in the circumstances and mental state of the patients, it is clear that the prescription is what it professes to be—infallible. If light, hope, and purity always follow; if "love, joy, peace, long suffering, gentleness, goodness, faith, meekness, temperance," always grow out of a personal reception of the Gospel, then it *is* " the power of God unto salvation to every one that believeth." Not from any doubt as regards its divinity, but as a deeply interesting study in the history of mind, I have narrowly watched the action of evangelical doctrine on the different classes of the community with whom I have associated, and the result has been as I have stated. "The Gospel" has uniformly been " its own witness." It has borne similar fruit, sometimes slowly and feebly, at other times rapidly and abundantly—sometimes thirty, sometimes sixty, and sometimes an hundred-fold; but the fruit was always similar in kind. Knowledge acquired thus, not from the mere belief of what Christianity says about itself—though I believe *that* unhesitatingly—gives confidence to the speaker, and enables him to say to his hearers, " What we have seen and heard, declare we unto you;" " we have not followed cunningly devised fables." It is a grand thing to be able to speak with certainty on a subject of such intense importance; a grand thing to say,

> " Religion ! thou the soul of happiness,
> And, groaning Calvary, of thee ! there shine
> The noblest truths ; there strongest motives sting ;
> There sacred violence assaults the soul ;
> There nothing but compulsion is forborne."

And, still further, the ability to express certain conviction on this heaven-and-earth-embracing topic has, in consequence of the law of mental sympathy, a powerful influence on the audience. The speaker must be sincere. He cannot avoid it. It is impossible for him to trifle or play with a subject that runs parallel with immortality ; and which must do its work during mortal probation, or fail ; and his hearers are arrested by and feel the power of his earnestness. Cowper has described this fact, but the lines are so well known, that I need not cite them. It is a fact, however, worthy of serious study, even by those who think they honour supernatural influence by speaking slightingly of all human instrumentality. The efficient cause of religious life is *not* in man. No one shall proclaim this proposition more loudly than I do ; but intelligent, settled, earnest, personal conviction is far more likely to be the medium through which the efficient cause acts than that of mere official formalism.

Sixthly.—I have learned that though Christianity should not be Divine, it greatly improves the physical and domestic condition of those who believe in it. That which increases man's happiness, as man, is valuable. Every true friend of man takes pleasure in the advancement of education, cleanliness, peace, and domestic comfort; and I have often been surprised that the adversaries of the Gospel, many of whom are professedly the advocates of these things, have not been arrested by the suggestive fact, that it *invariably* creates the desire for those things which they proclaim as so very desirable. And, as a matter of indisputable truth, it succeeds where all other agencies fail. I have seen evidences of this, enough to fill a volume. I have seen parents who had been brought up in ignorance, when they felt the power of the Gospel, denying themselves that they might be able to educate their offspring. I have seen the slaves of filthy habits seeking the comforts of cleanliness, as the acknowledged result of the same power. And I have seen peace and love reign in the domestic circle, where discord and wrath were supreme before Christianity entered. These are not theories, but facts. And, as facts, they should induce men who laud reason to pause and consider, and try to trace the effect to its cause, before they denounce the occupants of the pulpit as a brotherhood of fanatics or impostors. Men will doubt the sincerity of their professed patriotism and humanity, if they ignore that power which facts proclaim the most efficient auxiliary of the object they desire to realise. And reason will vote for the doubters. For, supposing that we have no first principles, and that everything is to be conducted on the finding of protracted experiment, the result of experiment condemns those who strike the Gospel out of the list of agencies fitted to improve the condition of men. The question concerning its divinity, its spiritual significance, and its eternal issues, may be safely waived for the time, so that the investigation may relate only to its bearing on general knowledge, youthful education, personal habits, and domestic peace. Conduct the inquiry thus, for example :—Does the belief of the Gospel darken the understanding, and make men the enemies of general education? Does it create hostility, on the part of parents and others, to Sunday, infant, and day schools? Has it been known to make a man of ordinary decent habits, careless, immoral, and filthy? Does it generally create—nay, has it been known in any instance to create—a desire for the public-house, the theatre, the fancy-show, or the immoral publication? Are the inmates of our prisons and penitentiaries persons who were decidedly under its influence when they committed the crimes and sins which brought them there? Is the savage, who beats and bruises his wife, and reddens his hands in the blood of his children, stimulated to these deeds by the lessons of the Testament or the voice of the Christian pastor? I feel it almost a crime against Him whom one of our Christian poets terms the

> " Great PHILANTHROPIST,
> Father of angels, but the Friend of man,"

even to propose these questions ; but I do so, because—

Seventhly,—I have learned that intellect, without supernatural influence, never receives the Gospel as a Divine message. This may seem a sweeping charge. If so, my design in making it will be realised. " The natural man receiveth not the things of the Spirit of God: for they are foolishness unto him : neither can he know them, because they are spiritually discerned." So far as my observation of men has gone, this is strictly true. I have known, and could name clever men, politicians, critics, editors, authors, schoolmasters, orators, and merchants —men of ability, intelligence, reputation, and taste—who are unable to comprehend those ordinary propositions of the Christian Testament, with the glorious import of

which all real Christians are familiar. Every idea emanating from a supernatural source seems either above or
below their powers of apprehension,—whether above or
below may be left to the reader's opinion,—and every
doctrine of special revelation seems to belong to a region
which natural intellect cannot embrace. "Why is it,"—
the question has been put to me repeatedly,—"why is it
that So-and-so, who is an able and intelligent man, does
not embrace Christianity?" It is, of course, very humilia-
ting to intelligence to hear such a question asked; but
that it should occasionally meet one is by no means
surprising. Christianity always improves and strengthens
the intellect; but, in the first instance, if my study of
facts has not misled me, it lays hold on the heart. It
subdues the perverse will, affects the inner man, and
changes the motives. If, therefore, that which we conventionally term the heart, or the seat of the affections,
be untouched, the mind, or rational powers, will remain
uninfluenced. Men have sometimes, by the mere force of
evidence, admitted that the Bible must be true, and yet
have remained unbelievers. This looks paradoxical; but
every day's experience proves that it is no paradox.

"The young man of whom I have been writing," says a
modern author,* " inquired what authors on the evidences
of Christianity I chiefly recommended. I told him that I
had a choice, but it was not so marked as to fix on given
volumes indispensably; that I did not fear the result,
provided he did not stop short of the given number,
although he might peruse those productions the most readily obtained, or the first procured. He told me that he
would read six or eight of the first books I should send
him, and the Bible afterwards, with Scott's notes. The
following are, as nearly as I can remember, the books

* Infidelity: its Cause and Cure. By the Rev. David Nelson, M.D.

R

which I obtained, and sent or carried to him, one as soon as he had finished the other:—Alexander's 'Evidences,' Paley's 'Evidences,' Watson's 'Answer to Paine,' Jews' 'Letters to Voltaire,' Horne's 'Introduction,' Vol. I., and Faber's 'Difficulties of Infidelity.' Before he was entirely through with these books, he told me, with a serious face and voice, that he had something to tell me of himself that was indeed singular. 'I am,' said he, 'in a strange condition. I will confess to you, frankly and honestly, that these authors have met, answered, and fairly overturned every difficulty and every objection which I had mustered and opposed to the Bible as being from God. Furthermore, I do acknowledge that I have found arguments in favour of its Divine authority so plain and so momentous that I am unable to meet or to answer them; *and yet I do not believe the Bible.* I cannot and I do not *believe the Bible!*'"

Substantially, my reply to the question under notice has been, that the representation of man's apostacy, given in Scripture, would naturally lead to the conclusion that the dark cloud which hangs over the understanding would preclude the entrance of saving spiritual light, except holy power were brought to bear upon and remedy his moral disease; that if Christianity has to stand or fall by the mere verdict of human reason, its claims to a Divine origin cannot be substantiated; and that its non-reception by intellectual men, whose dispositions towards God and holiness are unchanged, instead of forming an argument against its Divinity, proves the very reverse. But I have added the indisputable fact, that the brightest intellects that ever adorned humanity have belonged to men of humble and loving Christian hearts; and the equally well-known fact, that, other things being equal, the presence of Christianity, as a heart-power, has always tended to increase the brilliance of the intellect. And, without intending to bring a charge which cannot be fully substantiated, I may add here, in conclusion, that not a few of those who sneer at the Gospel, and point the joke at the expense of its advocates, claim credit for a degree of intelligence, culture, and mental power, to which they have not the remotest right. Generally, they are men most culpably ignorant of the literature of religion, the history of Christianity, the facts of the Bible itself, and the overwhelming number of witnesses, from all nations, that can be summoned to testify in favour of its truth. A few hacknied objections against the Bible, which have been answered a thousand times, and a few miserable gibes, at the cost of professing Christians, constitute their stock of weapons, with which they hope to put to silence the voice of prophets, apostles, evangelists, and martyrs, not to name the voice of the Son of God Himself. It is a forlorn hope. Would God that they were wise! for the wisdom of which they boast descendeth not from above, and its tendency is to deceive, enthral, and destroy!

But now I have done with the record of the past, and desire calmly but hopefully to anticipate the future.

Christianity has created a social home for man, the wanderer. That home is THE CHURCH. Within its hallowed enclosure multitudes have been gathered. The social instincts of humanity, consecrated to God, and mutually attracted by brotherly love, find here that which gratifies, gladdens, and purifies. The divided are made one. The sin-separated are united by holy principles. A common centre, Christ, like the central luminary of an astral system, draws them together. "To Him shall the gathering of the people be," is an ancient prediction, which has been in course of fulfilment for many ages and around Him they congregate, and find the best principles strengthened, and the loftiest aspirations encouraged. The heart needs a resting-place, such as the world, with all its paradises, cannot give; but it finds it in the Church. To invite the foot-sore traveller within its fold, to ask the heavy-laden to enter this enclosure and find rest, and to beseech the friendless, whose soul yearns for sympathy, to enjoy it in the presence of the brotherhood which he will find here, is the honourable vocation of the Christian minister. Benevolence, pity, earnestness, are the proper attributes of this vocation, and when the eye sees the multitudes of the perishing hastening to the ark, how cheering, how glorious the sight! In the act of inviting there is pleasure; but when the invitation is accepted, that pleasure is wonderfully enhanced. The true servant then forgets all his toil, and all that is of a merely personal or temporary nature, and participates in the joy which angels feel when sinners repent. He who feeds the hungry, or clothes the naked, or instructs the ignorant, does a good work; but he who instrumentally brings a prodigal son back to his Father, and induces the victim of moral disease to touch the hem of the Redeemer's garment, does a better. The open door of the sanctuary, within which he beseeches the sad brother to enter, is on Calvary, and when he has entered *thus*, he is

> " No more a stranger or a guest,
> But like a child, at home! "

The future will witness a great increase in the number of those who shall seek refuge here. The grace of the Great Friend of man will accomplish this; acting upon the conscious woes and wants of the restless human heart, it will realise its grand purpose, and secure multitudes from the night of storm and tempest which shall scatter the strongholds of evil, and carry desolation over the fortresses of the usurper. A bright day comes. Promise, prophecy, and gospel are committed to that; but first the oracle gives its warning in a voice of startling earnestness and great majesty :—

> " Go into the rock, and hide in the dust,
> From before the terror of Jehovah, and the glory of his majesty.
> The lofty looks of man shall be humbled;
> And the loftiness of mortals shall be abased;
> And Jehovah alone shall be exalted in that day.
> For the day of Jehovah of hosts shall be
> Against every one that is proud and lofty;
> Against every thing that is exalted;
> And it shall be humbled.
> Against all the cedars of Lebanon, that are high and lifted up;
> And against all the oaks of Bashan;
> And against all the lofty mountains;
> And against all the high hills;
> And against every lofty tower;
> And against every wall strongly fortified;
> And against all the ships of Tarshish;
> And against every sight of desire.
> And the pride of man shall be humbled;
> And the loftiness of mortals shall be abased;
> And Jehovah alone shall be exalted in that day.
> And the idols He shall cause utterly to disappear.
> And men shall go into caverns of the rocks and into holes of the dust,
> From the terror of Jehovah, and from the glory of His majesty,
> When He ariseth to strike the earth with terror.
> In that day shall a man cast away his idols of silver, and his idols of
>   gold,
> Which they have made to worship,
> To the moles and to the bats;
> To go into the clefts of the rocks, and into the fissures of the craggy
>   rocks;
> From the terror of Jehovah and the glory of his majesty,
> When He ariseth to shake the earth with terror.
> Trust ye no more in man,
> Whose breath is in his nostrils!
> For what account is to be made of him ? "

But the same prophet who thunders this doom of

destruction against all that is marked for judgment, has a note of consolation for those who have entered the home to which the weary are invited:—

> " And the work of righteousness shall be peace,
> And the effect of righteousness, quiet and security for ever.
> And my people shall abide in a habitation of peace,
> And in secure dwellings,
> And in tranquil resting places."

How exquisitely fine is that, and how it contrasts with the preceding! It stirs my spirit with the hope that I shall be permitted, again and again, and often, to take a sin-wounded human brother by the hand and to lead him to the place of safety, of which the Church is the emblem and the proof. If this honour and this privilege wait me in the future, then let me " press on!" Men *will* look forward. It is natural, it is proper, it is beneficial; but to enable them to look with something like certainty from a lofty position, and through a clear atmosphere, I would have them all to enter the true Church in the true way. The observatory erected there is the best, at present, in the world; and because I love the human brotherhood, I would say to them all,—" Enter, ascend, and look—all without charge!"

There is a singular characteristic of this home; it is temporary and permanent at the same time. Men enter it under the recognised character of lodgers and travellers, and yet they wish to be and are welcomed as— permanent residents. A mortal immortal knocks at the gate, and is admitted for a night and for ever. The scene and the locality, like a dissolving view, may pass from the sight, but the heart-union formed among the brotherhood will be durable as the years of eternity. The stranger, just admitted, may be a cold corpse to-morrow, but he is one of a family known in the language of heaven as the hosts of the Lord.

When I study the existence, the origin, the moral significance, the sublimity and the destiny of the Christian Church, I am overwhelmed with astonishment and grief at the lamentably inadequate and perverted opinions which prevail respecting it. Ecclesiastical hierarchies, doctrinal sects, religious fraternities — and do *these* comprise all that is meant by the Church? A State Establishment, a Dissenting Body, a Methodistic Society—does the meaning of these expressions terminate with the things they respectively designate? No, verily! There is a great thing among men, and they know it not; a wonder unwondered at,—a glory unnoticed! Is it generally known that a great problem is being solved by Infinite Wisdom; and that earth, in the first instance, and heaven, shortly, are the scenes of its solution? Have men, in any considerable numbers, recognised the fact, that a process of inconceivable sublimity is going on every day in the market-place, the streets, the fields, the houses, and the huts of this world?—that the Creator of the visible is forming, without rest or intermission, an invisible temple of living stones, which, when completed, shall be exhibited before the universe, as the most gorgeous and costly of all His possessions?—that heaven has really come down to earth, and brought into sympathy with its plans and purposes myriads of the human family, who are every day journeying to the city not made with hands, and growing in the likeness of Him who is the Head of all principality and power, and the Sovereign of life?—that, amidst the thorns and thistles of earth's deserts, grow flowers which are lovingly tended by angels, watered by the river of life, and destined to be transplanted to the garden of the Lord?—and that among those whom the world despises, as it did their Prince, are to be found men who shall ere long be acknowledged by angels as the sons and heirs of God? Is this known? Are these things considered when the word " Church " glides from the tongue? The street-passenger sees men going to some building consecrated to religious purposes, on the morning of the Lord's day? Does he think what that procession means? Is there not a hidden significance, a veiled glory, which will not burst upon his mental vision without the labour of trying to uncover it? May not that procession point to eternity, and signify the power of the invisible? Assume, for the sake of illustration, that the proper motives animate the travellers,—that they know wherefore they are moving thither,—that they understand the ultimate object of the holy convocation,—that they feel the solemnity of their profession,—and that they devoutly wish for the great things involved in their voluntary avowal of attachment to the Invisible King; and then, if asked by the passenger to explain all, what would they say? A correct answer would startle the querist, and very probably themselves; and a complete answer would convince him that his wisdom would be to go with them, and lead all to spend a day of rapt enjoyment and of exciting joy in the anticipation of the future.

Christian indifference and mechanical worship are the most melancholy phenomena in the world. Open wickedness and unblushing iniquity are not nearly so sad. *These* we expect; *those* are unaccountable, except on the hypothesis of non-consideration; but the want of consideration is itself a fault and a crime. How much there is to think about, and how strong the calls to thought, when the idea of a Christian Church rises before the mind! Originating before the world was, streaming along the lines of all history, and pointing to perfection and duration when the world shall flee away, and no place be found for it, the Christian Church really challenges the study of all thinkers. It is either an unprecedented imposture, or a magnificent embodiment of Divine love and wisdom. A thousand reasons prove that it cannot be the former; ten thousand demonstrate that it is the latter. Of course, I speak not of the Church of a nation, or that of a given brotherhood;—of the Church of the ecclesiastical historian, or that of the earnest polemic;—but of the Church of the First-born, whose names are written in heaven; and this, in its constitution, spirit, purpose, and destiny, is altogether a Divine thing. In this, earth has a visitor for whom heaven longs as a resident. "But, among conflicting sects, which is the true Church?" None of them, brother! The true Church is within the Churches. The visible is a poor exponent of the unseen. The robes are not the man. The body is not the spirit. The house is not the tenant. The nominal Church is wofully divided. "They parted His raiment among them." But the principle which prophesies union remains wherever the Spirit of the Lord is. And union is one of the predicted glories of the future.

> "The voice of thy watchmen!
> They lift up their voice together; they sing.
> For eye to eye shall they see, when Jehovah restoreth Zion."

The darkness which has so long separated the members of this true Church shall be dispersed.

> "And Jehovah of Hosts, in this mountain, shall make for all people
> A feast of delicacies, a feast of old wines,
> Of delicacies exquisitely rich, and of old wines well refined.
> And in this mountain Jehovah will remove the face of the covering
>   cast over all people,
> And the veil that is spread over all nations.
> He will abolish death for ever;
> And the Lord Jehovah will wipe away the tear from every face;
> And the reproach of His people will He take away from off the whole
>   earth:
> For Jehovah hath spoken it."

Alas! they have been a reproach; and, times without number, they have merited reproach. But, onward! the bright and beautiful future stands in its sure place, beckoning us on!

But there is another home in connexion with this holy socialism, and one, moreover, without which the latter is no sanctuary. My children frequently sing around their mother's knee the touching hymn, beginning—

"Behold a Stranger at the door!
He gently knocks, has knocked before;
Has waited long, is waiting still:
You use no other friend so ill."

The admission of this Stranger commences a new era in the history of the individual who admits Him, and conse-crates a new home on the earth. "Christ in the heart" is the secret of fellowship with the Church; but this secret, too, whilst it ennobles the man, points to the future. A sacred impulse is given to the recipient of this Divine Stranger, prompting him to go on unto perfection. A light has illumined his understanding, which enables him to see far into future worlds. The consciousness that he is exceedingly honoured, at once lays him in the dust and sets him in heavenly places. He understands now the meaning of the passage,—

"For thus saith the High and the Exalted One:
I dwell in the high and holy place,
And with him also that is contrite and of a humble spirit;
To revive the spirit of the humble,
And to revive the heart of the contrite."

And he feels constrained to obey the apostolic entreaty, "I beseech you therefore, brethren, by the mercies of God, that ye present your bodies a living sacrifice, holy, acceptable unto God, which is your reasonable service. And be not conformed to this world; but be ye trans-formed by the renewing of your mind, that ye may prove what is that good, and acceptable, and perfect will of God."

And then there is a third and a final home, to which the heart with its Divine Resident, and the Church with its redeemed brotherhood, steadily point as the result and development of them both. That home is HEAVEN. But who shall paint its landscapes, describe its glories, picture its inhabitants, or point out its locality? Prophets, poets, and evangelists have done much; but not enough to satisfy the cravings of curiosity. Like the holy of holies, into which none but the high priest entered, it is mostly vailed from the eyes of others; and "He who came down from heaven" has, undoubtedly from wise and kind reasons, said but comparatively little about the mansions of the Father's house. Yet metaphor, similitude, figure, with an occasional glance at a small opening, have excited expectation, and kindled the highest hopes. The language of the heart is eloquent on this subject. The future and the final home of redeemed men! It must be worthy of Him who is bringing many sons to glory! And what are all the cares, tears, anxieties, griefs, groans, and bereavements, in the presence of that short word "glory?" An apostle, the same man who was caught up into paradise, says—and in the very section, too, in which he speaks of the groanings of creation, "I reckon that the sufferings of this present time are not worthy to be compared with the glory which shall be revealed in us." He also writes thus:—"For our light affliction, which is but for a moment, worketh for us a far more exceeding and eternal weight of glory; while we look not at the things which are seen, but at the things which are not seen; for the things which are seen are temporal, but the things which are not seen are eternal." The heart set on that country may well bear up under the toils of this.   There is rest at the end of the journey, and whilst all its associations are not fully understood here, yet its essential character is known.   It is essentially peace in Christ.   How animating is such a prospect!   And its realisation is as certain as the word of the Faithful and True Witness can make it.   It is enough!

> "Then safely moored—my perils o'er,
>   I'll sing first in night's diadem,
> For ever and for evermore,
>   The Star—the Star of Bethlehem!"

*   *   *   *   *

Esteemed Reader! we are about to separate. We have journeyed together thus far, over some of the uneven passages of existence, we have seen sickness and health, poverty and plenty, youth and age, religion and wickedness, the outward appearance, and the workings of the heart; we have heard the song of gladness and the groans of grief; and, above all, we have had repeated illustrations of the great and consolatory doctrine of Divine Providence.   We are mutually strangers to each other, and in all probability shall remain so, until we meet beyond the confines of the present world.   I thank you for the patience with which you have listened to my simple narrative; and I sincerely hope that the facts it records, and the lessons it suggests, may not be without some use to others, as the review of them has touched the springs of deep emotion in my own mind.   Would God that my life in the future may correspond somewhat more with the proper deportment of one, whose whole history has been an evidence of His fatherly care, and of His long-suffering kindness; and may the writer and all his readers meet *in* HEAVEN!

19 DE 53

J. UNWIN, Gresham Steam Press, 31, Bucklersbury, London.

𝔅𝔬𝔬𝔨𝔰 𝔩𝔞𝔱𝔢𝔩𝔶 𝔓𝔲𝔟𝔩𝔦𝔰𝔥𝔢𝔡

BY

WILLIAM & FREDERICK G. CASH,

5, BISHOPSGATE STREET WITHOUT,

AND MAY BE ORDERED OF ANY BOOKSELLER.

Post 8vo., cloth, price 6s. 6d.

CURIOSITIES OF LONDON LIFE: or, Phases, Physiological and Social, of the Great Metropolis. By C. M. SMITH.

"Whoever has not read these [sketches, loses] the enjoyment of some rare pictures of human life, if he do not read them now."—*Manchester Weekly Advertiser.*

Post 8vo., cloth, price 5s.

THE WORKING MAN'S WAY IN THE WORLD; or the Autobiography of a Journeyman Printer.

"None can read it without feeling himself a better, a more cheerful, a more contented, and a wiser man. We cordially wish it all the literary success it so eminently deserves."—*Weekly News.*

"We are disposed to set a high value on the "Working Man's Way in the World."—*Tait's Magazine.*

"The stamp of reality marks out this autobiography."—*Leader.*

5, Bishopsgate Street Without.

Crown 8vo., cloth, price 4s.

THE HALF-CENTURY: its History, Political and Social, (1800 to 1850.) By WASHINGTON WILKS. With a chronological table of contents, and a tabular arrangement of the principal officers of state from 1800 to 1850. *Second Edition revised*, and containing a Supplementary Chapter.

" Containing an intelligent digest of contemporaneous history from the pen of a decided reformer and earnest thinker." — *Western Times.*

" A concise and well-brought together history, clearly written and full of useful information."—*Economist.*

" In a style at once unpretending and agreeable—full of well-digested information.—*Church of England Quarterly Review.*

8vo. cloth, price 8s. 6d.

THE HISTORY OF RELIGIOUS INTOLERANCE IN SPAIN; or, an Examination of some of the Causes which led to that Nation's Decline. Translated from the original Spanish of Señor Don Adolfo de Castro. By THOMAS PARKER. With a Portrait of the Author.

' *Ecclesiastically*, very richly suggestive; *Theologically*, a grand protest for spiritual truth ; *Historically*, the commencementof a rewriting of Spanish history."—*Nonconformist*

Cara Patria, Carior Libertas.

Foolscap, 8vo., cloth, price 4s. 6d., gilt, 5s. 6d.

MORNING DEW DROPS; or, the Juvenile Abstainer. By Mrs. CLARA LUCAS BALFOUR, with an Introduction by Mrs. H. B. STOWE, and Illustrated by ANELAY.

"No Sunday School Library should be without Mrs. Balfour's 'Morning Dew Drops.' Every teacher should read it as an admirable specimen of the best method of conveying information to the young. Though full of solid instruction and sound argument, no child can fail of understanding, and being fascinated by it. It is a complete epitome of total abstinence principles, pervaded by the spirit of true religion, and should be a hand-book with all the friends of 'The Band of Hope.'"—*From the Rev Newman Hall, B.A., Hull.*

8vo. cloth, price 1s. 6d., in paper cover, 1s.

"1793 and 1853,"

By RICHARD COBDEN, Esq., M.P. *A handsome Library Edition with a Preface by the Author.*

Foolscap 8vo., cloth, price 3s. 6d.

ESSAYS ON POLITICAL ECONOMY. By the late M. FREDERIC BASTIAT. Capital and Interest. —That which is seen; and that which is not seen— Government.—What is Money?—The Law.

"They are written with beautiful clearness, and from abundant knowledge. * * It is a small volume, but worth a large sum."—*The Leader.*

5, Bishopsgate Street Without.

Post 8vo., cloth, price 6s.

JUVENILE DELINQUENTS; their Condition and Treatment. By MARY CARPENTER, Author of the " Reformatory Schools."

" We heartily commend Miss Carpenter's performance, which will doubtless receive the earnest attention of all philanthropic and reflective persons who take an interest in the subject of which she is an apostle."—*Bristol Mercury.*

" To those of our readers who may desire to possess a compendious manual on Juvenile Delinquency, with an account of such remedies as have commended themselves to earnest and informed minds, we can well recommend Miss Carpenter's book."—*Athenæum.*

Foolscap 8vo., price

WORKING WOMEN OF THE LAST HALF-CENTURY: the Lesson of their Lives. By CLARA LUCAS BALFOUR.

Foolscap 8vo., price 3s. 6d.

THE SILENT REVOLUTION; or the future effects of Steam and Electricity upon the Condition of Mankind. By M. A. GARVEY, LL.D. of the Middle Temple.

" This is a plain, sensibly written, and eloquent Book concerning our social progress, from a condition of half-brutified people, to our present advanced state."—*Weekly Dispatch.*

5, Bishopsgate Street Without.

8vo. cloth, Library Edition, with a portrait, price 9s. 6d.

DYMOND'S ESSAYS ON THE PRINCIPLES OF MORALITY, and on the Private and Political Rights and Obligations of Mankind.

"The present work is indeed a book of such ability, and so excellently intended, as well executed, that even those who differ most widely as we must do, from some of its conclusions, must regard the writer with the greatest respect, and look upon his early death as a public loss.—*Quarterly Review.*

Another Edition, royal 8vo., paper cover, price 2s. 6d. Embossed cloth, 3s. 6d.

16mo., Illustrated, 4s. 6d., 18mo. cloth, 1s., sewed, 6d.

A KISS FOR A BLOW. A Collection of Stories for Children, showing them how to prevent Quarrelling. By H. C. WRIGHT. New Edition.

"Of this little book it is impossible to speak too highly ; it is the reflex of the spirit of childhood, full of tenderness, pity and love—quick to resent, and equally quick to forgive. We wish that all children could imbibe its spirit, then indeed would the world be happier and better."—*Mary Howitt.*

"This volume, of which it were to be wished that every family in the country had a copy, has been reprinted in London ; it is an invaluable little book."—*Chambers' Tracts.*

Post 8vo., cloth price 7s 6d.

THE LETTERS OF RICHARD REYNOLDS, with a Memoir of his Life. By his Grandaughter, HANNAH MARY RATHBONE. Enriched with a fine Portrait engraved by Bellin.

"In a spirit of reverence alike earnest and tender, Mrs. Rathbone has traced the few incidents which marked the life of this good man, and filled up the character by his correspondence. . . . The tone in which she has executed her task is unexceptionable."—*Athenæum.*

5, Bishopsgate Street Without.

16mo., price 1s.

VOICES FROM THE CROWD. Fourth Edition. Revised, with additional Poems. By CHARLES MACKAY, Esq.

" Bold and energetic—full of high thoughts and manly aspirations."—*Chambers' Journal.*

" These are the utterances of a man who has caught, and who expounds the spirit of his age. They are noble, and indeed glorious productions, teeming with the spirit of truth and humanity."—*Nottingham Review.*

Post 8vo., cloth, price 8s. 6d.

A MEMOIR OF WILLIAM ALLEN, F.R.S. By the Rev. JAMES SHERMAN, of Surrey Chapel.

" A. character at once so devout and humble, so just and generous, in a word so truly great, seldom, indeed, does it fall to the lot of the biographer to delineate. * * * The book is one of those productions which it seems impossible to read without becoming wiser and better."—*Bath and Cheltenham Gazette.*

" We can warmly recommend the book to all, both to those who love to trace the workings of genius, and to those who desire to be guided by the example of virtue."—*Literary Gazette.*

Foolscap 8vo., cloth, price 5s.,

THE PASTOR'S WIFE. A Memoir of Mrs. Sherman, of Surrey Chapel. By her HUSBAND. With a Portrait. Tenth Thousand.

" This constitutes one of the most tender, beautiful, instructive, and edifying narratives that for a long time has come under our notice. * * * We anticipate for it a very extended popularity and usefulness among the mothers and daughters of England."—*Christian Witness.*

" This volume deserves a large circulation, and we feel it a pleasure to commend its perusal to the various classes of our readers, especially to those whose sex may enable them to tread in Mrs. Sherman's steps."—*Nonconformist.*

Royal 18mo. price 3s. 6d.,

AUNT JANE'S VERSES FOR CHILDREN. By Mrs. T. D. Crewdson. Illustrated with Twelve highly-finished Engravings, from Designs by H. Anelay.

"This is a charming little volume, of excellent moral and religious tendency, and eminently fitted to call forth the mental energy of young people, and to direct it to a wise and profitable result. The pictorial illustrations are exquisitely beautiful."—*Evangelical Magazine.*

Post 8vo., cloth, price 5s.

CRIME IN ENGLAND, its Relation, Character, and Extent, as developed from 1801 to 1848. By Thomas Plint.

"We thank Mr. Plint for his volume. It is written in a philosophical spirit, and the inquiry to which he has devoted so much time has evidently been conducted with great patience and candour."—*Freeholder.*

"Mr. Plint shows the discrimination, accuracy and candour of a true statist."—*Leeds Mercury.*

"A work which we esteem the most able, dispassionate and conclusive, yet written on those momentous questions."—*Nonconformist.*

18mo., sewed, 1s., in packets, 1s., cloth, 1s. 6d.

"SISTER VOICES" FOR FIELD, FACTORY, AND FIRESIDE. Edited by Elihu Burritt.

32mo., sewed, and in packets, price 6d., cloth, price 1s.

SIXTY STORIES FOR SIXPENCE. For Nursery, School, or Fireside; or, Leaflets of the Law of Kindness, for Children. Edited by ELIHU BURRITT.

" These little stories are little gems : they are beaming with light, and their light is the light of Love. We have the most sincere pleasure in recommending this little packet to our readers."—*Friend.*

18mo., cloth, price 1s.

MEMORIAL OF THE LATE REV. ROWLAND HILL. Chiefly consisting of anecdotes illustrative of his character and labours. By the Rev. JAMES SHERMAN.

" Mr. Sherman has done worthily by his great and never-to-be-forgotten predecessor, Mr. Hill, in presenting this interesting little compend of the man of God, and the striking things that issued from his lips."—*Christian Witness.*

8vo., cloth, price 8s. 6d.

STATE CHURCHES AND THE KINGDOM OF CHRIST. By JOHN ALLEN.

Foolscap 8vo., sewed, price 1s.

AMERICAN PREJUDICE AGAINST COLOUR; An Authentic Narrative. By WILLIAM G. ALLEN, a Refugee from American Despotism.

12mo., cloth with a Portrait, price 3s. 6d.

THE WORKS OF ELIHU BURRITT; containing " Sparks from the Anvil," " Voice from the Forge," and " Peace Papers for the People."

" In every line coined from the reflecting mind óf the Blacksmith of Massachusetts there is a high philosophy and philanthropy genuine and pure. His sympathies are universal, his aspirations are for the happiness of all, and his writings are nervous, terse, and vigorous."—*London Telegraph.*

" The influence of the small work before us must be for good, and we wish it every success. The various essays it contains are written with natural eloquence, and contain many just and original sentiments."—*Scottish Press.*

12mo, cloth, price 1s.

A VOYAGE TO THE SLAVE COASTS of West and East Africa. By the Rev. PASCOE GRENFELL HILL, R.N., Author of " Fifty Days on Board a Slave Vessel."

" This brief but interesting narrative proceeds from one who has witnessed the horrors of the Slave-trade, as carried on in various parts of the globe. * * * The unpretending style in which the narrative is written, and the stamp of truth which it carries with it, induce us to recommend it to an extensive perusal."—*Standard of Freedom.*

Foolscap 8vo., cloth, 2s., sewed 1s. 6d.

ROGER MILLER; or, Heroism in Humble Life: a Narrative. By GEORGE ORME. Sixth Thousand.

This work has already had an extended circulation in all the States of the American Union, in Holland, (where it has been translated into Dutch) and in many other parts of the continent of Europe.

" A more worthy, diligent, kind, and useful person cannot be found in the whole circle of those who are engaged in the service of the poorer classes.—*Lord Ashley.*

5, *Bishopsgate Street Without.*

8vo., cloth, price 10s. 6d.

THE HISTORY OF CHURCH LAWS IN ENGLAND, from A.D. 602 to A.D. 1850; with a Sketch of Christianity, from its first introduction into Britain till the arrival of Augustine in A.D. 597. By the Rev. EDWARD MUSCUTT.

State of the Early Churches—Various kinds of Church Laws—Church Laws in relation to Things Civil—Church Laws in relation to Things Spiritual —Toleration and Religious Opinions.

" Any and every Protestant who can either buy or borrow this book—which has been the labour of years—may learn in a week the whole history and mystery of the DRACO CODE of craft and cruelty, and thus may judge for himself what the Vatican means by restoring Canon Law in England."— *Evangelical Magazine.*

Demy 8vo., cloth.

THE WEST INDIES, BEFORE AND SINCE SLAVE EMANCIPATION; COMPRISING THE WINDWARD AND LEEWARD ISLANDS.—MILITARY COMMAND. Founded on Notes and Observations Collected during a Three Years' Residence. By JOHN DAVY, M.D., F.R.S. &c., Inspector-General of Army Hospitals.

Post 8vo., cloth, price 5s.

LIFE AND ADVENTURES OF GEORGE WILSON; THE FOUNDATION BOY. By GEORGE GRIFFITH, Esq.

Foolscap 8vo., cloth, price 3s. 6d.

FACTS WITHOUT FICTION. By DR. HEWLETT, Author of "Thought upon Thoughts," &c.

Foolscap 8vo., cloth, price

LIFE AND TIMES OF JOHN PENRY, The MARTYR, 1559—1593. By John Waddington, Author of "Emmaus," &c.

Foolscap 8vo., price 5s.

ROYALTY AND REPUBLICANISM IN ITALY. Illustrating the late important and deeply interesting events in Italy, and containing Mazzini's Oration on the Death of the Brothers Bandiera; Letter to M. de Tocqueville and M. D. Falloux, &c., &c. By Joseph Mazzini.

" We fearlessly assert that there is no living writer of English to be compared with Mazzini in the rarest and most precious characteristics of original genius."—*Daily News.*

" Always dignified in tone, often singularly eloquent."— *Examiner, Oct.* 19.

2 vols., post 8vo., cloth, price 21s , (reduced to 10s. 6d.)

MEMOIRS OF THE WAR OF INDEPENDENCE IN HUNGARY. By General Klapka, late Secretary at War to the Hungarian Commonwealth, and Commandant of the Fortress of Komorn.

" This is one of the most extraordinary narratives of great and extraordinary military events that has ever appeared.— *Liverpool Mercury.*

5, Bishopsgate Street Without.

Post 8vo., cloth, 2 vols., price 14s.

HISTORY OF THE ANTI-CORN-LAW LEAGUE. BY ARCHIBALD PRENTICE, ONE OF ITS EXECUTIVE COUNCIL. Author of Historical Sketches of Manchester.

"Independent of the interest which will attach to the history of one of the greatest struggles of modern times, narrated by one of the actors in the movement, will be the utility of such a record, as an easily accessible reference, whenever any attempt may be made to revive, under whatever disguise, the system of protection."— *Manchester Examiner and Times.*

Post 8vo., price 6s.

HISTORICAL SKETCHES and Personal Recollections of Manchester; intended to illustrate the Progress of Public Opinion from 1792 to 1832. By ARCHIBALD PRENTICE.

"I have been reading, within the last few days, a book just published in this town, written by our excellent friend Mr. Prentice. It is a book which every man in Manchester ought to read and it would be well if every man in the country would read it; and I am sure I feel under obligation to him, and I believe other generations will, for the light he has thrown upon the progress of opinion in this great community.''—*J. Bright, Esq., M.P., January* 23.

Foolscap 8vo., cloth, price 3s. 6d.

ENTRIES: or, STRAY LEAVES FROM A CLERGYMAN'S NOTE BOOK.

"He is a shrewd, easy, spicy, clever fellow, who knows his business and does it well."—*Christian Witness.*

5, Bishopsgate Street Without.

Demy 8vo., cloth, price 12s. 6d.

THE FREE-SCHOOLS OF WORCESTERSHIRE, and their fulfilment. By GEORGE GRIFFITH.

"Hundreds of volumes have been written as to the wars, power, and grandeur, of the various eminent empires of the Earth, while few and far between have been the records commemorating the education of their sons, or their progress in learning and useful knowledge; thus the empire of reason has been overwhelmed by that of Conquest."—*Preface.*

Foolscap 8vo., price 2s. 6d.

THE CAMPANER THAL; or Discourses on the Immortality of the Soul. By JEAN PAUL FR. RICHTER. Translated from the German by JULIETTE BAUER.

" * * * Report, we regret to say, is all we know of the 'Campaner Thal,' one of Richter's beloved topics, or rather the life of his whole philosophy, glimpses of which look forth on us from almost every one of his writings. He died while engaged, under recent and almost total blindness, in enlarging and remodelling this 'Campaner Thal.' The unfinished manuscript was borne upon his coffin to the burial vault; and Klopstock's hymn, 'Auferstchen wirst du!' 'Thou shalt arise, my soul,' can seldom have been sung with more appropriate application, than over the grave of Jean Paul."—*Carlyle's Miscellanies.*

Foolscap 8vo., sewed, price 1s., cloth, 1s. 6d.

THE LIFE OF JOSIAH HENSON, formerly a Slave, as narrated by himself, with a Preface, by THOMAS BINNEY.

"We have seen and heard Mr. Henson, and listened to the narrative of his eventful life. His life, which this volume contains, is more thrilling than any romance we ever read. We have shed tears and smiled alternately as we perused its striking details."—*Evangelical Magazine.*

5, *Bishopsgate Street Without.*

12mo., sewed, price 1s.

SPARKS FROM THE ANVIL. By ELIHU BURRITT. The Thirteenth Thousand.

"These are sparks indeed of singular brilliancy."—*British Friend.*

"Reader, if you have not read the 'Sparks from the Anvil,' do so at once."—*The Echo.*

12mo., sewed, price 1s.

A VOICE FROM THE FORGE. By ELIHU BURRITT. Being a Sequel to "Sparks from the Anvil." New Edition.

"They deserve to be stereotyped, and to form part of the standard literature of the age."—*Kentish Independent.*

"We say to all, read it, imbibe its spirit, and learn, like the writer, to work for and with God, towards the regeneration of the world."—*Nottingham Review.*

12mo., sewed in packets, price 1s. each.

PEACE PAPERS FOR THE PEOPLE. By ELIHU BURRITT.

"We would rather have been the author of these six and thirty papers than of all the poetry which has dazzled Europe during the present century."—*Christian Witness.*

"If we wanted to put into the hands of young people a book likely to draw forth all that is generous in their hearts and solemn in their convictions, in favour of the cause of Peace, *this* would be the book.—*Nonconformist.*

Foolscap 8vo., price 2s. 6d.

THE PRIZE ESSAY, on the Use and Abuse of Alcoholic Liquors in Health and Disease. By W. B. CARPENTER, M.D., F.R S. Dedicated by permission to H. R. H. Prince Albert.

" We have now to congratulate the donor and the public on having obtained an Essay from one of the most eminent physiologists."—*Nonconformist.*

8vo., Sewed price 1s.

THREE LECTURES on the Moral Elevation of the People. By THOMAS BEGGS.

" The working classes ought to read them, that they may learn how much power resides in themselves ; the middle classes should read them, and learn that wealth confers increased responsibility on its possessor ; and even our nobles should read them, that they may learn that the downfall of *false,* and the reign of *true* nobility are alike at hand."— *Nottingham Review.*

18mo., cloth, price 1s.

TRUE STORIES; or Interesting Anecdotes of Children. Designed, through the medium of example, to inculcate principles of virtue and piety. Fifth Edition.

" No narrative nor anecdote is inserted in this little work, of whose strict authenticity there did not seem to be very satisfactory evidence.

5, Bishopsgate Street Without.

Foolscap 8vo., cloth, price 3s. 6d.

THREE YEARS IN EUROPE; or, Places I have seen, and People I have met. By WILLIAM WELLS BROWN. A Fugitive Slave.

"That a man who was a slave for the first twenty years of his life, and who has never had a day's schooling, should produce such a book as this, cannot but astonish those who speak disparagingly of the African race."—*The Weekly News and Chronicle.*

Foolscap 8vo. 2s. 6d.

THE LAW OF KINDNESS. Six Chapters. I. The Law of Kindness—Introductory.—II. The Law of Kindness in the Family.—III. The Law of Kindness in the School.—IV. The Law of Kindness in the Church.—V. The Law of Kindness in the Commonwealth.—VI. The Law of Kindness to other Nations and the Heathen. By the Rev. THOMAS PYNE.

" We shall rejoice to hear that it is extensively circulated." *Standard of Freedom.*

Post 8vo., cloth, price 10s. 6d.

PORTRAITS IN MINIATURE, or Sketches of Character in Verse. By HENRIETTA J. FRY, Author of the " Hymns of the Reformation," &c. Illustrated with Eight Engravings.

This little volume holds many a name dear to the best interests of society, like those of Elizabeth Fry, J. J. Gurney, W. Wilberforce, Hannah More, Bishop Heber, &c.

5, Bishopsgate Street Without.

18mo., cloth extra, price 2s. 6d.

ANGEL VOICES; or, Words of Counsel for the overcoming the World. Revised and partly altered from the American Edition. With an introduction by the Rev. JAMES MORRIS, D. D.

"The Wisdom and Piety of these Voices need no high Titles to recommend them. Their entire tendency is to exalt the human mind above the petty cares and anxieties of this world;—to teach us to follow the example of Him who "went about doing good," and to comfort those bereaved hearts which "alone know their own bitterness."—*Preface.*

Foolscap 8vo., sewed, price 1s.

THE FUGITIVE BLACKSMITH; or, Events in the History of Dr. PENNINGTON, Pastor of a Presbyterian Church, New York. The Eleventh Thousand.

"This entrancing narrative   *   *   *   *   We trust that thousands of our readers will procure the volume, which is published at a mere trifle—much too cheap to accomplish the purpose for which, in part or mainly, it has been published—the raising a fund to remove the pecuniary burdens which press on the author's flock. *Nothing short of the sale of Fifty Thousand or Sixty Thousand Copies* could be at all availing for this object   *   *   We very cordially recommend him and his narrative to the kind consideration of our readers."—*Christian Witness.*

Foolscap 8vo., cloth, price 1s. 6d.

HYMNS AND MEDITATIONS, with Additions. By A. L. WARING. New Edition.

"These Hymns and Meditations appear to us to be the effusions of a mind deeply imbued with the spirit of Christianity, and highly appreciating its blessings. The writer is evidently one who deeply communes with her own heart, and who cannot be satisfied unless she realizes the joys of communion with her Saviour. There is, too, a beautiful simplicity in the composition of the Hymns, which renders the perusal of them as pleasing as it is profitable."—*British Mother's Magazine.*

Foolscap 8vo., Cloth, price 1s.

LIFE OF A VAGRANT; or, the Testimony of an Outcast to the Value of the Gospel. To which is added, a brief and original account of ANDRIES STOFFLES, the African Witness. New Edition.

" When we tell our readers that we believe there are few among them who, if circumstances permit, will not be compelled to finish it at a single sitting, they will require no further proof of the interest we felt in it."—*Christian Witness.*

8vo., cloth, price 6s. 6d.

A POPULAR LIFE OF GEORGE FOX, the First of the Quakers. BY JOSIAH MARSH.

Compiled from his Journal and other authentic sources, and interspersed with remarks on the imperfect reformation of the Anglican Church, and the consequent spread of dissent.

The work abounds with remarkable incidents, which pourtray a vivid picture of the excited feelings that predominated during those eventful periods of our history—the Commonwealth and the Restoration.

Foolscap 8vo., cloth, price 1s.

A POPULAR MEMOIR OF WILLIAM PENN, Proprietor and Governor of Pennsylvania, under whose wise Administration the principles of Peace were maintained in practice. BY JACOB POST.

" Such a work, indeed, was much wanted at the present time. The dastardly attack by Macaulay on the well-established fame of this great man, has induced the desire in many minds to know something of the real character of the Pennsylvanian legislator."—*British Friend.*

5, Bishopsgate Street Without.

In a Case, price 5s.

CARDS OF CHARACTER: A Biographical Game.

"This Game, which is prepared by a young lady, contains much amusement and instruction. It consists of brief sketches of the lives and characters of about seventy of the principal persons of the past age, and questions corresponding in number with the Cards. The Game is well arranged, and very simple."

Foolscap 8vo., cloth, price 5s.

THE TRADITIONAL HISTORY, Legends, Wars, and Progress of Enlightened Education of the Ojibway Nation of North American Indians. By the Indian Chief, KAH-GE-GA-GAH-BOWH, or George Copway.

"We still must commend it as being what it aims to be, and as giving much interesting information relative to a tribe fast vanishing from the earth."—*Standard of Freedom.*

Post 8vo., price 3s. 6d.

ON NERVOUS AFFECTION connected with Dyspepsia. By W. BAYES, Esq , M.D. Second Edition

"We may therefore heartily commend this book as a very valuable contribution to medical literature."—*Morning Post.*

"No dyspeptic patient should fail to make himself familiar with the contents of this excellent little book.—*Morning Advertiser.*

32mo., in packets, price 1s.

THE WATERLOO SERIES OF CHILDREN'S BOOKS, containing Short Stories, illustrative of Peace and Brotherhood. Edited by ELIHU BURRITT.

∗ Containing Narrative, History and Biography.

5, Bishopsgate Street Without.

Post 8vo., cloth, price 5s.

JUVENILE DEPRAVITY. The Prize Essay on Juvenile Depravity. By the Rev. H. WORSLEY, A.M., Easton Rectory, Suffolk. To this Essay on Juvenile Depravity, as connected with the causes and practices of Intemperance, and the effectual barrier opposed by them to Education.

" The author admirably uses his statistics, and shows an intimate knowledge of human nature in its multifarious circumstances."—*Christian Examiner*, April, 1849.

18mo. cloth, vols. 1 to 6, price 21s.

SELECT MISCELLANIES, illustrative of the History, Christian Principles, and Sufferings of the Society of Friends. BY WILSON ARMISTEAD.

Foolscap 8vo., sewed, price 1s.

THE NATIONS. A Poem. In two parts. By T. H. STIRLING, Esq.

" This is the title of a short poem, in two parts, written by THOMAS HENRY STIRLING, Esq. The object of the poem is to decry tyranny in whatever country it is practised. It contains some spirit-stirring allusions to occurrences in Switzerland and other countries in later years, which have been marked by the most barbarous invasion of rights."—*Bell's Life in London.*

Crown 8vo., cloth, with a Portrait, price 3s.

MEMOIRS OF JAMES LOGAN. A distinguished Scholar and Christian Legislator. Including several of his letters, and those of his Correspondents. By WILSON ARMISTEAD.

32mo., cloth, price 1s.

A GUIDE TO TRUE PEACE; or, a Method of attaining to Inward and Spiritual Prayer. Compiled chiefly from the writings of FENELON, LADY GUION, and MICHAEL MOLINOS.

12mo., sewed, price 6d.

MEMOIR OF QUAMINO BUCCAU, a Pious Methodist. By WILLIAM J. ALLINSON.

18mo., sewed, price 4d.

AN INTERESTING MEMOIR OF THREE BROTHERS, (G., L. and S. Pierson,) who died of Consumption.

16mo., cloth, price 2s. 6d.

THE ART OF MEMORY. The New Mnemonic Chart and Guide to the Art of Memory. By W. DAY. Neatly illustrated with upwards of 200 Woodcuts,&c.

8vo., sewed, price 1s.

ELECTORAL DISTRICTS; or, the Apportionment of the Representation of the Country on the Basis of its Population; being an Inquiry into the working of the Reform Bill, and into the merits of the Representative Scheme by which it is proposed to supersede it. By ALEXANDER MACKAY.

5, Bishopsgate Street Without.

16mo., cloth extra, price 2s. 6d.

GEMS FROM THE SPIRIT MINE, illustrative of
Peace, Brotherhood, and Progress. With two en-
gravings after designs by H. Anelay. A New
Edition.

12mo., cloth, price 2s.

THE PEACE READING BOOK; being a Series
of Selections from the Sacred Scriptures, the Early
Christian Fathers, and Historians, Philosophers and
Poets—the wise and thoughtful of all ages—con-
demnatory of the principles and practice of war, and
inculcating those of true Christianity. Edited by
H. G. ADAMS.

12mo., cloth, price 2s.

DEFENSIVE WAR PROVED TO BE A DENIAL OF
CHRISTIANITY, AND OF THE GOVERNMENT
OF GOD. With illustrative Facts and Anecdotes.
By HENRY C. WRIGHT.

Foolscap 8vo., cloth, price 6d.

STRAIGHTFORWARDNESS ESSENTIAL TO THE
CHRISTIAN. By MARY ANN KELTY.

8vo., sewed, price 6d.

ECCLESIASTICAL COURTS. The History and Power of the Ecclesiastical Courts. By EDWARD MUSCUTT. Pp. 48.

18mo., cloth, price 2s. 6d.

A SELECTION OF SCRIPTURAL POETRY. By LOVELL SQUIRE. Third Edition, containing many Original Hymns not hitherto published.

8vo., 24 pp., price 2d, or 12s. per 100.

PEOPLE DIPLOMACY; or the Mission of Friendly International Addresses between England and France. Edited by ELIHU BURRITT.

Cloth 8vo., price 7s.

THE DEMERARA MARTYR. Memoirs of the Rev. John Smith, Missionary to Demerara. By EDWIN ANGEL WALLBRIDGE. With a Preface by the Rev. W. G. BARRETT.

"There will one day be a resurrection of names and reputations, as certainly as of bodies."—*John Milton.*

"The book is a worthy monument to the distinguished Martyr whose history forms its leading subject. * * * A valuable contribution to the cause of freedom, humanity, and justice in Demerara."—*Patriot.*

5, Bishopsgate Street Without.

PORTRAITS.

ELIZABETH FRY. A full-length Portrait of Elizabeth Fry. Engraved by SAMUEL COUSINS, A.R.A., from a Picture by George Richmond.

Artist's Proofs	. . .	£10 10s.
Proofs, with Autographs	. .	7 7
Proofs, with Letters	. .	4 4
Prints.	. . . .	2 2

ELIZABETH FRY. Engraved on Copper. By BLOOD. From a painting by Leslie.

Proofs	. . .	15s. 9d.
Prints	. . .	7 0

THOMAS CLARKSON. A Splendid Portrait of this distinguished Philanthropist.

India Proofs, First Class	.	£1 0 0
Second Class	. .	0 10 6
Prints	. . .	0 5 0

WILLIAM ALLEN. Drawn on Stone. By DAY and HAGUE, from a Painting by Dicksee.

India Proofs, First Class	.	£1 10 0
Second Class	. .	1 1 0
Prints	. . .	0 10 6

SAMUEL GURNEY. Drawn on Stone by DICKSEE.

First Class	. . .	£1 1 0
Second Proofs	. .	0 10 6
Prints	. . .	0 5 0

JOSEPH JOHN GURNEY. Engraved in Mezzotinto. By C. E. WAGSTAFF.

Proofs	. . .	£1 1 0
Prints	. . .	0 10 6

JOSEPH STURGE. Drawn on Stone by MILLICHAMP.

Proofs	. . .	10s. 0d.
Prints	. . .	5 0

HENRY VINCENT. Drawn on Stone by B. SMITH.

Proofs	. . .	21s. 0d.
Second Proofs	. .	10 6
Prints	. . .	5 0

www.ingramcontent.com/pod-product-compliance
Lightning Source LLC
Chambersburg PA
CBHW080858020726
47502CB00008B/2274